BLACK & BLUE

Love, Sports and the
Art of Empowerment

By Andra Douglas

For
Henry Clay Douglas Jr.,
my fearless dad
February 20, 1921-November 8, 2010
and
Christine Krusen Douglas,
my brilliant mom
March 11, 1926-September 8, 2018

and also for
Sue and Jin,
my two sisters
whom I love dearly.

And a special dedication
to the inspiring memory of
Sharon Pascale,
our friend and teammate.
December 14, 1973-December 25, 2001

ACKNOWLEDGMENTS

I would like to thank

Johnette Howard for her generous help and for believing in me,

Marcia Rockwood for her keen editing and genuine interest in my story,

Diane Krasne for her expertise of the written word,

Steve Mark whose remarkable website put the NY Sharks on the map,

Merle Exit whose ongoing PR work helped establish our place in history,

And last but furthest from least, Crystal Turpin and Dana Sparling, whose friendship and dedication to our cause kept the Sharks and me going.

I also want to thank every player, staff member, coach, volunteer, fan, and sponsor of our inimitable New York Sharks throughout our twenty seasons.

It was the ride of my life.

Fins Up!

"This above all: to thine own self be true,
And it must follow, as the night the day,
Thou canst not then be false to any man."
—William Shakespeare, *Hamlet*

WINGS OF FREEDOM

I grew up in the south. The freedom the south offers to its males is a singular experience. Gaining this freedom is a game of sorts. It is defiant and empowering. If you win, you become king of a world all your own. This is a world of self-sufficiency, of conquering the great outdoors and, above all, loving a sport called football. Football is the southern males' identity and if their team is no good, their kingdom is not whole. A winning team, on the other hand, is southern salve—the cure-all, and the key to the good life.

Had I been born a male, things would have been different. Aside from the obvious, the south would have engulfed me, seduced me and made me a child of its own. As a female, it still engulfed me, still seduced me, but then betrayed me as lovers do who end up bitter never repairing the scars of trust gone awry. I was as submissive as a good belle should be, but in a strong, male fashion. The woods and the freedom of the outdoors and, most of all, the love of football, won me over early. Dependence was not introduced until later when I could already take care of myself—after I had already been told the rules of the game and was playing it.

Man—was I playing. And I was winning.

It is this football I mention that became the problem. It was the part, I realized, that made me whole and it was the part my lover, the south, would not give to me. For everything the south gave me, it took something away. It is like that with dysfunctional lovers. It encouraged self-sufficiency, then slapped me for using it, taking away my dignity. It gave me a strong character, then told me it was useless, causing self-doubt. It gave me a world in which to lose myself, but it never came in to rescue me.

In truth, these words are pain on paper. But I'll tell you the story anyway.

BRAIDED TOGETHER

...as simply and carefully as the barbed wire fence,
glowing in the late fall sun.

I am 58 years old. I am slight in appearance, but strong. I am an athlete and also an artist. I tell the stories of my life in landscapes, cityscapes and portraits of some of the remarkable women athletes I have played with, and some I have managed, over the years. I tell my stories on canvases and palettes both vivid and pale. Sometimes I paint on skin so thin you can see all the way through to the back, other times, I work on canvas so thick, one has to search hard for the opening. But it's there. It's always there. You just need the right pair of glasses to spot it.

At this moment, I am standing in an elaborate high-rise art gallery in New York City. It is sleek, with a glass wall stretching across the back of the long room, and a view from the south end of Central Park down to the south end of Manhattan. I see the lower buildings of the east and west villages in the distance and those that rise taller and taller and crescendo before me, the Empire State, the Chrysler, the old Pan Am. The cityscape is dramatic and beloved, my New York City, and I stare at its peculiar perfection until I hear voices behind me, and turn around to re-focus. The large room is filled with "BRAIDS," my one-woman art opening, something I have been working and reworking for many years.

More people have arrived. Amelie, my life-partner, and I are expecting several hundred guests; friends, family, collectors and football players. Amelie is also my agent and the producer of this show. Tonight, she is dressed in a captivating Cynthia Hendel custom printed black dress and is shimmering around the room, landing deftly at various groups, like a migrating monarch butterfly. I have on a stylish pair of black pants, a fabulous white T-shirt replete with kerchief pocket, and a men's-cut long black tailored coat.

More people arrive and move slowly around the 65 pieces of my artwork. It is a retrospective; ten large canvases, as much as 10 feet tall, that feature K-Bar ranch in Florida where I grew up. Fields and tractors and cows and palms and oaks and things that have disappeared from my world. Or did I disappear from theirs?

My mom and two sisters will be here soon, as well as cousins, a niece, nephews, great-nephews, in-laws—a whole arsenal of familial support. I wish my dad and grandma could see this, but they are both gone. Fifty-eight years of friends and acquaintances will also percolate throughout the evening. Some curious, some supportive, some who've come to quarter and critique. And there will be collectors, too. Ha! I never thought my inner mechanics—because, to me, that's what artwork is—would be of value to anyone. Especially the football series and, oddly, they are the most popular of my works. Forty pieces in the show focus on the faces of football players. Female football players from sixty teams across the United States wearing helmets and pads and grins and grimaces. They all have a particular energy. There's a player from the Pittsburgh team, whose green eyes seek acceptance. A New York Shark with a white-toothed grin on her uptilted face claiming her place on her team. I can hear the D.C. defensive back laughing before I even see the image of her head tossed back, arms outstretched towards the sky.

One of the images is larger than most and, unlike the other close-ups, it shows a group of players rapturously celebrating. The piece is not abstract, I don't really do abstracts, but the image is over-painted in crude paths of baby blue strokes and daubs of green and black. A viewer can easily discern emotion with an element of the game to it—you can see football players and liberated energy, emotional smears of colors, joy and disbelief.

I walk over to one of the large K-Bar pieces and examine it closely, using my last minutes wisely before the fray gets cranked up. A fence with twisted barbed wire stretches partway across an autumnal field, rose-colored in the sunlight. As an artist and an athlete, I know that this gracious ranch has allowed me to find the person I wanted to be, my own freedom braided together as simply and carefully as the barbed wire fence, glowing in the late fall sun.

CHAPTER 1

NEIGHBORHOOD FOOTBALL GAME

I am last to be chosen. I am hurt. I am frustrated. I am a girl.

I am nine years old. I am slight in appearance, but strong. I am tall and quick. My hands are good for catching. I have a good arm for passing. I know the game of football. I am standing in a group of neighborhood boys watching carefully as sides are chosen. The number seven on the front of my orange and aqua Miami Dolphin jersey is palpitating as my heart grows heavier, angrier while captains keep choosing and choices of players become few. I stand tall, accentuating my height. Taller than the others. I, wearing matching orange and aqua sneakers, become impatient and take a step forward, firing a pleading glance at the captain whose turn it is to choose. He looks past me and calls Pete Ahrens instead. Pete is a short, timid boy of scapegoat nature. I am last to be chosen. I am hurt. I am frustrated. I am a girl.

I am not new in the neighborhood. Nor am I new to admit my interests. I do not like lace. I hate cooking. I am too young to wear a bra and burn it, so I take Betsy Wetsy and set fire to her diapers. I think girls are stupid much like all the boys in the neighborhood do. I show signs of domesticity in much the same manner as my pet squirrel, who imbedded her long, yellow teeth clean through my mother's middle finger one morning, and bid a fast adieu while running towards the terra firma of the great outdoors.

I am not perky. Or loud. My father says I am "bullheaded." I am. My views, though seldom verbally expressed, are communicated through other means. I usually get my way because I can badger with amazing results. My grandmother says it's like being "nibbled to death by a duck." Usually, I am pestering her or my mother for things like Matchbox cars or G.I. Joe's. Or art supplies. I like to draw and paint and have won first prize at the Pendle County Fair for the last four years in a row. Today, however, after my grandmother has heard "for the last time, child!" the plea for a football of my own, she grabs my arm, takes her car keys off the kitchen table and pulls me out to her silver Cadillac to take me to the Western Auto. This car is the size of Rhode Island. It could hold every kid in the neighborhood, but we are all too embarrassed to ride in it. It is so big and so silver. Its two fins sloping up on each side of the trunk take up way too much space when they come slicing through the hot, gray asphalt of Fifth Avenue like a pair of mutant sharks. I am mortified now as we shimmer through town taking up the entire width of the avenue. Slunk down low in the seat, I am eager to dash from the Cadillac into the store as soon as we angle park right in front.

The Western Auto is run by Mr. Timmons. He has two daughters — one in each of my sister's grades--six and eight years ahead of me. I have been in the store a lot lately. I stop in on my bike after school and pick up each football separately and have made a decision on just the right one. Somehow, it just feels better than the others. I run to it now—I have it hidden behind the basketballs—and fly up to the counter with it. My grandmother is just getting inside the store.

"Hello Bob," she says.

"Good day, Dottie. I bet I know why you're here!" he grins and adjusts his thick glasses. He looks just like Mr. Potato Head. He has a mustache right in the center of his long, bald, head, which has strange dents all over it just like potato "eyes." Except his ears are too small.

"I'll bet you do too. I don't know what this child is going to do with a football, but no one will rest until she has it."

"Cain't wait 'til Christmas, huh?!"

"Can't even wait until dinner, Bob! How much?"

"It's eleven forty-nine."

"Fine. Here." She pays and sends her 'hello' to Laureena —Mrs. Potato Head—and we leave. Our house is only about a mile away. It sits on the edge of town. Western Auto is smack in the center of town. Gives you a good idea of how big the place is. It's not. Plain and simple. But today it feels like we drive twelve bazillion miles before I get home and out in the yard to play with my new ball. This ball is going to change my life. Football is ALL anyone talks about in this town. Especially my dad. The varsity team, the junior varsity team, the Pee Wee league, the Gators up in Gainesville, the Dolphins down in Miami. Plus, all the fun around here is when the boys play football every afternoon and all weekend long. They get to wear jerseys and cleats and don't have to do stupid, embarrassing things with dolls. Or roller skates, or jump ropes. Or food-related tasks like cooking and washing dishes. And just from watching, I know the game. But I am tired of watching. I am tired of not being taken seriously when I ask to play, of never being chosen when sides are picked. I want things to change. All of life is a pigskin pie and now, with this ball, I'm gonna get a slice.

But first, I gotta get out of this car! My oldest sister Annie says, "It is not important how you depart from that godawful tank, it is only important that you depart." I recall this as I leap without grace from the front seat.

"Thanks, Grandma!" I say.

"Well, dear child...I hope it makes you happy." She walks to the edge of her driveway and watches as I run with my new ball through the field separating her house from ours.

CHAPTER 2

MY DAD

He shows me proper grips on the ball
and how to have a soft touch when I catch it.

I am radio-hosting my own game in the front yard when my dad drives up in his Chevy Impala. It is brown and has a special engine in it so he won't get stuck when he drives people who want to buy his cattle around the ranch. He says it holds more people than a pick-up truck and has a better air-conditioner in it which makes them more comfortable, which makes them more likely to buy his cows. I like it because no matter how often he washes it—which is never—it is always encrusted with mud and cow plop. It's not like anyone else's car in all of Zephyrhills. My sisters call it "Shitty-Shitty-Bang-Bang," but they can't say it except when there are just kids around, because if my mother hears "language like that" her toes will curl. So, says my oldest sister, Annie. But I like "Shitty-Shitty." My dad always stands out no matter what he does. Even in his car. When he gets out of it, I run to him with my new football and ask him to play catch. He grins and puts down a bag of oranges he has pulled from the back seat. They are from his groves.

He shows me proper grips on the ball and how to have a soft touch when I catch it. He shows me some moves a wide receiver uses, lets me fake him out, then challenges me to a race to the goal line where he tackles me on the one. He laughs but falls down anyway when I try to "bull" him over on his goal line stance. We play until it is too dark to see.

The next day after school, I go out to the field over by the airport where the boys play. Walter has the flu, which makes the sides uneven, so reluctantly, they let me take his place. My dad told me since most boys would be bigger than me, I should grab the ball carrier by the back of the jersey and orbit him around me until the "mixture of balance and gravity sends us both slamming to the earth with a loud thud." This sounds like fun to me, so I do it on the kick-off of today's neighborhood game. I am not allowed to kick. I can outrun most of the boys, and I do. I catch the one with the ball and mercy is not in my heart. He is orbited venomously and slammed to the ground. He hits with a thud just like my dad said he would. My opponent is slow to get up but eyes me with new admiration.

Somehow this small success gives me a shot of confidence. Maybe I really can be good at this sport. At dinner that night, I announce my plan to become a professional football player on the Miami Dolphins. I sit next to my father who is at one head of the table. My mother is at the other. My oldest sister, Annie, sits across from me and my sister Jan, the middle daughter, sits next to me and closest to my mom. Six and eight years older than I, neither of my sisters' interests are like mine. Even when they were my age, the ranch, hunting, fishing, and sports were not a part of their world. My father always wanted a boy and finds it appealing in an amusing kind of way when I make my grand announcement about professional football. He hides a smile as he cuts his rare steak.

"How are you gonna do that when you're a girl?" asks Annie in her usual snotty tone.

"Because I am as good as they are. Better even!" I say, learning at a young age to defend my worth.

"I don't know why you want to play with boys like you're one of them!" Annie continues while already primping for a date she has that night. "Especially if you're any good 'cause then they won't ask you out on a date. You should always let them win."

My other sister is not interested in either of us and says nothing. My mom says Jan was the only one of her three babies who would entertain herself. Annie and I were "obstinate and impatient." My mom is watching me as Annie continues her babble.

"You're just a girl! You aren't even allowed to play on teams. That's a stupid idea!" she swings her long brown hair around to the back of her head and adjusts her hair band. Somehow the word "just" in "you're just a girl" doesn't sit right with me and I begin to get heated.

"It is not a stupid idea! I bet I am smarter than they are!" I fire back.

"Well you better not let them know that, either, or you really won't get asked out! If you're so smart, you better play stupid." She has all the answers, she thinks. All clamped under her long horsetail of hair by that stupid hair band.

"I don't play stupid for ANYONE!" I shout as I push my chair back and run out the back door into the yard. My mom comes out later to find me. I am up in the holly tree feeling scared of my sister's words. Scared that they might be true. I look at my mom standing at the base of the tree and she wants to speak but doesn't know what words to use. Her own life has been mixed with the reality of my sister's words and her struggle against them. She wants to tell me not to listen. Wants to tell me that they are all lies. But she can't. All she can do is put her arms out towards the top of the tree.

She studies me as I get lower to the ground. When I hop from the lowest branch into her arms, she tells me how talented I am and how blessed I am to have these talents.

"Don't forget that. That you're a talented little girl and don't you ever take a back seat," she says. "Don't ever do that to yourself."

My mother is good at seeing a simple truth. A truth that is sought by many but rarely found because people often become sightless. It is hard to ingest daily observations without becoming numb to some truths and insensitivity takes over. So many people are sightless and numb, but that never happens to my mom.

CHAPTER 3

BECOMING A PEER

The anger over those days when they rejected me has dissipated,
but it quickly returns when I am not playing football.

Months pass. I make great progress. I am revered. When I am not playing, I am conjuring plays to outwit the others. The plays are both solid and cunning. They work. I have built an empire becoming a peer with these boys and life is good. The gang appears at my house each afternoon after school and sides are chosen. These days, I am always a captain because I will beat the tar out of anyone who protests. For some reason, they enjoy an occasion which calls for this and often even instigate such events. I oblige to entertain. They like me and I like them.

The anger over those days when they rejected me has dissipated, but quickly returns when I am not playing football. My two sisters believe I am strange. I am. My father, though amused, is also proud at my power over the neighborhood of boys—some older than myself. Others younger. It is an earned power. Kingly respect. Yet I am dethroned once the teams have disbanded and each has gone home. I savor last minutes until the sun has snatched its final glow beneath the horizon. Then I must leave the football field and return to a world where I do not fit in. A world that I do not understand.

It is Saturday night. My mother and father are out for the evening. This allows my sisters, Annie and Jan to ride to Dade City for "a few minutes." I would prefer to be in my room working on my pencil portraits of Miami Dolphin players. I have a big, white, round table in the middle of my bedroom and I spend hours drawing with pencils, pastels and painting with watercolors as my art teacher taught me. I tell them I want to stay in my room and promise not to leave, and I mean it, but they say they can't leave me by myself. Besides, my sister, Jan, likes me a lot and asks me to come along. I say yes so as not to disappoint her. They tell me we will only circle the Royal Castle and return. So they say. The theme song from Gilligans' Island runs through my head. The part about the "three-hour cruise." Several hours later, and only minutes before my parents are to return home, we depart from the Royal Castle. All windows in the Chevy Nova are down. To "air it out" we drive 72 mph—which is proven to be the Chevy's top speed—because, according to my oldest sister Annie, the more air circulating throughout the car at a crosswind, the less noticeable the marijuana and beer smell. I marvel and wonder out loud if I will be as wizardly as she is when I am a teenager. She informs me that it is doubtful since intelligence levels decrease with each child a mother births. She is the eldest. I am the youngest. I am left to figure it out.

It is not very late when my parents get home. They have been down at the Home Theatre to see The Odd Couple. My mother says Jack Lemmon is cute. My father says nothing. He goes straight to their room and packs to go to the hunting camp he belongs to with his friends. It is only about thirty minutes away. Sam and Howard are undoubtedly already there, and I can tell he is impatient to be gone. My sisters and I are on the couch dipping lemon wedges in bowls of sugar and sucking on them while we watch T.V. Mom is curled up in a "pajama-ed" ball in her favorite black leather chair when he comes in to say goodbye. We three give him big hugs even though our eyes never leave the T.V. Mom doesn't take her eyes off the T.V. either, but I can tell it is not because she is so interested. Her hug is a hollow one, and when she sinks back into her chair, it looks like her arms are still around someone, but nobody is there. I take my lemon wedges and a bowl of sugar and offer her one. She puckers her lips and smiling, says it's all too sour for her.

When Sunday morning rolls around my mother and grandmother are in the camellia garden picking camellias to float in bowls. They pick each bush clean. Not a single one is left. My cousin must be coming to pick camellias. My cousin loves camellias. They must not love my cousin. Even at the age of nine I am perceptive.

"What about Cousin Betty?" I say while pushing a floating red blossom around the perimeter of a candy dish as if it had a motor on it.

"Hush or you'll get nothing for Christmas," says my mom never looking up from her task of arranging a large group of white blossoms with stems into a cut-glass vase.

"I remember one Christmas all I got was a big bag of coal and a bundle of switches," my grandmother says. She doesn't look up from the flowers either, but she is smiling.

"Must have been a good year," adds mom.

Soon the house is on camellia overload. They are floating in punch bowls, ashtrays, coffee cups and candy dishes. My cousin, with sharpened garden shears, should arrive momentarily. I pick up the football my grandmother bought me down at Western Auto and go outside. The neighborhood gang will be arriving soon. We will pick teams and play all day until angry mothers stand at screen doors and yell. Or send stupid sisters to fetch their brothers.

When I get in from my neighborhood football game, my father has returned from his hunting camp. Even though it is close to Christmas, the temperature outside is warm, so my whole family sits at the patio table for dinner. Me, Mom, Dad, and my two sisters. The topic, for some reason, turns to cats. My father; not a fan of them, expresses a desire to "stomp" cats, and also to "shoot dad-burn" armadillos and— "I'd like to fix those 'blame raccoons' once and for all!" he adds, getting peevishly worked up over animals he deems to be pests. Raccoons get into attics and "mess" on everything and "army's" root up his fresh, planted grass fields.

My mother indicates her feelings about this by declaring her desire to "haul all of those... GUNS out back and throw them into the...POND!" Jan says it would be the cause for a divorce. Annie says the divorce would be secondary to the murder that would take place. I am not sure who would kill whom, however as the unloading of those......GUNS into the ......POND would no doubt serve as a catalyst to express the suppression of my mother's discontent. We change subjects because the dog is preparing to knock over the Christmas tree. My dad says he would like to "BOOT that... daaaaam dog!"

The "daaaam" dog is my mother's twelve-year-old Boston Terrier, named Wink. We call her "Stink" because she does, and her eyes already bug out without my dad planting a shoe up her can, so I get up and take her outside. There is a large roach legging it across the pavement of the driveway. Without thinking, I squash it then feel suddenly guilty. Not because I killed the roach, but because I should have let my dad kill it—he being so anxious to kill something all evening. He is standing next to me only moments after the incident, asking with great envy: "Did you STOMP 'im?"

"Yes," I answer. His back is hunched and he is observing the dead roach.

"Hmmmph." He turns silently and disappears.

CHAPTER 4

DAD'S HUNT CLUB

When the terrain gets too rough, I climb on his back and
survey the surroundings like a tiny queen, untouchable.
I know life doesn't get any better than this.

My father was born an Alabama boy. His life revolves around hunting wild turkey, deer and hog, or fishing for largemouth bass in the rivers and ponds of Florida. Always has. He belongs to a club where others share his passion. Altogether, there are about twenty passionate ones. They are all good friends. They formed a hunt club, leased the land, and have been hunting and fishing on it since before I was born. It is all men. Only men. No women or girls are allowed. But my father listens to me beg to go to the club with him. For weeks I beg and I am relentless and finally, one Friday afternoon, which is the day he always leaves for the camp, he decides to take me. He says I am no bigger than a gobbler and feistier than any boar hog we might encounter—what harm could be done? My mother says "Oh DOUG!" and she puts a hard emphasis on the "Doug" part just like she did to the "Christine" part of her statement the day I brought home two Mallard ducks I caught in a nearby pond. This familiar emphasis means he is in trouble, but I am not sure why, so I wait in the car until we leave. And when the other men see me and learn that I will be staying for the weekend, they say nothing at all.

Original in their thoughts, they have named the camp the Ponderosa. It is no more than a word under an oak tree with several trailers pulled around an old wooden cookhouse, and in the cook house is a black man named Robert. He prepares the game the hunters bring to camp. My mother says she'd like to strike a match to ALL of it, but this camp is pure magic to me. And everything about my father is wizardry. He can track any kind of animal, shoot any gun put in his hands, and can always catch fish from any pond or river. I want to learn how to do this, and he says he will teach me. But first, he will take me to Monroe's Country Store. My mom tells him it is pronounced "mon-ROES, not MON-roes—you've got the em-PHAS-is on the wrong syll-AB-le" but this does not change my father's pronunciation.

The following Monday he picks me up after school and takes me there. To MON-roes. We pick out camouflage things like my G.I. Joe's wear. He buttons the front of each jacket I try on to make sure it fits properly and will keep me warm. Then he stands back admiring our choices. Khaki colored levis, a green long-sleeve t-shirt, wool lined camouflage jacket and a camouflage cap. My official Red Wing hunting boots extend above my ankles to protect me from snakes and water, and when we get home, my dad waterproofs them with mink oil, laces them tight and pats me on my toes while asking me how they feel.

They make me feel eight feet tall, and all I can think about is Friday and going with my father to the Ponderosa to kill my first turkey. When Friday comes, I ride my bike home from school as fast as I can. I pack all of my things in a khaki duffel bag and stand in my Red Wings by the back door holding my football and impatiently waiting for my dad to get home. When he finally arrives, we pack the car with our hunting gear—a 30.06, his favorite twelve-gauge pump shot gun and my .410. Because I am so small and the gun is heavy, my father has cut the wood out from the middle of the stock, which makes the gun lighter and provides a "handle" for my hands. I carry the gun across both arms as I try with every ounce of energy to match his long strides through the Florida swampland and across the oak-studded hammocks. Sometimes I bring my arms up tight to my chest, locking the .410 in place and I jump from one of his steps to the next. When we come to water where even he has to jump, he kneels down, and I instinctively know to get on his back. Soon it becomes a game, and when I see him drop to his knees in front of me, I get a running start and leapfrog onto his back. We cross all kinds of terrain like this. I survey the surroundings from his back like a tiny queen, untouchable, and I know in my heart that life doesn't get any better than this.

It is 8 a.m. on a school day. My dad has let me skip school to hunt and we are sitting in a turkey blind at the Ponderosa drinking coffee and eating sugar cane from a stalk Dad is peeling. We wish for another stalk, as it becomes shorter and each knuckle becomes sweeter. Dad tells of a time he was duck hunting. How he hit one that was flying so high, it split when it hit the ground. "His guts came out his butt!" he adds. I take a sip of coffee because I have no idea how to respond. It is 9 o'clock now, and we cautiously peek out into the field where the birds should be. We see whoopers and small white cranes better known as cowbirds, but no turkeys are in sight.

"Hmmmph!" states my dad. "That 'ol gobbler was here by this time all week long. With a little 'ol hen not worth SHOOTIN.' Wonder where he is?"

"Maybe they found a cheaper restaurant," I throw out, but get no response.

We get antsy, all out of food, and ride around in his Impala. We visit all the feeder sites where round, metal feeders are hoisted up long poles with ropes that lower and raise them, like flags in the home camps. The ongoing battle between hunters and wild animals continues.

"They've been here," announces my father who is peering down at the ground with the same interest one would have looking through a glass-bottom boat. "Turkey turds all over," he picks one up and squishes it between his fingers. "Yup. Still warm. They were here." He ponders, then says "You know," and he cocks his head and looks at me and I suspect he is going to say something important, "Turkeys don't have a schedule. They might show up at ten—maybe at noon. You can't tell what a turkey is gonna do!" I nod in total agreement and stare at the turd-dotted ground, but I don't want to pick one up, so I don't.

On our way to the next feeder, we spot four turkeys running like their backs are on fire across a field towards a small cypress pond. "Those could be the ones that were at the feeder," he says. "Maybe not. You can't tell a turkey." He is full of profundities this morning.

We stop behind the small pond. He abruptly points a long finger out my window, barely missing my nose and says that he has always found a covey of quail—as long as he can remember—down the ridge of this pond. For some reason, my father points with his "bird" finger, and now it is only inches from my face and twitching as it emphatically extends towards the pond. I grip my football lying in my lap and draw back in my seat, but turn to see where he is pointing. "Patches always knew where they were," he says "Do you remember Patches? She was a good bird dog."

"Yes," I answer, "I remember her." I don't, but I say I do because it always makes a memory sweeter if two are in on it. Then, as if on cue, a covey of quail burst like fireworks from the Palmetto bushes and head towards Porters Creek.

"There they are, Dad!" and there's almost disbelief in my voice "There's your quail!"

"Yup," he says solemnly and watches them until they disappear into the pines.

We are easing out across "Number 3" rye field when we spot four turkeys again. "These aren't the same ones," he says slowing down to helplessly watch them as they duck into the dog fennels and are gone from guns' distance. "But, hell," he adds "maybe they are. Maybe they lit out running from back at Rattlesnake Pass. They'll be at the front gate next time we see them! You can never guess a turkey." We peel and eat an orange from a wild tangerine tree and notice what nice December weather we're having.

Later that week on a Saturday morning, my father and I drive the Impala near the pond head called Jam-in-the-fence. We listen to the CB radio, and the voices we hear are mostly my father's friends. Our friends. My mother has a CB in the house in case she needs to contact my father or the other way around. It sits on the top of the refrigerator and chatters throughout the day until she becomes disgusted with its noise and twists the knob sharply to stop it. She says they "squawk on that dad-gum radio all day long and why-on-earth don't they get SICK of it?" She says that radio might as well be the center of the universe to them and she doesn't know why they don't give it a rest!

We are nearing Coopers Bend when we hear a voice coming from the center of the universe. It is Dooley, our ranch hand whose voice is sharp and hard to understand. Not because of the CB, but because his southern words come at you quickly, like a round of ammunition. They are rich with an accent and sprinkled heavily with local flavoring. He says he fired (furred) at a seven-point buck and is on his way to run 'round the pond to collect it. Then he hears two shots comin' from the other side (sad). He says he finds the two Smith boys and one of their kids (kee-ids) standin' over his deer (dur). He tells them it's his 'dur' and they say:

"No, we shot it!"

Dooley says he shot it first. His 'dur!'

The Smith boys say "No. Nuthin' wrong with the dur. Ain't was wounded when it run past."

"I hit the 'dur' first!" argues Dooley "It would have fallen even hadn't you not shot it."

"No other shots in this 'dur!'" say the Smiths and they punctuate the argument with the word "Ours!"

They decide the only fair thing to do is to count the holes in it. So they stretch it out spread-eagle on the ground and count the holes in it like it is Jesus fresh off the cross. And they count three holes. Smith boys only shot twice. Dooley's 'dur'. But it is Christmastime. Dooley gives them the 'dur.'

I am playing football in our field that same afternoon and trying to forget the fact that my cousin's wedding is this very evening. It is a dreaded day, and I have lost sleep over its arrival. My mother, for the very first time in my young life, has failed me. She has bought a white eyelet dress with a high collar and puffy sleeves and expects me to wear it. Everyone expects me to wear it. I would eat beets to avoid this.

And it is the third quarter of a very important neighborhood football game. The call is a pass to Walter on a right end 'flat and go' and I am to zip it to him crisply in the right corner of the end zone. He is in a three-point stance on the line of scrimmage when I notice the left guard looking towards my back door. He has a strange look on his face like someone trying to convert Fahrenheit to centigrade, while their house burns down. Then I see it, too. My sister Annie. Staring at us from behind the glass door. She is a nightmarish apparition, and she is waving the white eyelet dress like a war banner. In one heroic act, she has reduced me to infinitesimal fool status amongst my peers. My players.

"Put it DOWN!" I scream, but nothing comes out because there is nothing left of me. Humiliation takes over, and I realize how fragile and precarious my kingdom is. Embarrassed for me, the other players skulk away like moose that have discovered a friend's head mounted on a bar room wall.

I am an unhappy sight at my cousin's wedding. I don't say a word. HATE them all. Only a flicker of a smile appears when the bride—the cause of all this!—prepares to throw her bouquet. I take a three-point stance despite the white eyelet dress and run a post pattern through the pompous crowd of onlookers. She throws short, and I don't know why. I am wide open in the middle.

CHAPTER 5

HURT AND REJECTION

...you're a girl, and the club is for men and boys...
and some of them have complained...

Turkeys have become the obsession of my dad's and mine, and all week long at the dinner table, or while we are watching T.V., we discuss strategies to get close to the large birds. What time should we arrive at the blind and how long will we sit and wait for them? We promise ourselves that we will wait for those birds ALL day if we have to, and sometimes we do.

And it is finally Friday, and I am standing by the back door with my football, guns and duffel bag looking like a miniature war hero when my dad pulls up. He has an odd look on his face, and when he bends down in front of me and our blue eyes meet, I know something is not right in our world.

"Toady," he begins—my family calls me Toad because I used to sleep in a ball as a baby and my stupid sister, Annie, said I looked "Just like a TOAD!"— "Toady," he begins "I have to go alone tonight, ok?" I nod my head ok, but it is not, and my lip quivers and tears cloud my eyes.

"Will you come get me tomorrow?" I manage to squeak out.

"Well, I don't know, I have a meeting to go to tonight."

"I can wait in the trailer..."

"Well that's just it, Toady....the meeting is about you, you see....you're a girl, and the club is for men. And boys...and...some of the men have complained....so I'm going to go to the meeting and see if I can't straighten things out, ok?" I nod my head again, but it is absolutely NOT ok, and tears stream down my reddened face and my mouth is wide open and not a single sound comes out. My father picks me up and carries me inside. My mother takes me from him and says she'll take me to Lamb's toy store to pick out a Matchbox car for my collection, but this treat fails to entertain, and my misery continues. If I am no longer allowed to go to the Ponderosa, I will no longer be able to breathe. From rejection and disappointment. And when my mother puts me to bed that night while my dad is at the meeting, I grasp my football with all my might and hold my breath until I nearly pass out just to feel what it will be like.

It is late when my father returns. I have thought things over and have come up with the perfect solution. I am not going to be a girl any longer. I will say prayers right now, for God to make me a boy and by morning this whole problem will not exist. And even though my father is not in the room, I say "Daddy, I will fix this problem for you—watch this!" and I pray: "God..." I say "...you do a real nice job on nearly everything I can think of, but this problem I keep runnin' into...well...something just isn't working. If you'll just make me into a boy, so many things would work a lot better around here. I'll be able to play football on Walter and Alvin's Pee Wee football team, my friends at the Ponderosa will like me again and...and I won't have to ride a bike with no bar in the middle. That's so STUPID!" And I start to get worked up right there in front of God, so I apologize and say please at least two hundred times before I figure he probably has the message, so I tell Him "Good night—see you in the morning..."

It is nearly midnight, but I am instantly awake when my father enters the room. He sits on the side of the bed and begins his tale.

"Well, they were all there. Sam, Howard, Ben Johnson, and his crew. Even the Brooks showed up. A few of them said it just wasn't right—you being a girl and all—that you shouldn't be in our camp. That Tyler fellow had quite a campaign against us. They said you couldn't come out anymore." He paused and I wondered if this is where I would stop breathing.

"So..." and he sighed, "I told them that if you couldn't come out...then I quit the club! —and then ya know what happened?" and I saw the makings of a grin on my handsome father's face. "When I quit, Sam quit. And when Sam quit, Howard quit. Then James said he wasn't coming if Henry and Howard and Sam weren't gonna be out there....so..." and the grin was full-blown now... "get some sleep. I'll be waking you at five so we can be in the blind by sun-up. Gotta get a turkey before the season ends!"

I took a deep breath and canceled my prayer to God. For now, all was right again in our world. But I had gotten the message. The whole world thinks girls are stupid!

CHAPTER 6

A FEW YEARS OLDER

I have to defend my every move.
It makes me constantly second-guess myself.

'My mind often feels captive as I try to understand the direction it moves—towards freedom, a point of escape, a feeling of satisfaction and self-approval to where I know I can rest. But never attaining that feeling, I strive to create it and that will to create extracts an inner being and tosses about its pieces until I am all around myself. And again without escape.'

I write this down one day in the middle of stinking Home ICK class. I don't know where it comes from, but I read it a few times and think I might have written something profound. I wonder. So I make the mistake of sharing my possible profundity with my high school English teacher, who shares it with my mother, who shares it with a therapist. There is, in fact, a lot of unprompted sharing going on and now that everyone has a damn slice of me, they want me to talk about it. Since most people have the attention span of a Cockatoo, I figure it won't take long.

But it is hard not to become angry. So I do.

"I am angry," I say to the therapist my mom has taken me to. "I'm angry because I have to struggle to be who I am. I am uncomfortable with how I have to dress, talk and 'play pretty.' It's not in my blood. I'd rather kick ass (I emphasize the word 'ass' then I pause to get her response to my cursing. It is a new habit, and I intend to wear it out) in whatever I choose, but instead, I am taught that I have to please people. I should be demure and cautious. It's not my nature! It doesn't feel good to be 'demure' (new word memorized from my vocabulary test), and it doesn't feel good to be angry about it. It doesn't feel good to be constantly slighted.

And I'm not feeling my blue-ribbon best about talking to you either, because talking to you just reinforces it all! I mean, if I were a boy I wouldn't be in need of your services, now would I!"

If she were a turkey, and I was shooting at her, the wadding from the shell would have been imbedded because I am in close range and not holding back. She should consider herself blasted with buckshot and it's the first thing that feels good in a long time. Plus, I think she is actually listening. Which makes me feel strange because she is the first to hear my inner voice. It's as though I have just admitted something awful. That the unjust treatment I have received for being a girl is now real! Before, it all stayed in my head and now, announcing out loud my displeasure with the world and its prejudices makes me feel vulnerable and even more inadequate—and somehow dirty. I want to refill with a fresher substance—a little more bubble, tingle and spark that will clean off the tarnished spots and let the value of my true being show through. I feel so trapped. Even if I could escape my surroundings, I am still stuck inside myself, unable to express the feelings and emotions that are so complicated yet so simply....me.

"Do you have any examples you can give of why you might feel this way?" she asks.

"Yeah. Lots of examples. Up my ass on the second shelf!" It is a line I learned from Alvin. I like it and am delighted to have found an opportunity to use it.

"You sound hostile."

"I'm a teenager. It's what we do."

"Do you always do what everyone else does?"

"If only I could!"

"I see," she says, and she pauses before she continues as if she gets it. Yeah. Right. "So why do you think you might feel this way—this...inadequacy, this anger?"

"There's no 'might' in this. These feelings are...all I am." I am bold in my communications, and it surprises me. I might even be profound again. I continue. "I have to defend my every move. It makes me constantly second guess myself."

"So you feel you have no self-confidence?" says the therapist.

"I wonder why!" I say and shove a photo at her that I brought just to demonstrate my point. The photo is a group shot of my sixth grade Christmas party. My mother has it in a frame and I have stared at it for years and suddenly, on the very day I am to speak to this therapist, I discover why that photo makes me writhe with shame just to walk past it. My hair is rubber-banded like two poodle ears and gaudy, bright ribbons adorn each 'ear.' A short, flowered dress with long puffy sleeves and a crinoline looks very out of character on my small body whose face frowns with embarrassment. White patent leather shoes cap off skinny white legs and yellow lace socks stick out of the top of the shoes like tissue paper—as if my feet are a hidden present. All in all, I look like a human birthday cake and I am mortified to be amongst my boy peers who are allowed to dress like respectable people ought to dress. They wear neatly pressed pants, inconspicuous jackets with simple, comfortable shirts underneath. Their socks are dark and do not set their ankles ablaze with bright, inappropriate colors, and their shoes are miniature versions of grown-up shoes. They are both subtle and admirable in appearance. The boys look like small men. The girls look like fools.

The therapist studies the photo blank-faced. "Are you mad at your mother?" I give her one of those frosty teenager looks that should give her an indication of how unworthy she is to be alive, but when I answer her, my words come from a depth of which I am unaware and it startles me so that I begin to cry.

"It is not my mother who did this to me. It is society." My mother has, in fact, waged her own war with society. She is a victim of her time, and I feel the need to defend her. She had no choice back then, but today, she has her own war going on. Daily battles. But even to her it's confusing. It's hard to know who your opponent is.

After it is over, the therapist tells my mother she thinks I am bored with life, which just happens to be what Mrs. Wright, my second-grade teacher wrote to my parents in the notes section of my report card. That I seemed bored. And I was. And oh, so tired. As a teenager, I am already tired of struggling to be allowed to do things that come naturally to me. After seeing me so unhappy conforming to these female precedents, my mom allows me to shop in the boys' section of Otto's department store in Dade City where I buy all of my back-to-school clothes each fall. They are practical. Simple. Jeans, t-shirts, sports socks and button-downs. These clothes allow me to be me—even if I do look like a boy and my mother decides not to give a speckled pig's ass what others think. But she does not say 'speckled pig's ass.' She says she "doesn't give a darned tootin' what anyone thinks! She's donated enough to the church and that ought to be good for something."

But sometimes, even my parents are forced to conform. In my head, I have albums of collected snapshots, which resemble the photo of the Christmas party. I am either dressed ridiculously, spoken to patronizingly, or ignored altogether and slowly, my self-esteem is whittled away.

Despite my wanting to be one of the guys, two of the guys are at war over whose girlfriend I am. No one has asked me. Instead, they begin treating me differently. Our afternoons after school, which are normally spent playing football, discussing realizations of how stupid everyone is, and telling jokes about them, are suddenly off limits to me. I feel this because the jokes, though not directed at me, are now about me since I am a girl and when I walk up to join the group, a hush falls over them, and their eyes are full of guilt. Especially Walter and Alvin, the two who are arguing over whose girlfriend I am. I tell them I don't want to be anybody's girlfriend, or else nothing will be the same. It will all change. And it does.

CHAPTER 7

GUNS AND GOLF

Tell them about football, too, Dad, I say to myself.
I can really play football! Don't forget that.

My mom wants me to play golf. She says at least I'll be in nice surroundings, and also, women can play professionally if they are good enough. I still only want to play football professionally. Even though I know it is an impossibility, I still wish to be the first girl on the Miami Dolphins. This golf crap doesn't interest me. Until my mom and my grandmother bribe me with the promise of the motorcycle I have been pestering her and my father about. It is a Suzuki 185 trail bike. Orange. I have to have it. So I go to the range. Golf seems even more stupid from there, but I hit at the ball anyway, until I am asked by the girl's golf coach if I would play on the golf team in high school. There isn't a team—she wants to start one—and she isn't a coach—she's our English teacher—but the men's coach refuses to have 'anything to do with such a silly notion as the girl's having their own team. Wasting time...' So Mrs. Jordan has volunteered to 'coach.' She doesn't know anything about golf but thinks the girls should have a team. She thinks I should play for her. For the school. For that motorcycle. So I play. Golf.

Gick.

I am standing near the first tee of the Zephyrhills Community Golf Course. I am watching our neighbor's son and daughter tee off and waiting for my turn. They are both excellent golfers. The son is dressed smartly, looking sharp and handsome in his white polo shirt, khakis and traditional golf shoes. Then I endure the appearance of his sister in a ridiculous looking sweatshirt with a silly-shaped word sewn across the front: PASTA. And I am confused. The outfit does not improve as my eye moves south. I see the shorts playing host to other silly and meaningless motifs: a fork twisted full of spaghetti strands. A bowl. And capping the end of her slightly over-weight body is a loud pair of socks sagging limply around tri-toned deck shoes. She is playing golf. This is not a circus or a costume party. This is not how things should be. I am already aware of this. She is teeing off. A beautiful drive. Especially for a thirteen-year-old. Her hair wrung into a rope and squeezed into an eye-blinding yellow band is sticking straight up as she watches her beautiful drive pass the two-hundred-yard marker. I notice, to my horror that the hair band matches her socks....which makes it even more embarrassing to watch the diffident yet talented girl. Would anyone feel confident wearing this clown suit? Despite the two-hundred-yard drive! She can beat most boys of any age, yet she squirms when she does something good and says thank you effusively when complimented. Because she is a threat, does she have to reduce her talents with ridiculous apparel and this insecure behavior? I am confused by society's expectations of girls and boys, men and women. Who declares these roles? I wonder. And I don't understand.

But I keep playing. And my first real tournament for this game called golf is at a Cattleman's convention at the Marriott in Marco Island, Florida. I am out by the pool. Apparently, there are no meetings in progress because many cattlemen are encircled about the pool. I can tell they are cattlemen because even though their shirts are off, their jeans and boots are still on. Despite the ninety-seven degree temperature and tropical surroundings. I am reminded of the Italian myth concerning Venetian fishermen who will not take off their shoes for fear of disclosing webbed feet. Do cattleman's boots encase hooves? I wonder.

I am at this convention because my dad said the cattlemen and their families hold a golf tournament every year. No one in our family plays golf, but mom says I should 'go and have fun.' And now the annual golf fun is over. I sit beside the pool with my football and three very tall trophies—the longest drive, low net and closest to the pin. My mother is glad I beat the other women participants because "If they had brains at ALL, they'd be idiots!" My father is eager to boast because I have once more outdone his cronies and their sons.

"She can flat play some golf, now!" he beams from under his straw cowboy hat and mentions 'all three trophies' to anyone who will listen. In winter, he wears a gray, felt hat, but it is summer. He wears straw.

"You should see her shoot!" he continues with a laugh. "Killed a big 'ol gobbler last season. 'Bout a ten-inch beard. Yup—she's my huntin' and fishin' partner." His grin is so wide; his ears nearly touch in back of his head. He points it down at me as he pats my shoulder.

Tell them about football, too, Dad, I say to myself. I can really play football! Don't forget that. I finger the leather around the laces on the football I am holding, and figure the driving range I warmed up on earlier would make a perfect football field.

There's a group of people standing around my dad. Him, me, some guys and one wife, named Eadie. They start talking about lying on the beach. I hate lying on the beach. The sticky suntan oil, the sand, the salt and... WHY I wonder, am I here? So

I stand there, staring bug-eyed at the ocean, but I do not see the ocean. They are chatting about boring subjects until my dad's friend, Will, brings up the subject of playing beach football. Another guy named Simon grabs my football, and the guys immediately follow him to the beach.

"Three against two." An idiot named Bert who has only counted the males of the group is the first one to openly assume that Eadie and I don't want to play.

"Don't forget us!" Eadie insists.

Simon puts his hands in the air and faces Danny. "Who gets stuck with the girls?" And the word 'stuck' immediately makes me mad. How deflating it is to hear such derogatory words. Phrases like 'you're just a girl' or 'girls aren't allowed' kindle a rage that flares outward like the flame of an after-burner on a fighter jet. This cauterized anger is from hurt; the malignity of the world to its females.

"Let's make it three guys versus two guys, plus the girls. The girls can have Bert. He's the quickest." Says Simon-Short-and-Fat.

"That's fair. Unless we can get some other guys to play, then we don't need the girls," remarks Going-Bald Danny. I would like to skewer both of them with the beach umbrella, but I say nothing and simmer in the silent rage that is familiar to me. Eadie detects my anger and tries to break its grip.

"The trouble with men is, they're so...unevolved. Don't you mind them. They're just proof that evolution can go in reverse."

I appreciate her efforts, yet am pissed that I have to be allied with her. Always the underdog. Always the inferior group. Always the "unchosen."

She yells to Marco who is playing catch with the two sub-humans with MY ball and the other two who haven't commented. "I'll play with the others, but Christine will be on your team." Eadie and I walk onto the sand.

"I think the girls want to play," says Cousin-of-Einstein Kenny. Will has said nothing yet.

Teams are chosen. Bert, Marco and I are one team. Simon-Short-and-Fat volunteers to kick off to us and is surprised when Eadie grabs the ball out of his hands and kicks it towards us. He is complaining about this when Marco picks up the ball and runs straight at him. Simon is reaching to tag him and complaining at the same time when Marco laterals it back to Bert who scampers another fifteen yards before Going-Bald-Danny shoves him into the sand. Our ball. First and ten. We huddle up. Marco, after a tip from my dad, tells me to be QB. Bert's eyebrow goes up, but he is quiet as I tell Marco to do a corner and him to run a buttonhook just over the goal line.

"Make sure you come back for it!" I tell him before we leave the huddle. We line up. I take an imaginary snap, drop back, fake pump to Marco and fire a twenty-yard bullet into Bert's gut. Touchdown.

"HAAA!" Will shrieks. It is his first comment, and he points at Simon-Short-and-Fat. "She can throw better than you!" Bert is attempting an end zone dance while Not-so-Bad Will continues to taunt Simon-Short-and-Fat. "Plus, that was your man. You got outsmarted! By a girl!" For some reason, he is elated over this. Why do men find it so appalling to be outdone by a 'girl'? I wonder.

"Chris!" he says and I feel the need to correct him.

"It's Christine." I give short unembroidered replies, my voice useful for concealment more than connection.

"Sorry. Christine, throw me one, ok?" I pick up the ball and fire it at him. He catches it. Throws it back. "Throw one long," and he takes off down the beach as I drop back, set up and throw a bomb. His stride is unbroken as he gathers it in. Meanwhile, Will is causing such a noise that others have gathered.

"Look at that girl throw a ball!" I hear one man remark.

"I have never seen a girl do that," says a woman next to him.

In some respects, I am flattered. In others, embarrassed. Like I am an oddity. Like I am something unnatural and not necessarily good. Did circus people of long ago ever feel this way? I wonder.

CHAPTER 8

JESUS LOVES YA

All I did was win at something I am good at, yet suddenly,
I am ashamed of my talent. I want to be invisible.

When we get back home my father and I immediately ride around the rye pasture at our ranch. A common pastime for the two of us, because we are inseparable. Today, a dove is foraging in the tall rye grass. The dove is small. Her eyes are bright and keen. My father took me dove hunting for the first time when I was eleven. I killed the first dove that ever flew by me. I enjoy the thrill of the hunt and delight in pleasing my father. So I continue to kill them. I am a good shot. Better than the sons who accompany the other men. This particularly pleases my father. The more pleased he becomes, the more birds I kill. It seems a small sacrifice to see his beaming face and I would shoot the mayor to see my dad grin.

Saturday my father is having a dove hunt. He makes calls constantly all week to men he knows to invite them to come to the dove shoot. "Bring anyone you like," he says, "there's plenty of birds." The words repeat themselves as I watch a dove in the field silently, gently in search of something to eat. She doesn't know that I am only fifteen yards away. If she does, her instincts alert her to no harm. The birds on Saturday will not know there are men near. Not at first. The men will arrive by the dozens in pick-up trucks. They will be wearing camouflage caps with words written across the front: John Deere, Evac-u-bowel, or for those of sharp wit, a cartoon drawing of a woman where ninety percent of her is comprised of breasts and large nipples with a clever phrase off to the side: 'My wife thinks I'm at work.' They will find this hat so clever that it will be passed around much of the afternoon becoming increasingly more clever as the beer supply becomes less plentiful. The pockets of their camouflage vests will begin to bulge with dead birds. Dead doves who didn't know they were there. Doves who flew innocently past the pointed barrel of a gun carried by a grown man who will have had too much beer and will be angry because a football game which he is listening to on the AM radio in his 'door-to-door-shit' pick-up truck is announcing his Gators as losing. A grown man who finds it amusing and feels powerful to kill two of these birds at once. A grown man who will get bored when more birds don't fly within gun reach after several minutes and, to 'keep 'em flyin', will crawl into the cab of his filthy, Eau de manure truck and ride across the pasture with great purpose. The tin of chewing tobacco and the No. 2 buckshot shells which are carelessly thrown onto the dashboard will slide from side to side as he winds his way through the rye grass. The innocent doves will be flushed to their deaths. I don't understand.

What I do understand is that my first job is a really stupid job and it is all Jim Brooks fault. Jim is from Dade City and comes to all of my father's dove hunts. The job he gets for me is an order taker at the first neon sign company Zephyrhills has ever had—or seen. His grandson owns it. It is called Glowworks. With two "w's". Why don't they combine the "w's" to make it 'GloWorks?' I wonder. Shortly after I start, I get fired.

Not to be left behind or outdone, everybody in town is ordering their signs and having them delivered and installed. I am to take down all the info. Somehow I switch the installation addresses of the Ezekiel First Baptist Church and the Pendle County Savings and Loan Bank. Installation for the bank is completed on a hot Wednesday afternoon in September. On top of the bank and pointing downward, a 16 ft. neon pink arrow with neon green letters boasts that "JESUS SAVES."

I don't apologize to the bank, but one afternoon in a fit of guilt, I do go over to Reverend Timmon's house which sits appropriately on the corner of Nowhere and Now Here Lanes. He isn't as mad at me as he is at my mother and grandmother— staunch Methodists—who, ever since the sign switching incident, laugh like escaped mad women whenever and wherever they see him. That same afternoon he coaxes me into going to his church. With a fat, sausage-like arm around my shoulders, he tells me it would "do Jesus' heart good ta see me com-mone down and join some fine, honest people." This whole act is a passive-aggressive Baptist revenge tactic aimed at my mother and grandmother. I know it even now. But I don't say anything, so he continues.

"Plus, there's a ping-pong tournament for recreation afterward. Do you play ping-pong? Wooodja like that?" Even his voice is pudgy, and his greasy words make me want to throw straight up.

But the ping-pong sounds real interesting.

My father is an excellent ping-pong player. Learned it when he was young and played a lot of it in the war. When I became tall enough to see onto a ping-pong table, my dad set one up on our porch. We would get up from the dinner table nearly every night and play. Initially, he would play with his left hand—a handicap of sorts—until

I could beat him. Then he switched to his right hand but eliminated several crippling shots from his vast collection. Until I could beat him that way, too. Soon I matured into a player who rivaled his best game. Arch competitors, we played ping-pong back and forth, point for point, deuce, ad, deuce—in DEATH matches until we would finally fall into the swimming pool for relief from the heat we worked up.

When I show up to Reverend Timmon's sermon on Sunday, I tell him it is "cause I am concerned for Jesus' heart and want to do it well." I don't say a bit about the ping-pong. After the sermon, when I mercilessly beat the tar out of the reigning champ who is also the head deacon, my attendance is never again solicited.

Embarrassed for the deacon, the good Reverend pays a visit to my mother to tell her how "inappropriate it is for a young girl to win!" and he would like to stop his sentence, but he adds "with such violence!" Then he continues.

"Jesus is comin' and he will frown on such a..... a.. an....." he is clearly floundering, but finally comes up with the mot juste -- "aggressive...young lady. It's not right and I'm tellin' ya right now..." and he hisses out his grand finale: "Jesus is coming!"

"Better look busy," comes my grandmother's voice, hissing back from the doorway. She is displeased with this Baptist intruder. "My granddaughter hasn't an inappropriate bone in her body, and if your Jesus is going to condemn her for beating the socks off your lousy deacon at ping-pong, then we must be familiar with two different Jesuses."

"Which would make them 'Jesi' in plural form," throws in my always-a-stickler-for-proper-English-mother.

I am visibly wincing at his description of me. All I did was win at something I was good at, yet suddenly, I am ashamed of my talent. I want to disappear into the worthlessness from where I feel I came. I want to be invisible. I can't be these words. Violent. Aggressive. I am always told by mom to 'play pretty.' She said it was what her boarding school roommate's mom used to tell them when they would go out for the evening. I can only assume, but with a fair amount of accuracy that these adjectives are not on that other mom's 'pretty' list. Nor on my own mom's list.

So I have to say that my mother's response to Timmons surprises me.

"One should never place the ball high and outside on her left, or she will do just as she was taught—SMASH IT!" I could tell she delighted in saying the 'smash it' part especially when he turns on his little pig 'hoof' and leaves without a parting grunt. The best part of the whole incident though is learning that my mother actually watched us play. I never knew she watched my dad and I play. I never knew she watched.

CHAPTER 9

HOMECOMING QUEEN

For the first time ever, I am on the field looking out but not playing football.
I am not wearing shoulder pads. I am wearing a God-bless-ed dress.

I don't know where my obsession with football began. There is so much that I don't understand and this is no exception. The truth is, when it comes to life, I wouldn't know beans if the bag were open. All I know is that it is Friday night and I am standing on the football field that my best friends—boys—are playing on. The score is 14-3, and Clyde Denson scored on a quick reverse that I devised. Oh, don't misunderstand. I am not playing. I am not even allowed on the sidelines.

Because of a petition that my friends—male and female—drew up and signed begging Coach Southwell to let me play football for the varsity football team, I am thought of as a troublemaker, and in our small school, many teachers and coaches consider me an upstart. I don't care. I just want to play football. So I wait after school for the answer from my friends Walter and Alvin who have taken the petition to the coach. Everyone has gone home, and I am leaning on the lockers midway down a long hall outside of Miss Baker's art room. It is dead silent until I hear the double doors swing open at one end of the long hall. I know the petition has been denied when I see them walking towards me. They are shuffling through the empty halls and their heads hang low in a guilty fashion.

"He's an asshole." Says Alvin quietly as they get closer and lean against the lockers next to me. Walter and I nod in agreement and the three of us are wordless for a minute as if to offer a moment of silence for yet another death of a football dream. Then we shuffle down the freshly mopped green linoleum hall and out the other end of the school towards home.

And here it is at halftime, Homecoming night which is a big event in this small town. And, for the first time, I'm on the field looking out at all the towns-people who have come to watch their boys play. But I am not playing football. I am a candidate for Homecoming Queen and thrilled in the knowledge that my fellow students have nominated me, but twisted because here I stand on the fifty-yard line of Edward B. Krutchen Memorial Field—donated by my family and named after my uncle—and I'm not wearing shoulder pads. I'm wearing a God-bless-ed dress.

My mother, who has succumbed to my propensity towards unfeminine things, tries to make donning the evening's attire less painful for me. At the mall, she picks out a 'sporty looking combo'—a foxhunt kind of getup with a long plaid skirt and a black jacket with velvet lapels.

"This is sharp!" she says "And it will keep you warm. It gets chilly out on that field!" she exclaims as though she has experienced it first hand and the imagery of this thought almost makes me smile. Other outfits we have seen are so asinine — sleeveless garbage, with horrid floral patterns. I momentarily eye the suit Mom holds and realize that it is as good as it gets.

"I'll do it," I say, silently thanking the god of untold humiliation for sending something with sleeves and back. As I dress for the evening's events, my mother comes into my room and lays a set of my father's thermal underwear on the bed.

"You might want these. It's chilly out there on that field! No one will see them, and it beats being cold." I put them on.

We are lined up on the field and sure enough, Cindy Peters, another candidate for Queen, wearing a ridiculous spaghetti strapped, floral nightmare of a dress, complains of being cold. I take delight in hiking my skirt way off the ground, exposing my thermal underwear. She squeals with both horror and delight, and we try to regain composure, as Mr. Clements gets ready to announce the winner.

When he announces my name over the scratchy, small-town mic, tears run uncontrollably down my face. It means a lot to me, I know this, but winning gives me reason to release the rejection I have faced, the defiance I feel, and also to accept the love my fellow students have shown. I cry. And I look at my mother and father in the stands, knowing how happy it makes them and I mouth the words, "We did it!" And I look at the head cheerleader, who is smiling at me sweetly.

The traditional Homecoming song is playing— "Tonight, tonight, won't be just any night..."—and as the announced queen, I am supposed to kiss the cornerback, Danny Gavin, who is our new Homecoming King. But I don't want to kiss Danny Gavin. I have faked out Danny Gavin on an end around at least eight times—he is too stupid to kiss. Plus, he's ugly — all big and sweaty in his shoulder pads and cleats. Gick. No, I DO NOT want to kiss Danny Gavin. So I focus on my friends Christine Stewart and Karen Ross who are in the stands pointing at me and saying "I told you so!" and I look at my mom and dad again sitting in the rickety bleachers and as I turn my face away from Danny Gavin's nasty ol' lips, all I can think of is how my dad promised my mom a brand new T-Bird if I had been born a boy, and when I popped out a girl, my mom didn't get her T-Bird.

CHAPTER 10

SCHOLARSHIPS ARE FOR BOYS

I am a better player than most of the guys going to college to play.
Why do I have this ability and no outlet to use it?

By the time springtime rolls around, I am saddened as several of my friends—boys—are getting college scholarships. Some basketball, some baseball, but mostly football. Florida is big into football, and even the small schools like ours are heavily scouted. I am happy for my friends, yet furious.

I am in my room complaining to God. I tell Him that I am a better ball player than most of the guys going away — especially that sorry-ass Billy Laver. He's the size of a Chrysler and can't even block! Why do I have all this ability and no outlet to use it? Why?

The door to my room is shut, while I listen to deafening music and await God's answer when my mother comes in. She is saying words, but all I see is her lips moving because David Bowie is singing 'Fame' at a decibel just under jet roar. I reluctantly turn it down. She tells me that the song sounds like a junk wagon coming down the road and then she tells me that my father wants to take us to dinner at the Valencia—a fancy restaurant—with Billy Laver's family to celebrate his scholarship to Gainesville. Home of the Florida Gators! The University from which, judging by my father's behavior, all life springs forth. I am not impressed, and I'm hurt that Billy gets the opportunity with half the talent I have, so I make light of the entire scenario.

"What's so great about playing for the stupid Gators!"

My mother stands in mock disgust. "Hail to the Gators, for thou shalt put no other god before thee!"

"Amen!" I say.

"Your grandmother is going, too. Call her and tell her to be ready at six. We're taking your dad's new camper so we can fit both families."

My father's camper isn't exactly 'new.' It's new to him and to our family, but it's an old model on which my father insists he got a deal. Truth is, this camper is nothing but a blot on the landscape. And now he wants to take it and all of our 'dressed-up-edness' to the Valencia. With Billy Laver. And his ghastly family. Sometimes I don't know what my father is thinking. Nor does my grandmother. When we pull up in her driveway, she is wearing a chic cocktail dress and on her head is my grandfather's old duck hat with the earflaps hanging down on each side of her head.

"I'm gonna have to protest the hat, Dottie," says my father from behind a wide grin.

"Doug, you're not into protests. Although you did protest getting thrown out of that English pub last summer." She wears the hat all through dinner and diverts the conversation several times from football to other topics.

"Six of our boys got scholarships this season, Henry," says Mr. Laver.

"Did anyone see the article on the Silverback Gorillas in the Tampa paper?"

"No," says my mother "But I hear they may bring one down to Busch Gardens soon."

"That's right, Christine. That's right. Has anybody been to Busch Gardens lately?" With the topic changed, my grandmother cuts a nice slice of her steak and passes it to me. "I can't eat it all dear, but you can."

"Thanks, Grandma." And I grin at her like I am part of her conspiracy.

Later I find out that she did all this to cheer me up. She knows my disappointments, my hurts.

"Dear, dear child," she says, "you can't dwell on what will never be."

"I can't help it, Grandma. So much in life is unfair and it makes me crazy! I'm gonna end up in the nut house with all the nuts."

"Well, that's not the worst thing that could happen, dear. After all, everyone is nuts. They're just the ones who got caught. Besides, you are going to graduate next month and move on to bigger and better things in life! You're going to do things and go places you've never even thought about!"

My mother agrees with her. My mother says I need to get out of my hometown. Farming and ranching are my only opportunities here, and she says there is "nothing appealing about poking something into the ground and watching to see if it comes back out." In this way, I take after my mom, and since she is usually right, I listen. She tells me I am a very talented artist. She says I should take that talent and find adventure. She says in Zephyrhills, "nothing is happening every minute of the dad-gum day. A week's rest can be accomplished in half the time, and people chat on the phone for thirty minutes even when they dial the wrong number." On Friday nights she invites the 'undead' over for drinks. There is no adventure in my hometown because there is no place to go where you shouldn't. And how can you be adventurous with everybody watching? She says leaving will be a success story in itself, and I should plan to see the world, so I figure I will. Even if I have to change buses to do it.

And when I get a call from an art school known as Pratt Institute in New York City saying I have been accepted, the first thing I pack is my football. Even before my pens and pencils. Even though I know my passion to play the game has just been a silly fantasy.

"I'm proud of you Toady," says my dad on the day I leave for New York. He has to take a Venezuelan to see his bulls and can't go to the airport. As excited as I am to leave, I want to get in his car and go with him. He hugs me so tight it hurts, and he gets choked up, but that's not unusual. When we finally let go, he says it again.

"I'm proud of you."

"I love you Dad." I answer, and I do, but what I want to say is 'I'm proud of you, too.' But I figure he wouldn't know why I'd be saying that, so I don't.

My mom drives me to the airport. It is time to board the plane. I tell her goodbye. My sensitive and intuitive mom, who is bitter about life. Her grief is spoken in wrinkled sentences across her forehead. In the slowing of her step. In the deliberateness of her gaze. My mom. Who has given to a fault. Who has received comparatively little. Who needs to be reconstructed a queen. It would take so little. I can orchestrate each step, yet I cannot do it myself. A hard lesson to learn. We hug.

"I don't know what I would do without you, Mom."

"You'd do just fine."

"No, I wouldn't," my words cut hers short. My carry-on bag is heavy. We have been sharing the load — each carrying a handle. She releases it and places my coat across my other arm. I walk away. We are crying but say nothing. Just a few tears. Liquid words. I board the plane.

CHAPTER 11

NEW YORK, NEW YORK

*I walk around a lot, looking at things so foreign to me
and missing my small town.*

I have never seen New York City. My friends back home take bets on how long I will last. And with good reason. I didn't 'fall off the turnip truck' as some would say. I was pushed! Pushed by ennui and my mother. So I am trying to find a place to live in New York City.

The five dogs on my family's ranch back in Florida live in a kennel, each having their own room, which is about four feet wide and ten feet long. I always felt sorry for them, all cramped up in there, so I let them out every chance I got. They ran around the pastures, ducking under barbed wire fences, racing from hole-in-the-ground to fencepost to whatever stench they could find. They bark-bark-barked and wag-wag-wagged until, tired of their idiotic behavior, one of the cowboys would coax them back into their pens. Letting them out annoyed our main hired hand, Dooley, but realizing he had no control over my actions, he posted a handmade sign on the telephone pole, which stood in the middle of the circle of dirt driveway in front of the ranch. The plywood sign had a black background and in white hand painted letters, these words: 'Speed Limit: 10 1/2 miles an hour and don't run over the damn dogs!'

My pity for the 'damn dogs' dwindles and the term 'kennel' takes on a new meaning during my search for an apartment. I read an ad in the New York Times, which goes something like this:

F/T or P/T rmmt for E side,

SE, grt lgt, chrmng 1br w/dw, wbf

sm grn, sblse 6 mts. NO FEE!

The ad under that says something like this:

Long list of affordable studios

Call Miriam at 212-555-7689

Miriam is a woman of considerable size who says she will give me keys to several 'charming' (chrmg) places but she can't climb the stairs. She waits outside the building and smokes a cigarette while I go take a look at the first 'affordable studio.' This particular building, located on 23rd street, has five studios in a row no bigger than the kennels at the ranch. They are on the 4th floor. Each has a Murphy bed which, when pulled down, covers the whole damn studio. A hot plate on an ugly brown shelf is deemed 'the kitchen' and closet space consists of how much you can fit on your own person. The paint on the walls has by-passed beige and gone headfirst into brown which starts my oldest sister Annie's decorator voice in my head:

"I will never use the color brown! For anything! Brown is...it's... well, brown just makes me MAD!" The rental prices make me mad. And there is no bargaining with these folks. The landlords in New York City have hearts the size of kitchenettes. It just goes to show, you can't have everything. Where would you put it?

When I finally take an apartment, it is in an area called Gramercy Park. Miriam tells me artists live here, so I figure I might fit in. I wince when she says the word 'studio,' but she promises it is "nice space, great light, (grt lgt) — and it's on the SEVENTH floor, a good sign! The building has a small 'community' roof deck and..." (she is very excited to tell me this) "It has a fireplace! It doesn't work, but the look is 'Tres chic!! Tres, tres chic." I don't know a word of whatever language she is speaking but I take the apartment. And it is small. More like a 'compartment.' But it is now my home and there's no place like home. Especially when you're not invited anywhere. So I walk around a lot, looking at things so foreign to me and missing my mom and dad, my friends and our small town. I notice the gorgeous cut flowers for sale outside on the sidewalks of the corner deli's. I think of Mom and Grandma in the Garden Club and the arrangements they used to make from flowers I would bring to them, and I stare at a cluster of daisies until they take me as close to home as I can get.

I see my father coming home at night. He empties his trouser pockets full of change into a dish on the shelf in his closet, before showering for dinner. The dish overflows with dimes, nickles, some quarters and lots of pennies.

My pockets are heavy with these coins as I pedal my bike to Jillian Biggs Florist, the only florist in town, and conveniently located—as everything is—about a mile away. I lean my bike against the yellow cinder block building and go in. Jillian herself is behind the counter. She is ancient and I think her head is shaped like a T-Rex, which my mother thinks is funny so we all call her T-Rex instead of Jillian. But not in front of her. I wave shyly and head for the big walk-in refrigerators, full of all different kinds and colors of beautiful flowers. T-Rex appears next to me while I peruse. This is not my first visit and she is familiar with the drill.

"I'll have some daisies and an iris in each bouquet, please." I am getting two bouquets, because I can't get one for Mom, without getting one for Grandma. It wouldn't be fair. I tell this to T-Rex who agrees and plucks several daisies and two iris out of the large water buckets on the floor and begins to form the bouquets.

"I think a snapdragon would be nice," I say, and T Rex pulls several stocks of bright yellow snapdragons.

"How is your grandmother doing?" she asks.

"Grandma is doing great! She's having a party this weekend." I say.

"Yes! I know. I am looking forward to it. Please send my regards." I smile up at her and point to a bucket of Gerbers and ask her to add a yellow one for Mom and a red one for Grandma. I look around some more and T-Rex tells me what kind of flower each bucket holds. I am mesmerized by the colors and I look at them for a long time.

"They are all beautiful to me, but I guess that'll do it," I say and make my way to the counter. The top of it is at eye level so I reach up to unload several handfuls of sweaty change from my pockets, while T Rex wraps the bouquets in green tissue and ties them with a white ribbon.

"How much are they Mrs. Biggs?" I asked timidly, always afraid I won't have enough. She eyes the piles of coins and fingers them into groups: eleven dimes, six quarters, sixteen nickles, and many pennies.

"This covers it just fine. Tell your mama and your grandma hello."

"I will. thank you!" And I skip out the door to place the two bouquets wrapped in green floral tissue paper in the basket attached to the handlebars of my bike and pedal home. I deliver the bouquet to my Mom first, then run down to Grandma's house. They both 'ooh and ahh' over the flowers as they choose one of their many vases to arrange them in. Then they put them in the place of honor, which is usually right in the middle of the kitchen table. Their arrangements are works of art to me, and it pleases me to see them every time I go in or out of either house.

I wish I am there today, as I am jolted back to reality. I buy a bundle of white tulips, simple perfection, for my own apartment and set them in the place of honor on my small gate-leg kitchen table. The arrangement does not have the flare that my grandmother or my mom would add, but they still give me a sense of being home.

I am too naive to have any fear. Or maybe just too damn ornery. I walk through every borough, neighborhood, and street of New York City, wondering where in "Sam Hill" I am. But it isn't nearly as big as I thought it would be, this New York City. Not nearly as tall. That doesn't mean I'm not cautious. Everybody from home warned me about the Big City and its perils, so while I walk around, I concentrate on street-wise advice given to me by friends who have none.

— Don't walk too close to the building—someone will grab you.

— Don't wear anything nice—someone will ruin it.

— Turn your rings around—someone will steal them.

— Cling to your purse—someone will mug you.

— Don't let your chains show—someone will slit your throat for them.

— Don't go to Chinatown in the rain—the Chinese are short
   and they'll poke your eyes out with their umbrellas.

— Don't take the subway—you'll be shot.

— Don't use public facilities—you'll catch a disease.

— Don't make eye contact with anyone—they will follow you home.

If all of this is true, then a block party is out of the question. But it is an adventure and for the first time in my life, I'm not bored. Honestly, I don't know what I am looking for here, but the sight of the New York City skyline gives me chills, and every time I see it, I zero in on the World Trade Center at the south end of the island and say "Come through, New York, come through!"

Come through with what, I'm not sure. But I am sure there's some sort of a special dream waiting to unfold. Some great success story even greater than being a pro football player! Would I become a famous artist? The CEO of the next hot company? What is it that the magical city is supposed to deliver? Not at all sure, I none-the-less keep repeating the words, and directing them right towards the World Trade Center. "Come through New York, come through!"

Occasionally my sisters call in from their busy lives. Jan is always interested in what's going on in the city and promises to come see me. She says I am 'her little hero' for moving here all alone.

"You should have been the one, Jan. You're the one with the looks and the flair for fashion. You should have moved to New York." Annie has looks, too but she seems only interested in William, the man in Tallahassee she's been dating. She is very focused and doesn't have the time to have a go at New York City at the moment.

I call home a lot. Collect. My father accepts the charges and immediately gives me the weather report. How much rain he's found in the rain gauge nailed to the fencepost—to the 32th of an inch. How Dooley had to pull a big 'ol gator out of one of the ponds, so it wouldn't get a calf. He says he saw a whole bunch of baby turkeys round the corner down by Dan's old place and he is filling my mind like a tip jar while I listen and 'see' home. He is launching into the pea crop report, when I hear my mom grabbing for the phone and saying how 'sick she is of hearing about the peas, peas, PEAS!' Then the phone is hers.

Her tone changes when she speaks to me. "There is an art exhibit at the Met that you should go see." These reports excite me and I am eager to hear her news and suggestions. In reality, all I need to do is open the paper to learn of the many things offered around the city. But I prefer my mom's findings.

"I saw the Georgia O'Keefe exhibit, Mom. And the paintings were beautiful!"

"Yes, and you should go see Radio City. I don't care what's there. Just go see it. I went to see the Rockettes on my way to Alfred one time. I was 18. Mother put me on the train right here in Zephyrhills and we chuuuugged all the way to New York where there was an all-night layover. She told me to get a cab and go over there and get a ticket, so I did and I loved it!" I smile thinking of my mom loose in New York City. She has no fear and though timid at times, she is one of the bravest people I know. The ranch and Zephyrhills is all she's really known, but she's so much bigger than that. It holds her heart, but it has also held her back. I know that's why she had the courage to leave me here in this city alone. As much as she has loved her life, I believe she is still looking for a 'her' she never found. Maybe she sent me to find her. Or maybe I am her.

"I went back to Grand Central after the show to wait for the train," she continues. "There was a big, roped off waiting area and I remember one of the black porters kept an eye on me all night until I boarded the train to Alfred early that morning. I'll never forget him."

I never ask about the successes or failures of my male friends who are playing scholarship football for different universities. Even though I played along side of them until the day I left for New York City. Even though I know my dad obsessively reads every published word and the phone calls going from house to house across my hometown are constant, reporting every football incident as though the world would quit spinning if not for these boys and this game. It isn't that I don't care about my friends, but hearing about them would make me feel the exclusion all over again. So I don't ask.

"You are not missing out on ONE thing around here!" my mom says every time we speak, but I always believe that I am.

When my dad finally gets the phone back, he bellows into it. "Turnips are comin' up...and I saw a flock of baby turkeys down in the rye field the other day." He doesn't ask much about the city, preferring to remain innocently in his agricultural realm. After I hang up, I stare out my window, which looks directly into the side of a large, wooden water tank silhouetted by the glow of red and blue lights from the Empire State building. I miss his simple, southern world.

The next morning, I get on the E train to go to class. Find a seat, sit down. I notice as I glance towards the other end of the car, a man wearing a cowboy hat. A gray, felt cowboy hat, just like my dad's. A little worn with a feather hatband—pheasant, if I'm not mistaken. As I stare, I notice that the man also has on an all-weather coat—putty colored—as I have seen my father wear to so many cattle conventions. His felt hat and overcoat, his khaki slacks and boots, his tall, slim figure—the combination exuding such purpose, such importance. I remember this so well. Those conventions were such a part of my life. Our lives. I stare at the man and notice that his pants are pin-striped and his shoes are shiny, very business-like, very city-like—this cowboy on a New York subway. I stare. And when he finally feels it, he looks up, his felt hat point-ing straight at me and we make eye contact. Through glasses not unlike my father's, he stares back at me. I smile, embarrassed because I have been caught. Because he looks nothing like my dad. Just his hat. His overcoat. I look away. I miss my dad.

Two stops later I stand to get off the train. So does the cowboy. He is short. Not at all like my tall, handsome father. The cowboy is going up the escalator in a crowd in front of me and the only thing I can see is the hat. The overcoat. My father.

Outside he turns left and goes up Fifth Avenue. His top half a perfect cowboy. His bottom half the perfect New York businessman. I guess nobody is ever all of one thing. Sometimes it shows more than others.

CHAPTER 12

LONELINESS

In New York, you are always an arm's length from another human being,
but that doesn't mean there is anybody there.

May Sarton aptly worded it: "Loneliness is poverty of self, solitude is richness of self." At first, richness of self is abundant and I am very, very rich. I spend it quickly, however, and feel so poor that any human interaction is like pennies from heaven.

Loneliness is hard to admit when the city itself seems alive. At nights the skewering lights of cars pierce the steam emanating from manhole covers. Underneath the streets lives the bulk of the huge rock monster that either bestows its riches or shares its woes. Afraid of the latter, dwellers are wary as the monster peers through the steam. It reaches towards those who scurry on their way, never making eye contact with each other, afraid that if they do, it will somehow affect their own fate. I buy fruit daily from the same vendor yet, months later, he still doesn't acknowledge that he has ever seen me.

This could not be any less like my experience with Hubert Watts, a man who sits in an old green 1952 truck on the top of Grace Hill, a piece of land that belongs to my family, a place where Hubert sells watermelons. Supposedly it is the highest hill in Florida, but it's hard to tell because the hills along that part of Highway 301 ripple up and down, and every time you get to the top of one, you can see either Zephyrhills or Dade City, depending on which way you are headed. Grandma says it's a great way to spot who's in town in case you want to turn around.

The bed of Hubert's truck is full of watermelons and there is a long hand-painted sign propped up on the back wheel well of the truck that spells out 'watermelons.' No price, just 'watermelons.' Hubert has spent a lot of time in the Zephyrhills clink because he is a bootlegger. His stills have dotted the orange groves for decades, and sometimes Chief Carter has to arrest him just to keep things official, but everyone at the jail knows him and they make him comfortable until he can leave. Then he goes back to his stills. My grandmother says back in the 30's when Hubert was running his moonshine, he had a big Buick and the trunk would be loaded up with the stuff.

When he would make the run on 301 from either direction, he'd get going so fast the old Buick would leave the ground as it topped each hill.

My grandfather offered Hubert some money and a field where he could grow watermelons so that he could make an honest living. He told Hubert he could sell them right up alongside 301 on Grace Hill, because lots of people passed by and they would buy his watermelons. So Hubert did just that. He grew the most delicious watermelons in the world and every summer, he still sells them from his truck on top of Grace Hill. But he never gave up the stills.

Hubert can spot my dad coming a mile off over the rolling hills. By the time my dad pulls in, he has the 'finest watermelons from the patch' set aside. He is old now and walks with a limp but always insists on loading the watermelons into the backseat of my dad's car.

"Naw, Mr. Doug. You let me load these here melons in for you." A chewed cigar stub hangs from his lips as he talks and he points to one. It's not the biggest one, but Hubert can tell details about each one. "You give this 'un right here to Mrs. K. for me, ya hear? Tell her it's the purtiest one in the patch jest for her."

"I'll let her know. Thank you, Hubert." We drive away as he sits down in a patched-up lawn chair to whittle a branch from an orange tree.

Back in New York, I often walk through a neighborhood called Hell's Kitchen. Familiarity is its only endearing quality. I see a cornucopia of crime and abomination performed on the streets. After a short time, however, my eyes no longer protrude in the manner made famous by snails, but my eyebrows constantly raise and lower allowing, like a drawbridge, the absurdities to sail in and out of my mind. I ask God to bless the people in the soup line on 29th and 9th. By human standards, these prayers are necessary, but maybe God thinks they are doing just fine.

I am passing Bryant Park at 42nd Street one afternoon when I suddenly feel exposed. So many people, so many eyes, and I know my raw feelings, my insides, some expression of who I am must be showing. I wonder what it looks like. I have been here for months, and I wonder if I look different here in New York than I did at home. I sit down on one of the benches and cry, and I feel stupid because I am crying out loud, but I don't care because I just want to go home. I reach into my backpack to retrieve a small package that has arrived from my sister, Jan. I tear into it now, as if she's inside, and if I let her out, she, like a genie, will take me home. That is my wish. That is all three of my wishes. Take me home, take me home, take me home. I unwrap a small, gold, refillable perfume vial that contains my favorite essence—one she and I discovered together. I hold it tightly to my cheek and feel a roughness on one side.

When I inspect it more closely, I find 'My little hero,' inscribed on the vial, and I cannot hold back the tears. I try to speak to myself through gasps of air, but the thickness of the city and the tangible isolation I feel prevents my own communication. In New York, you are always an arm's length from another human being, but that doesn't mean there is anybody there.

So I sit, trying to spill words about 'home,' but they never come out. I know that the only way to go there is to feel it in my mind. Even if for a moment. I open my address book to run my fingers over the raised ink of my home address, hoping it will transport me there. I see other addresses with crossed out street names and new zip codes attempting to pinpoint the proximity of change. How do you hold on to a nostalgic moment that gives you only an instant to remember? A whiff of summers past. A word. A sound. How do you mesh one moment into two and pull the past into today?

My fingers are pressing the paper as blindness reads braille, trying to pry open the door to home—just a bit wider. I want to return so badly. I haven't been away that long, but I feel a sense of panic, especially at the thought of my parents aging. It's as if somehow, everything has already changed, and I am responsible. I fear the day when this very moment will be a nostalgic one, and I will yearn for it, as I do now for 204 21st street in Zephyrhills, Florida 33599. Holding time is like trying to hold a cloud as it forms. Or trying to squeeze it into a different shape. I cry from this longing. For the loss. For knowing I can never return to exactly what I left.

CHAPTER 13

INVITATION TO PLAY

I stand in the heat of the day, thinking this must be a mirage!
I look again: a group of women is playing football!

I am sorting socks one day and thinking that all of them can't possibly belong to one individual when I realize that there are two companions I have overlooked—Me and Myself. After this realization, I view my existence as three entities sharing space in one body. It is a type of schizophrenia that I find comforting. Plus, it explains all the socks.

Time passes quickly and living in New York City means paying the Piper. It also means paying the doorman, the coat checker, the cabbies, the "super" in my brownstone and that foreign woman giving out hand towels in the bathrooms of fine establishments. Life in New York City moves so fast that it seems as though events overlap. Unlike my beloved game of football, there are no time-outs, no half-times, not even any two-minute warnings. Even the traffic lights mean nothing. And all the horns honking make it so noisy. At home, the things with horns say "mooooo." In New York, there are lots of nasty and maladjusted people. They swear loudly from the middle of the streets and write rude words on walls. The rudest thing on the walls back home was the day the "l" dropped out of "public" on the building we know as the Public Library. Nevertheless, I navigate this city well. And it is slowly becoming home.

"Come through, New York!" I say, aiming my words at the beautiful skyline at the southern end of the island. "Come through…"

Then one day it delivers something. A group of women who play football. I don't remember exactly, but somewhere I hear that beach football is played on Fire Island. So one Saturday I take the ferry over from Sayville out on Long Island. I sit down in the sand holding my football like a security blanket and look for the football action.

Suddenly, like an apparition, Jessie appears next to me. Twenty-nine, slim, muscular and quite beautiful, until she opens her mouth, at which point you know for sure she is a true Brooklynite. Everything you hear is unruly and the opposite of what you might expect from her full and opinion-giving lips. She swaggers; even her gestures have an accent.

I take notice of her curly, unruly shock of short hair. She takes notice of the football in my hands. Then she speaks.

"Seen ya bwall," she says.

"Yeah?" My slight southern dialect is not nearly as distinguishable as her 'Brooklynese.'

"Wanna play wit us?" she romps around me in the sand like a puppy.

"Yeah. Ok." Of course, I want to play! Who's "us?"

"Zat ya football?" Stupid question number two. Doesn't matter. Just want to play.

"Yeah." No one was gonna elect me to the debate team.

"Ok. There's more of us over there."

"Ok—good!"

I follow her down the beach and see a group of about fifteen women throwing a football to each other. The heat of the day, the sand…this must be a mirage, or a dream and Jessie is the ghost of football past. But as we approach, I can see that they are still there. An entire group of athletic women and they are playing football! Jessie introduces me.

"Hey! Found another player for the game today. Maybe for the Sharks, too!" They greet me with sandy handshakes, and soon they are telling me about their team named the Sharks in a league in Brooklyn where they all live.

"It's flag football," announces a woman named Sarah who says 'flag' like she's just discovered rancid milk in her lunch pail. She is sitting in the sand putting a pink band-aid on her toe, and her long blonde hair drapes around her knees as she leans forward. Flag football. Alright, maybe it isn't the spot on the Miami Dolphins I dreamed of as a child, but at least I can play my favorite game and meet people, too.

"But it IS full contact," Sarah is quick to throw this in, as if embarrassed that they don't play tackle. They all nod in agreement, grateful that Sarah has pointed this out. She is the EF Hutton of the group. Everyone listens. Calm, jocular and in control of herself, Sarah is revered by the others. Her confidence is contagious. She seems to be a bit younger than some of the others, yet clearly a leader. "It's really fun and competitive. You'll love it!" she looks up from the band-aid application, gives me a big smile and unabashedly shifts her pink, mid-thigh length tights by sticking her hand down the front of her pants and centering the crotch and waistband. "Plus, it's all we have." She adds as a light afterthought. "So…let's play…is it Christine or Chris?"

"Christine." She stands up and her stature is not nearly as big as her presence. About 5'4", Sarah has a thin, athletic but curvy body. She begins to trot away from the group and puts her hands up signaling for me to throw her the ball. I feel like I just reached heaven and as I whip the football in her direction, I hear several murmurs and a grunt of approval from Jessie,

"That lil' 'ol skinny arm can send that ball!" she says and Jessie grunts again, but is smiling. Someone named Dulce is waving for me to throw the ball to her, so I zing one her way. She catches it effortlessly and grins at the others.

"Aiiight!" she says, and Sarah is kind enough to translate.

"That's 'alright' in Puerto Rican, Christine." Then she laughs as a cacophony of 'aiiights' fill the beach air. We play most of the day and the only reason we stop is because Sarah's dad, Thomas, is picking a group of the players up at the dock in a boat. I sit in the sand after everyone is gone, tossing the football in the air against the blue sky, reliving moments that made my adrenaline flow: Jessie catching my pass in the end zone and rushing back to the huddle full of excitement. "I didn't think you saw me!" But I did! Or after I was flushed out of the pocket and ran for a long gain; as we returned to our side of the ball, Sarah flipped her long hair around and, in a playful taunt, told the defense I was the fastest one on the field. These are the things I want to feast on, and the more I eat, the hungrier I become. I lie down in the sand to digest the delicious moments. The clouds form the X's and O's of the playbook in my head. I will go home, gnaw these memories to the bone and be ravenous in the fall when I play flag football in Brooklyn with my new friends.

CHAPTER 14

THE LONG ISLAND SHARKS

I just want to play football all day, every day.

When it gets close to the beginning of practice for the upcoming season, I unfold the piece of paper I have carefully stored in my art supply box, and call Jessie for information. We exchange pleasantries, and she launches into the directions. She is articulate.

"So... if you're coming from lower Manhattan, it should take you about thirty minutes—unless the traffic's fucked up, then it'll take you, I dunno...a long time." and I can hear her shoulders shrug through the phone. "Leave early since you don't know where you're going. S'good idea." and she adds an 'r' to the end of the word 'idea' and I understand what happens to them when they disappear from her other words.

"I don't have a car. I'll have to take the train."

"S'easy. Take the R train all the way to 86th street in Bay Ridge. When ya come up outta the hole, go west for two blocks and north for one block. That's Bay Ridge High School. We'll be there 'trowin' de ball.'"

"I'll be there!" The 'R' train. Of all letters.

For months I don't miss a single practice and now I'm am batting back butterflies hours before the first game of the season begins. I have called my mom and dad before the game who, amused by the way I often mimic a Brooklyn accent, tell me to 'trow da ball' well. I take the R train from Union Square and arrive in plenty of time but I hold up for a few minutes before walking to the field. I don't want to be too early. When I get to the Bay Ridge High School football field, I feel very shy and somehow out of place. The only thing familiar is the number 7 on my jersey, the same number of the first jersey I ever owned—orange and aqua— the one Mom let me order from the Sears and Roebuck catalog. I nervously touch the threads around the numbers' perimeter. It's my identity right now so I make sure it's sewn on well and won't come off.

I feel even more out of place when Coach Tony puts me on defense at safety instead of quarterback, and though I am delighted to get into the game, everything about it feels strange. After I intercept two passes, I am starting to feel much better.

"So, you must have played in Florida. You're good!" says Dulce.

"I never expected that kinda play when I first saw ya," says Jessie.

"Thank you," I say, knowing it is what my grandmother would call a 'back-handed' compliment.

After the game, Sarah is the first to invite me to the small bar on 4th Avenue where all of the players are going for Sunday afternoon beer drinking. I say "Sure," and all I can think is that I wish Sundays would last forever. I tell them this at the bar and they laugh and agree and raise their beers high to football.

CHAPTER 15

MANY YEARS PASS

We don't have to sit in the bleachers and watch
and we aren't anybody's damn cheerleaders!

I have been 'trowin de ball' in the Brooklyn Women's Flag Football League for many years. Players and coaches for the eight teams appear and disappear like cheap ink on scrap paper, and the start of each season often finds the deck of players shuffled onto different teams. But the core group returns every year because our very existence revolves around the game and our league. My team is called the Long Island Sharks, and everyone on the team except me is from New York. They have the accents to prove it.

Long ago, in this same Brooklyn neighborhood, many of these women were children who played ball in the streets and playgrounds. Today, the high school field where we play, and the grimy little bar that sponsors the league has become their playground. Our playground. Every Sunday of every fall, from warm-up to last call, we, the flag football players are free to express our passion for a so-called man's game. We can be the adolescent, juvenile-acting youth football players who were, as young girls, never allowed to emerge. Our "inner-football players" are loose at last. We don't have to sit in the bleachers and watch, and we aren't anybody's damn cheerleaders! Whether we suck at the game or not, we are catching and diving and rooting around after the ball with the same aggression and passion as the boys.

Nothing deters us even when we know the ambulance will be called at least once every Sunday. Today is no exception. Kim Darren is down after having a mid-air collision with a wide receiver. Kim Darren is a 5' 2" 210 pound, thirty-eight year old professor, who always argues a point even when you agree with her, and her sandpaper voice never stops, even after she wins.

She's quicker than she looks, in wit and athleticism. Wendy, our safety, calls her a "fat son-of-a-bitch." The 'fat son-of-a-bitch' plays middle linebacker on the team, she also coaches in her argumentative, browbeating fashion. Her wild, jet-black hair streams out behind her, undoubtedly from zipping around on a broom. She can catch, too. Squatting in mid-field, Kim looks like a mutant toad and just as a toad seemingly has a 12-foot tongue to catch unsuspecting insects, so Kim has her stout little arms. She has 'licked' several of my passes from the air, devouring play after play, but she is never satiated. Winning only keeps the beast at bay. For once, as she lays still on our borrowed football field of rocks and broken-glass, she is not trying to argue with the refs.

The players from both teams have circled her as they would any downed player. We know each other so well and despite wanting to annihilate each other's team, we are aware that a serious injury could happen to any one of us. So we gather to stare and needle and make childish remarks, which in reality, only mask our fears.

"She got filleted like a salmon.....heh-heh!" comes Wendy's caustic voice from the middle of the group. Wearing number 31 and her signature bucket hat, Wendy is one of the most notorious women in the league. At 5'5," 145 pounds, the twenty-eight-year old ruffian plays free safety. She is sinewy, muscular, has long black hair and an off-kilter personality that bubbles like battery acid.

Eve is the best all-around athlete to play the game. At thirty-three years old and 5'4", 130 pounds, Eve is the toughest cornerback and the truest quarterback there is. It is said that Eve could play Division 3 college football and do well. She has a tremendous arm, is a smart scrambler and never misses demonstrating her unparalleled wit. The unfortunate side of Eve is an amazing case of hyperactivity, which brings along, as a side dish, the attention span of a cockatoo.

Ironically neither Eve nor Wendy are big enough to look menacing. They are rough, crude and excellent football players, albeit two demented people who wreak havoc on their friends. The fact that they both live on copious amounts of candy does not help either of their unfortunate maladies. They criticize and make cracks at everyone including each other. Some of us laugh, others find them offensive, and Kim incessantly argues with them. So Wendy and Eve are gleeful to see Kim quiet for once and move closer to hurl a few barbs, before she inevitably erupts back onto her feet.

"Kim, you ok?" asks Sarah, who is genuinely concerned. The medics have a penlight and are shining it into her eyes.

"She'll be fine," clucks Eve. "I'm sure we'll find her spleen around here somewhere." Eve congratulates her own humor, by mimicking the Heisman trophy stance, and chirping a quick "Oh!"

Kim can barely squeak back at her.

Bobby, the ref who has been reff-ing the league since its inception many years before I arrived, shoos us away. "Let her have some air you guys. Kim, if you can get off the field, we'll get going. We still have two more games to play and the days are getting shorter and shorter this time of year."

"Yeah, roll your cheap size triple x's off the field! We have games to play and it's 3:00 on the dot," Eve can't help herself.

"Thank you, Big Ben," Kim responds. The bickering resumes and we are back to our competitive selves.

CHAPTER 16

VISUALIZATION TECHNIQUE

My mom can heal anything.

My heart flutters as each Sunday approaches, and I imagine myself scoring touchdowns. My dad taught me this 'visualization' technique and I think back to when I first realized how effective it could be.

I am eleven years old. I am in our front yard throwing my football and trying to make it go through a hula hoop. I have hung the hoop over a magnolia branch. My dad drives up in Shitty-Shitty Bang-Bang, and comes over to see what I'm up to. I show him by dropping back and firing the football at the hula-hoop. It doesn't go in.

"Toady, if you visualize yourself doing something, you can do it easier when the time comes to do it. It's almost like making it happen." He takes the ball from me, closes his eyes for few seconds, then opens them and throws. The ball goes right through the hula-hoop. It makes sense to me so, besides throwing the ball accurately, I 'visualize' myself doing lots of things. One is holding a goose at Zephyr Lake. There are so many of the big birds and I wonder how it would feel to wrap my arms around one and lay my head on its back kind of like I hold my pillow at night. I 'visualize' hugging that goose tight, the creamy, soft feathers doused with the scent of clean air.

A few days later, Karen and I are cruising around on our bikes after school when we spot an injured goose by the lake. Without hesitation, I scoop up the large bird, leave my bike in the park—no one ever bothers anything in Zephyrhills—and hold the big bird tight, while balancing on the seat of Karen's bike as she pedals us home to Mom. My mom can heal anything. She has revived and raised baby squirrels that have fallen out of their nests high in trees, bunnies nearly run over by lawnmowers, a possum that came riding into the house on our collie's leg, a preemie goat, a fawn with a broken leg, motherless calves and even a broken-winged turkey that my dad 'visualized' as the perfect dinner as it healed, but couldn't get past my mom.

"That birds been through enough without you filling it full of lead. What is wrong with you that you want to do such a thing!" she says to him. Once the turkey got better, she made sure my dad was nowhere around and we drove it to the ranch and turned it loose.

The goose drapes it downy neck over my shoulder while I cradle it, whispering into its air-fresh feathers to 'hold tight—help is a few pedals away.' "Hurry Ka! He's not going to make it." And he doesn't. When we come to a stop, the goose is limp and his eyes are closed. My mom comes out and pronounces the goose dead, and Karen and I cry and so does my mom. We bury him in the back yard and Mom puts some of her homegrown rose petals at the bottom of the grave and a few whole roses on top.

But it isn't until the hummingbird incident that I realize how powerful the 'visualization' tool can be. I am fascinated with hummingbirds. They move so quickly that I can't study them the way I want to, so I 'visualize myself' holding one, petting its little head and stroking the frangible wings and microscopic feet. Several days later, my sister Annie, home for the summer from college, yips that there is something stuck in our pool screen. I run to where she is pointing and disentangle the long beak of a dead hummingbird from the screen, then hold its little body in my hand. I pet its tiny head, stare incredulously at its wings, and marvel at the birds' minuscule feet. Then it hits me. I have done this. I have 'visualized' holding the bird, but I never specified that it should be alive.

It is my fault that the hummingbird is dead! I killed it! And I killed the goose, too! I wail to my mom, confessing my sin to her and my two sisters. Jan and my mom try to soothe me, assuring me that it was God's will and Annie agrees, saying that the bird 'rammed its beak into the screen because it was his turn to die.' Then she takes the hummingbird body out of my hands and puts it in the freezer. "Let's save it. Maybe we can have it stuffed for you." We don't and my mom eventually buries the tiny bird next to the goose and other unfortunate creatures who have passed away in our care. From that point on, I am very careful about what I 'visualize.'

Today, I can't imagine that by visualizing myself scoring touchdowns, I could cause anyone's death, so I feel safe doing that and I 'visualize' myself into the endzone three times to chalk up another win.

CHAPTER 17

GAMEDAYS

We are all twelve years old again, genderless and free.

Players from the eight teams, regardless of which team we end up on, know each other, and we study team tendencies like the NFL studies game tapes. Our studying, however, is usually done at a bar after a Saturday practice or a Sunday game.

One Sunday, the players from all eight teams head to Walters, the grubby little sponsor bar on 4th Avenue in Bay Ridge. The television above the foosball table has the Giants game on, as we push through the metal door and take seats at the long bar or put quarters on the pool table to claim "next." A typical afternoon involves recapping, taunting, teasing, laughing and often punctuating the day's end with an argument. Today is no different. I am sitting with Tanker listening to Wendy's perpetual grumbling.

"She sucks!" mutters Wendy about a player on another team. "She's slow and if she scores on us next week, I will never speak to you whores again."

"Yea! She runs the 40 in 4-ever!" says Eve with her follow-up fold into the Heisman stance. "Plus she's got hands like feet. OH! She needs to 'retiah," she adds in her Long Island accent.

Tanker bristles at this remark. "Hey now, don't you be talking like that about that girl. She's put in too many years to be getting no respect from you two clowns."

Kindness is the highest form of intelligence. I don't know who said this, but I do know that Tanker is kind. Leah 'Tanker' Woods is a 300-pound dreadlocked African-American woman playing both sides of the football. She's that good. Tanker loves her mama, football and the kids she teaches, with Mama always coming first. Special Education teacher by day, bouncer by night, Tanker speaks from the gut and her laugh, in addition to being contagious, is organic. She fears nothing, especially life, and she is able to bear hug every drop from it.

One of her students, Lily, is a problematic child who lost her mom to a drug overdose, and was being raised by her grandmother. This was hard because Lily was extremely hyper and had a propensity for hitting other people without prompting.

Tanker, in an attempt to reach Lily, sat her down one day, and told her all about football. Lily was amazed to hear that girls played football.

"Yes! Girls play football—kinda like the NY Jets and Giants!" says Tanker, and she showed Lily a flag belt and her jersey from the Sharks.

"Only girls play on your team?"

"That's right!" answered Tanker. "There are teams for everyone now. Football's not just for boys!" After Tanker explained the game to Lily, she started to teach her math, using the numbers of the players on the field. "If three players leave the field for a water break, and there were only eleven to start, how many ya got left?"

Lily wound up with a good score in math, but was still beating up on the other children in class, so Tanker took her out to recess.

"Now, I'm gonna show you the only time you should be hittin' someone and how to do it right." She showed Lily the 3-point stance of a lineman on a football team, and then showed her how she could come up out of the stance and hit people. Hard.

"No!" said the child "When I hit people in school, they tell me I am mean!"

"Not in football!" answered Tanker "That's the game, but if you want to play, you have to promise to only play with me. You can't hit other people in class. That isn't football, Lily. That really is mean!" Lily agreed.

On offense, Tanker plays center because of her size, but she can catch and kick also. On defense, she plays tackle and those who know her are not shocked to see her large body suddenly horizontal and high off the ground, as she dives for a flag. A parallel observance would be seeing an Orca breach the water to pick a small fish from a trainer's mouth. Ironically, Tanker only eats fish. More ironic still is the fact that the Sharks' entire frontline, each one large enough to enter in a rodeo, are vegetarian. You can't make this stuff up.

Today, Tanker proudly wears a thick gold chain with a large cut-out 'Tanker' hanging from it.

"What does this signify?" I asked her when we first met.

"That's my name!" she said

"I thought it was Leah."

"Don't nobody call me Leah no more! My name is Tanker. Leah 'Tanker' Woods."

"How did you get that name Tanker?"

"One day when I was playing against the Killer Bees, I was a pulling guard and I came around the end and launched a few people into the air. Someone in the stands yelled down that I hit like a Tanker truck. So that's my name ever since. Leah 'Tanker' Woods!"

Just then, Sarah walks over to our group: Wendy, Tanker, Turpie, Eve, Piper, Dulce and myself. She reads aloud from a flyer she's found about an upcoming National Flag Football Tournament in Key West in February.

Sarah reads enthusiastically, her pink hair tie clinging to her ponytail, as though even it was exhausted from her energy. "A 'National' tournament! The defending Champions are the Maryland Crabs—they'll do in a pinch." She laughs, then looks at us seriously. "We're gonna go and we're gonna win! Those Crabs might as well stay home. Save the gas," she says in her flip manner, and tosses the flyer onto the bar. Case closed.

"What do jew all think?" says Maria "Dulce" Rodriguez, our 5' 6," 145 pound Puerto Rican cornerback from Staten Island. She is a divorced substance abuse counselor, with long brown hair and a thick accent. Dulce loves motorcycles, men and football.

Her young daughter, Charlotte, always attends practice with Dulce and sometimes acts as water girl. Kim says Dulce sucks, but she doesn't. She is a good player and a passionate one. Wendy says Dulce has the brains of a squash, but she doesn't. In fact, I am in awe of Dulce. She is the eighth child of eleven. Raised by a gambling-addicted mother and an alcoholic father, by the time she was twelve she was already on the road to a twenty-one-year drug addiction until two of her brothers intervened and cleaned her up. She has been clean and sober for many years now.

"We are going, right?" Dulce asks. No one replies because it is a moot question. Of course we are going! She starts gathering her scattered trinkets on the bar putting them into her purse: lipstick, small mirror, cell phone and sunglasses. We know by watching her that she is going into the bathroom to ponder the question that no one is answering. In the bathroom is where Dulce has 'thoughts' as she calls them. "I had this thought..." or "A thought struck me today." Seems like Dulce is always being struck by thoughts and now, as if she felt one coming on, she whirs like a fleeing pheasant towards the bathroom, her purse bulging with girlish items and seals herself inside with a click of the lock.

"I don't understand why she has to go into the bathroom to contemplate things!" I state in a querying voice. Tanker stares at the door momentarily then turns to answer me. "What do you expect from someone who spent puberty in there. It's the only place she feels secure."

Twenty minutes pass before Kim legs it across the room from the pool table to the bathroom and splats against its door, since Dulce has it locked. She spins around to see who has witnessed her crash and observes our group.

"Jerks," she grunts at us. "Why didn't you say someone was already in there?" Just then, the door flies open and Dulce emerges. A strong, sweet scent tumbles out behind her not unlike potpourri gone awry. 'Potent' is an adjective well placed here.

"HOOOOEY! What did you do, roll on an old perfume bottle?" says Kim as she wrinkles her nose in disgust.

Turpie, ever the polite one, tells Dulce that the scent is nice, which evokes a wide grin and Dulce points it right at her. "You are soooo sweet to me. Always have been and in case you're wondering what it is so you can get some for yourself, it is called Beautiful. I mean—that really is the name of it" she is smiling coyly. "It is made by Este Lauder—and I promise you, when I have it on I AM beautiful!"

"Too bad Este doesn't manufacture 'Intelligence!'" Eve says flatly. Always quick-witted, she can't resist the shot at Dulce. The Frigidaire is re-opened and Dulce's cold stare glaciers across Eve.

"Eve Edwards" says Dulce as she rests her hands on her hips "Sometimes I have a good mind to jus tell you what I think!"

Turpie, always trying to patch things up, follows her. Turpie is the 'fixer' of our world. Her soothing manner and persuasive skills are the glue for our tattered, bickering souls.

"Dulce, you know we all put up with them. They don't mean anything."

"They are always saying mean things. Even to that girl who doesn't have an arm and was trying to play." Turpie ponders the statement, trying to identify which of the Sharks does not have a full complement of limbs. She comes up blank. "The one who broke her arm at work, but came to practice and tried to play." Dulce reminds her, and the cloud slowly passes from Turpie's mind. "They said she sucked and was stupid and then gave her a Notable."

"Dulce, what's a Notable?"

"Those two give out awards like when we were seniors and got voted on stuff? Like Most Likely to Succeed and all? They voted her 'Most Likely to Have her picture in the yearbook again.' I hate them."

"I know," says Turpie. Then she and I go sit with Tanker.

"Look at Fat Fuckin' Kim," says Tanker, and I do and I look around the bar as we immerse ourselves in long ago desires that were, and still are, in reality, our true selves. We jeer and taunt, loudly and obnoxiously. We hate and love simultaneously. We drink, sing and often stream out of the bar and into the street interrupting traffic and not caring. We are all twelve years old again, genderless and free until our fall Sunday slowly dissolves and suddenly, without choice, we are someone else.

CHAPTER 18

TOP TALENT IN THE COUNTRY

*I fit in well enough, if for no other reason than the fact that
we all love the game of football.*

Just as Sarah predicts, the swaggering Sharks win the Women's Flag Football League's National Tournament in Key West, Florida. This earns us a name in the world of women's flag football. To be exact, the name is: "Those Goddam Sharks," but we are touted as the top talent in the country! Rude, top talent, classless, even, but respected in a fearful kind of way. We are New York! There is no other city like us. There is no better women's flag football team! And, yes, it is only flag football, but that is ok. I am over the tackle thing anyway. I am pushing forty and playing in this league with my friends is all I expect from the game of football. No more letdowns and rejections from naive childhood dreams. My sister's words of long ago were right. I am "just a girl." That's the way it is and what the hell, this is fun, this flag gig. It's competitive, yet offers a camaraderie that is my glue. I fit in well enough, if for no other reason than that we all love the game of football.

Underneath it all, however, is a rivalry and a seriousness that no one cares to admit. We are competitors and we crave the opportunity to prove ourselves. For some players, rivalries go back as far as elementary school. Rivalries no one ever had a place to showcase in an athletic arena. Scores that were never settled because there was never a way. So you see, as a Shark and in our small world of flag football, winning does matter. It isn't at all how you play the game.

CHAPTER 19

THE PHONE CALL

There's a man from the women's tackle football league on line seven...

I have manifested a wonderful life in New York City. Though people told me I was crazy, I purchased an 1837 brownstone on Bank Street in Greenwich Village. I have a partner I adore and feel secure with, and I have great friends in the entertainment industry. I have a green and yellow Senegal parrot named Dina who has bonded with me and we are best friends. I love my job at Time Warner as Vice President of Creative Services. When interviewed, I was asked by a woman in Human Resources, what I liked doing best, and what my strong points were. I answered her as best I could, and she told me Time Warner wasn't in the market for a quarterback. I told her I was only kidding, of course. I'd play halfback if I had to. She liked my humor. I got the job and I was especially pleased to tell Mom and Dad.

"I got the salary I asked for and, Dad, I even got a signing bonus!" They both sounded very excited for me.

"Well, Toady, we are real proud of you, but we sure do miss you here!" says my dad.

"My buttons are just popping off down here! You know, Christine, sometimes you just have to toot your own horn!" says Mom and a few days later I get a manila envelope in the mail with a horn in it. It's about eight inches long and has a rubber ball at one end that looks like a clown nose. When you squeeze it, it honks. My mom's handwritten note inside tells me it's for a bike, but it's all she could find and that she and my dad are 'all smiles about my new job' and that I should 'toot my own horn more often.'

For my job, I travel to Los Angeles frequently to direct photo shoots and to meet with design studios, and in New York, I am building a top creative group of artists for our in-house program of packaging and marketing music. Our offices are in

Rockefeller Center, and every morning, as I come out of the subway and make my way to 1290 Avenue of the Americas, I tell the universe how happy I am! I tell my mom and dad too, when I call them to give updates.

"I don't know Toady," says my dad. "I'm not much for that big 'ol city, but I'm glad you are having fun."

"It didn't take too long to win that big city over. We are real proud of you!" adds Mom.

My life-partner, Ellen, was not as easy to win over. Tallish and slender, she has the biggest blue eyes I have ever seen, like those of a china doll; clear and deep; conversation-stopping. She glides in and out of rooms, conversations, lives with beguiling sophistication; and a calm nonchalance as if to atone for yesterday's boorishness. We met through a friend at a dance club, which is ironic since I can't dance. But I can drink scotch and she wasn't bad at it herself, so we stood there and embalmed ourselves with Dewar's, while others we knew jerked their appendages around in the center of the room. One night, while watching Ellen's slender fingers clutch the scotch and water, I asked her out.

"HA!" was her surprising response. I thought she liked me, despite the nine-year age difference. "Call me when you're thirty."

The next year, I turned thirty and called her. As they say, the rest is history. We had been together for four years when we bought the brownstone.

And now, it's a Friday morning and I am on my way to work. Sunday's game is less than 48 hours away and my mind is on nothing but that. We are to play Kim's team and I hear Wendy's crude voice: "Fat son-of-a-bitch." I am thinking of the plays we will run and as I walk down the crowded sidewalks of the city, I play my made-up game of 'Team Pedestrian.' I am the ball carrier. Everyone going my direction is blocking. Everyone coming at me is trying to tackle me. I hit holes, stepping up my pace and I slow behind lead blockers, waiting for the right opening to break. I cut left. Right. I lean sharp up the middle. If I am touched by a pedestrian (tackler) or if I break stride, I am down.

I 'radio-host' my progress as I work my way to the office remembering how I used to do it in our front yard at home. Donning my Sears Roebuck orange and aqua jersey and my Miami Dolphin sneakers, I run to the front yard for a quick game before dinner. There are two small magnolia trees about forty yards apart that are the goal-lines and I place pine cones that have dropped from the tall pine by the circular drive as ten-yard markers. Then the game begins. Some have imaginary friends, I have imaginary teams, usually jammed with New York Jets or Oakland Raiders since I am a Dolphin and they are the Dolphins biggest rival.

"Davis goes left on a keeper, dodges a would-be tackler and breaks for the sideline. Great block from her big pulling guard and she springs ahead for another four yards, hurdling a linebacker, and then, switching the football into the other hand, she cuts across the field towards the middle. A quick move puts her down the seam and OH NO! ... from out of nowhere, the free safety brings her down after a gain of 37 yards and a Dolphin first down!" Today's play-by-play announcing is exactly the same. Only the setting is different, and the people are not imaginary.

We have to win Sunday and with these new plays I am conjuring, we can take Kim's team! My favorite is the inside reverse. I run the sweep a lot, which takes me around the ends. I expect Kim to overplay the outsides, thinking I am sweeping and that is when Dulce will take a handoff and cut up the center of the field. Tanker, playing guard, will pull around the center and make a path for Dulce to run to daylight.

I am picturing it all in my mind and become so excited my heart is beating fast. I am nearly running without realizing it and I have passed the street where my office is. I turn around and tilt my head towards the tall buildings downtown and say, "Come through New York, come through!" Though I have been in Manhattan for many years now, I am still chanting my plea and awaiting results.

I have a beautiful office, lots of perks, a staff of seventeen with an unlimited stable of freelance talent stretching from coast to coast. I am on the verge of self-actualization, something I have only read about when, on this same Friday afternoon, while sipping a three-o'clock cappuccino in my neatly decorated office and listening to Balanchine CD's for which my staff is creating the packaging and promotion, the phone rings. It is not unusual for the phone to ring and it does this continually throughout the day, but this ring has a certain octave, a tininess, unlike the others. As usual, one of my two assistants on the other side of my closed door picks up. Moments later, she buzzes me over the intercom.

"A man from a... women's tackle football league?...on line seven." she says feeling certain she has heard wrong. I am puzzled and stare at the phone. I recall Wendy and Eve's version of 'Senior Notables,' those things in high school yearbooks like 'Most Likely to Succeed', 'Best All Around,' things like that. As a senior, I had received two: 'Most Artistic' and 'Most Athletic.' But only one could appear in the yearbook, so I honored my passion for football and chose 'Most Athletic.' The picture in the yearbook shows me on Paul Filmore's shoulders stuffing a football through a basketball hoop. I look pleased even though I had, at age seventeen, received society's brutal assessment of athletic women loud and clear. Passions and dreams had become synonymous with pain and rejection and although it had taken nearly twenty years, "Most Athletic," had finally faded and "Most Artistic," was doing very well in Corporate America.

And now that silly passion for playing "real, tackle football" was knocking from the far side of the glass ceiling. I sit at my desk and repeat my assistant's announcement: A man from a women's tackle football league? On line seven...that's my jersey number, the one I've had since I was a kid at home...number seven.

I push the button and say hello. A man introduces himself as Kendall Covington and tells me about his two partners, Joey Minor and Trent Rankin. He tells me they have formed a football league for women. He says it was several months ago that this football idea crossed their minds. I suspect it hadn't been a long trip, but I say nothing. They held try-outs somewhere in Louisiana or wherever they were, and filled positions for two full-contact NFL style women's football teams. He tells me hundreds of women had shown up and two teams, replete with 45 players, a staff of coaches and the three of them, were born. All at once I become skeptical, because of the past; angry, because I am now too old to play and excited because of the concept. Mr. Covington, however, is not a good salesperson. He sounds too smooth, he mispronounces words, and I begin to suspect he wants either dates or money. Still, I listen.

They had christened the two teams: The Lake Ponchartrain Minx and the Louisiana Vixens. I have a bad feeling about the name 'Vixen' so I look it up while he embellishes his successes on speakerphone. Here's what I find:

Vixen/vik'-sen 1. evil person, 2. a shrewish, ill-tempered woman: witch. LEECH

Then I look up 'minx' because he tells me the logo on their helmets is a curled up fox-like thing. However, knowing what 'Vixen' means, I am fairly certain the 'Minx' they have in mind is not a fox. Here's what Webster says:

Minx/min(k)s 1. a pert girl, 2. obs; a wanton woman.

'Wanton'...aw, dammit, now I have to look up 'wanton.' I always have to look up some word. My years of high school were some of the best times of my life, yet I did not depart campus a cornucopia of knowledge. Being in New York has made me wonder how my life would be different today if I had gone to a private school. Surviving New York thus far, has taught me that I'm not stupid--just extremely uninformed.

Now, 'wanton'...where, where, where is it, as I thumb through the dictionary. There it is.

Wanton/'wont-n/ *adj* deficient, wrong, 1. hard to control, mischievous, 2. a: lewd, bawdy b: causing sexual excitement: lustful, sensual.

BINGO! There is the intended translation. I shake my head at the not-so-subtle suggestion that there is something shameful about being a woman in this society. The sense of outrage rises like a high tide across my body. While he continues his diatribe, I utilize Google, the new way to search the web, to see if there is any info on 'Kendall Covington' and his football league. There is. The first is out of the Medford Courant and i scan the article and quickly find this:

The WPFA's league office – "Nation-Wide Sports" -- is based in Monroe, Louisiana. It is staffed by an answering machine that apparently isn't checked often, which might explain why league officials, CEO Kendall Covington and president Joey Minor went a month without returning phone calls from The Courant.

But as the story goes -- and the league has gotten its share of national press -- Minor came up with the idea of the WPFA while serving as a tour manager for the Women's Professional Bowling League in 1992. He approached Covington, who was running an NFL wannabe, the Mid-Atlantic Minor Football League. Covington called a friend, Alex Newelle, who invested $40,000 to birth the baby.

Of course, there may be another explanation for the reluctance of Covington and Minor to talk up the league: The fly-by-night nature of Covington's managerial past, a long list of unpaid debts, broken promises and lawsuits chronicled recently by the Pierre Press, does little to engender confidence in his ability to keep a promise.

"It's not like I'm saying I'm never going to pay," Covington told the Pierre Press about debts estimated at $40,000. "I am going to pay...when I get the money."

Uh, boi....

Though the two teams have, I see, played in several different arenas across America, the three founders, Kendall, his partner Minor, and his other partner Rankin, according to the accounts of many people quoted in many articles, are scoundrels.

Fresh from the West Sentinel:

Kendall Covington and Joey Minor run the league. Minor came up with the concept as tour manager for the Women's Professional Bowling League in 1992. He submitted a proposal to Covington, head of the Mid-Atlantic Minor Football League for NFL hopefuls.

The league was in trouble from the start because of a lack of money, then was further damaged when news surfaced about Minor and Covington having checkered pasts. According to Louisiana court documents, Covington has been arrested nine times, mainly for unpaid services involving his minor league football operation in the state.

Minor spent time in a Louisiana prison for two assault convictions in 1986 and 1989.

Uh, boi...

But I am still listening, as Covington, Crook Number One, tells me he has heard of our Sharks. He had, in fact, found us from an article in the New York Times, which listed my name as the quarterback of a team of very talented athletes despite our big mouths and unruly behavior.

Goddam Sharks. And now, Crook Number One wants to combine his Vixens and Minx (which would give you, according to Websters, evil shrews causing sexual excitement. Whoo-hooo! Bring the whole family!) and come to New York to play us. He is challenging us to a tackle football game. A REAL tackle football game! AND the possibility of "forming" a women's pro football league. A REAL Women's Professional Football League! I am shocked. I am thrilled. I am forty-fucking-one years old! NOW the fat bastard calls? Jesus H. Chrysler with a flat! He is twenty years too late!

"So, let me get this straight." I say while skimming articles about their multiple frauds. "You want the Long Island Sharks, along with the other players of our flag league to come up with enough women to field a tackle football team? And you will send us a coach, pads, helmets, uniforms, pay for a field, drive your team to New York and play a TACKLE FOOTBALL game?"

"Yes!" says Crook Number One and for an instant, one lost instant, I am without sense.

"You are so on!" I reply and the saga lurches into motion.

CHAPTER 20

WORD GETS OUT

Will players who've been rivals in the past,
come together as a team?

Life changes. It changes in particular, for my friends and me in the Brooklyn Women's Flag Football League and, it changes on this Friday. All because three guys in Louisiana have come up with the idea of a women's professional football league and they name it the Women's Professional Football Association. They have created two teams. And now, these two teams and coaching staffs, along with these three suspect guys, are traveling around the country playing each other to take America's pulse about women playing football. The Sharks will play an exhibition game in New York against the Louisiana Vixens, a precursor to seasons of women's tackle football across the nation.

"That sounds like fun!" says my partner Ellen, who is half listening to my story as she reads her mail. She pays only slight attention to my flag antics and this is no more than that. "The New York Times declared that football has usurped baseball as America's favorite past-time." She adds, always one to be up on current Times reports.

I scratch Dina's head as she leans into my neck from my shoulder and remember reading through Ellen's report on Senegal parrots before I got this tiny bird. Ellen, a student of meditation, serenity, chakras, pita, vatta and all that, was not a fan of boisterous birds and their propensity to communicate in voices that penetrate rain forests.

"There's a small kind of bird from Africa that doesn't screech so loud. The South American ones are louder for some reason," she says and I'm not sure if that is true. Then, on a long weekend in September, she and I walk into a parrot store in Stamford, Connecticut. There, swinging from a rope attached to each corner, is a wooden tray packed with Senegal parrots. At least twenty of them. Swagged in green, gray and yellow, clown-footed and bright-eyed, they all watched as I approached the tray. And they all walked away in their little pigeon-toed steps, except for one who requested my finger. She wrapped a little clown foot around it and helped herself onto my shoulder. That was ten years ago.

She sits on my shoulder now, while I leave answering machine messages to players on the teams in our league with the info and quickly receive their replies.

"Oh my GOD!" is all Sarah can say and she repeats it many times before she drops the phone and goes running off somewhere to tell her dearest confidant, her dad, Thomas, a retired NYC cop. Sarah is the youngest of Thomas's four girls. The other three are married and otherwise occupied with life, but Thomas and Sarah have full and fast-paced lives due to her boundless zest.

"A message from God is what I was waiting for, and I found it on the answering machine," says Tanker.

"God answers prayers," says Dulce, our fervent Christian. "He told me I would have something new to do and he doesn't care 'bout some of the 'de odder tings' I was planning. I gon' do this. I am in." She tells me God talks to her all the time and recants pieces of their conversations. I notice that He speaks without much thought for the rules of spelling or grammar, but it seems many of us, including God, think the league, in theory, is a really good idea.

Unfortunately, Larry, Mo and Curly are at the helm. I hope they don't steer the vessel right down the toilet. At least not before the league is in place, franchises are sold, schedules are made and the New York Sharks Women's Professional Football Team, from a long-standing passion, is born.

CHAPTER 21

FLAG TURNS TACKLE

Relatively tall, I habitually hunch over, so my height won't attract attention and sometimes I am quite certain no one knows I exist.

I try to think of us, the players from the eight flag football teams, as free agents. I like to use that term, because it is an NFL term, and sounds important. An announcement is made and the interested players from the eight flag teams agree to meet at Cow Meadow Park on Long Island to see how many want to play the tackle game. Then we will, after a short, informative meeting, have a practice.

It doesn't go smoothly.

The eight teams in the Brooklyn Women's Flag Football League are like tribes that have been warring since the Indians traded Manhattan for baubles. How do you tell eight tribes of women that they must cull and combine to form one big tribe for one huge war? A war where the stakes are about so much more than football. What if we really do get to play? What if it really happens? Suddenly, I feel visible and extremely self-conscious. A girl—no it is worse than that—a grown woman wanting to play tackle football, to be a quarterback, no less. In the south, even the word 'woman' has negative connotations—one who isn't a proper 'lady' gets called a 'woman'. As far back as I know, girls are barely entitled to occupy space on this planet.

There was a horrible event long ago in a town near Zephyrhills where a young girl disappeared while walking home from school. It was all over the news and everyone in town talked about the progress of the search. It felt personal since she lived so close to us and a few people in town knew the family. One night I am at Heidi's house for dinner. Her mom has made a fresh pitcher of iced tea and is pouring it into tall glasses at each setting on the table. Her father has just gotten home from work so we are ready to eat dinner. The TV is on in the background, and we are listening to the update of the search for the girl. Heidi's brother, Larry comes out of his room and casually pulls his chair out to slide in behind his plate.

"I don't know what the big deal is. It's just a girl." Heidi and I don't say anything because it feels strange that he said that—like even if it had been one of us, we were not important enough for anyone to care. Girls have no value. Her mother never stops pouring the tea, but tells Larry that what he said 'isn't very nice.'

Her dad laughs out loud and reaches across the table, stabbing the largest piece of roast on the platter. He gives it to Larry, because 'he's a growin' boy' and offers Heidi and I the small overcooked end pieces. He doesn't serve his wife at all, and I think to myself that Larry may be 'a growin' boy,' but not in the right direction. I don't say anything though. This is just one of many similar incidents and speaking up will only stoke my temper.

Through the years, I have attempted to blend in with my surroundings. Relatively tall, I habitually hunch over so my height won't attract attention. I tend to say very little, and sometimes I am quite certain no one knows I exist. I have worked hard at invisibility and at soothing a corrosive anger, but now as I wait in the Cow Meadow parking lot for my friends to arrive, I feel there is surely a neon sign over my head. A big purple neon arrow with the silly-notioned words WOMAN QUARTERBACK above it, and it is no doubt illuminating every crevice in the five boroughs with a glow of foolishness. Even when I sleep, its lumens will seep in and make me feel... silly. Admitting my desires makes me feel embarrassed. Can anyone tell? I wonder and suddenly I don't know what to do with my own hands. They twine around my slender build from front to back and side to side. I want to unscrew them and put them away. They are just a nuisance to me, as I stand and watch players from the eight tribes arrive.

Bigger than life, both literally and figuratively, Leah 'Tanker' Woods shows up to Cow Meadow with a big grin. She tells me she has just come from work as a bouncer for a bar in Hell's Kitchen. She has been bouncing there for 20 years and everyone in the neighborhood calls her the Mayor of 51st Street. She knows all the dogs and all the people who walked the dogs and today, when she sees a few players with scowls on their faces, she tells me they look just like a very grumpy woman named Miss Eileen.

"She hated everyone! Especially the gays and the music that played too loudly at my bar. I said to her one day after she walked by and wouldn't answer my 'Hello,' I said "Why you so so mean Miss Eileen?" She doesn't answer, so I say "If you will just talk to me, I promise to help you be less hateful!" Tanker is laughing now. "She was a nasty ol' woman, lemme tell you! But she finally started talking to me. Miss Eileen complained about the music being too loud, the sidewalks too crowded, and all the bad characters that roamed her neighborhood because of the bar. So I told her I'd help her, and I got the DJ to turn the tunes down a li'l bit, and I put up a sign to make people be a li'l quieter when they left at night. Four months later, I was working on Thanksgiving Day and Miss Eileen showed up with a plate of food for me."

"No way!" I say.

"Yes way! She even said thank you. Ya see, I believe you always gotta treat people with respect and a li'l understanding. In over 20 years, I never had a physical altercation as a bouncer. Well....," she says, "except these two gay boys who were going to get into a fight at the bar. They were little gay boys and I lifted each one up with one arm and set them gently on the sidewalk outside. "Now you boys settle this out here and when you're done, come back in and drinks are on me. Only one drink though because I only make 150 a week!" she lets out a guffaw and throws her arms in the air. "They didn't laugh, but they did come back in. I just had to make 'em stay in their lane!" says Tanker. "That's respect. Stay in your damn lane. Some coach gonna make these savages stay in their lanes if they don't start smilin' and being grateful for this opportunity. But it don't matter who you are, I LOVE my teammates!" She hugs me so hard my feet momentarily dangle off the ground. Then she begins her teasing. She looks me over and, judging from my comparative low weight, asks "Which dwarf are you?" I don't find it funny, but I grin and wish for 30 more pounds. She continues.

"It ain't so much the up and down Christine...ya got some good height. But the side to side is gonna kill us!" She emits her signature belly laugh, and tousles my hair. "It's all good, my friend, it's all good. I ain't mad at you at all."

I am 5'8" and 120 pounds. Tanker may know big and bold, but I know fast and furious, and have every intention of proving it. And I am always able to outrun her, though not without effort. For a large person, she can move.

"Remember, Christine can run," says Turpie who always asked me to stay after our flag games to practice pass routes. She wanted to be better and I never tired of throwing the ball, so she ran routes and I passed until we were both tired and satiated. Then we would sit around in our cars, telling each other versions of the stories of our lives; those that were factual, those misremembered, some true, some invented and shortly, we understood enough to feel protected by each other's company.

Tanker scans my feet and rolls her bugged brown eyes. "If I wanted to hear the pitter-patter of little feet, I'da put shoes on my cat." Then comes another belly laugh.

"Ignore her," says the raspy voice of Kim, chief of the ancient tribe of 'River Rats.' "The aliens forgot to remove her anal probe when they dropped her off." It is awkward for some of us because we have such intense rivalries on the field, yet we always acknowledge each other in civil settings.

Nearly all of the flag players gather. 'Little Toni,' chief of the Rottweilers. Stoic Piper from the Raiders. Deb, Jessie and Snacker from the Killer Bees. 'Queen' Louise from the lost tribe of Hawks, Disco-ball Carol from the Breakfast Club. Big Dot and Juana from the Inferno. They all come. More than enough to form the New York Sharks Women's Pro Football Team, even if only for the one upcoming game against the suspect trio's combo team.

But the tension between tribes is intense. Even after the trio's appointed coach arrives, a former New York Jet named Johnny Belmont, the newly melded team is difficult to control. There is a good bit of chilliness floating about everywhere and Coach Belmont's senses it. He calls everyone together. His voice is boarding school confident and clear.

"I'm Coach Belmont and I understand you want to be football players. Well, I'm going to turn you into football players if you will let me. But you're going to have to do as I say. Can you handle that?" He looks around at the group of women. Black, white, gay, straight, large, small, Northern, and well...me, Southern—a strange concoction of personalities. We are uncommonly silent as we digest his statement.

"How many here love the game of football?" We all raise our hands. "How many here love your teammates?" only a few raise hands. "How many here love your teammates when you're on the field?" a few more hands go up but not all. "I don't see everyone's hand and until I do, we won't be a great football team. We can be a good football team, but I'm not here to coach a good football team. I want us to be a great football team. If you want to win, you are going to have to let Cupid shoot that arrow straight through your hearts because when you are on that field, you better damn well love your teammates."

Cupid had truly shot us straight through the heart even though some of us show it differently. Some loved the game but also loved divisive behavior. It is lodged in them somewhere dense and malodorous as if Cupid had aimed at their hearts but their asses were so much bigger.

"Let's start with some drills so I can see how each of you move. We have a game in two months, so I won't waste time we don't have." We follow his instructions and eventually move into a quick scrimmage.

"That was a good read," he says to Sarah after she stays home as a good linebacker does and makes the play up the middle.

Big Dot, not the recipient of his kind words, speaks up. "You didn't compliment me, Coach. I just did the same thing. Why don't I get a compliment?" We await Coach's response, which is slow and deliberate.

He looks her up and down. "You have nice socks," he says and turns to Dulce, whose hand over her mouth helps suppress a squeal.

"The swim technique," he continues, "is one way to avoid getting 'chucked' off the line when going out for a pass." Big Dot is silent, but even silence for Big Dot is loud. Feeling the tension, several of the players become jumpy as if a series of specters has recently been appearing to them and they might be compelled, at any minute, to put in some fancy footwork and leave. But Big Dot says no more as Coach Belmont assesses our skills.

Talent is abundant. We have speed, good throwing arms, good hands and, several besides Tanker weigh in at a 'svelte' 270 pounds. This is comforting when visualizing a front line, but the truth is, we are losers. I know this from our first day. Not in our abilities on a football field. But in our maturities as women and athletes. Since childhood we have harbored dreams of being recognized for our athleticism, but in reality, none of us have received that acknowledgment.

When I received MVP of the high school volleyball team my senior year, my art teacher came up to me after the banquet, hugged me and told me how proud she was that one of her best art students was also good at sports. My teammate, Susan, standing next to me when my teacher told me this, didn't speak to me for three weeks. Finally, she confessed to me that it wasn't the award she wanted. It was someone to tell her that they were proud of her. Some compete just to win or for love of the game. She competed for acknowledgement. For simple recognition of her efforts.

Even today, competition surpasses simply earning a position on the team. The Sharks fight over jersey numbers, helmet sizes, practice shirts, practice shorts, which size football to use, which one of the footballs to use, what field to practice on, which end of the field, which sideline to stand on, who should stand on which sideline, where on the sideline shall the 'anointed ones' stand, where will the rejects stand, who are the 'anointed' ones anyway, and who are the rejects, who should be captains, who shouldn't be captains, who should be on the field at kickoff, who shouldn't be on the field ever in their lives, who should or shouldn't suit up, who should have never, ever even had the audacity to show up, who should die immediately for their sin of showing up and, last but not least, which ones are worthy to do the killing!?

As Coach Belmont lines us up in potential positions, Wendy mutters under her breath.

"I'll kill 'em all!" she finally coughs into the air with her deep voice, then continues to mutter complaints and insults about the coaches and her teammates. Her blurts and tantrums are famous within our league of flag players and we have learned to ignore her outrageous insults, which are directed at no one and everyone. Helmet throwing is high on her list, accompanied by repeated information that we are all stupid, talentless and are wasting her time.

"I could be doing something to make money instead of watching you try to teach these people who are NEVER going to be any good." she says to Belmont as she stands, arms crossed at her self-appointed position of free safety. "I'm playing here in case you didn't know."

"You'll play where it best suits the team," says Belmont. Wendy rolls her eyes at the coach and sits down on the grass, the proud pilot of an improvised life.

Many years ago, after we had been playing flag a long time, Wendy's brother, Phillip, passed away. A few years older than Wendy, he had been in an accident when he was a teenager that left him paralyzed. I meet Wendy's mother and father for the first time at his wake. Wendy's father tells me about Phillip's athletic prowess before the accident. How quick and how big and smart an athlete he was. He talks about Phillip's good friend Max Bryce, a former Giant's player and how, even in 4th grade, Max was so much better, bigger, stronger than most boys.

"Phillip was like Max." he says. "He could have gone all the way." I glance at Phillip in the casket and bring the conversation back to Wendy and how amazing her athletic skills are. Like Phillip's must have been. And how Wendy's are. Today.

"She must have gotten that from you." I say. He grins and agrees, but isn't serious. Sincere, just not serious. Like her talent doesn't matter, her skills don't count. No wonder her rage can propel her into the end zone. No wonder her anger flirts with self-destruction. She has weighed the value of her ability against the value the world has assigned it and knows she got gypped.

"Can we fuckin' play some football now!?" Wendy spouts holding her arms out to gain support from her teammates.

"A strain of Tourettes...you'll get used to it!" Kim says to Coach, as she legs it to her assigned position of defensive end.

Kim and Wendy are at constant odds, but today, Kim shows tolerance. Must be due to her excitement. Wendy, the loveable malcontent, continues splattering deep-seated issues on us like Pollock paints a canvas.

Big Dot from the Inferno is assigned center on the offensive line. Big Dot, —245 pounds worth of large—has an even larger personality. Yearning to be an actor or a club singer—she's undecided—she is always looking for an audience and will create one even if she has to be unsportsmanlike. She decides to taunt Carol, the Rotties' large, African American nose guard whose pear shape is greatly accentuated by the bright yellow football pants the Rotties have worn to the practice. Big Dot and Carol are lined up across from each other. Semi-talented, temperamental and notoriously lazy, Big Dot is always causing uproars.

"Hey. Lil' Black Sambo don't look so lil' in those 'fugly' yellow pants!" Big Dot is starting on Carol. "You gonna be chasin' round and round after these runners today 'til you turn into butter, Lil' Black—I mean BIG Black Sambo, so them yellow pants is gonna mean more 'cause they are yellow like butter." Her taunt turns into rambling, and I am thankful to see Carol taking her three-point stance and ignoring her. When the ball is snapped, Carol gets around Big Dot and stops a dive up the 'A' gap. Quick to point fingers and blame others, Big Dot turns on Jessie, our assigned left guard.

"Ring, ring." she says and her hand is next to her ear with an imaginary phone. "It's the Lawd. He wants to know if you need a path parted to the gym so you can get fit enough to make your block. You gotta MAKE those blocks now, Jess. Come on!" Big Dot has a hard time owning up to her own mistakes.

"That wasn't my fuckin' block!" Jessie's eyes get big and she puts her hands on her hips. "I block OUT on a dive one! Carol is your block!"

I have been placed at quarterback for the temporary set-up. "Huddle up!" I command and they gather around and lean into the circle. I call an inside dive. "One-fifty-two. Dulce hit the hole and bounce out. Big Dot will nail the linebacker, right Big Dot?"

"You got it. Let's go!"

"On two." I say and we begin to line up.

"Ring, ring!" Big Dot is back on her imaginary phone. She is calling poor Carol and making fun of her pants again. "It's the Lawd again. He says he's looking down on this field and he's seein' something down here lined up across from me that's yellow and bigger than Rhode Island! He wants to know if he should make it a state and call it Yellow?!"

Carol comes out of her three-point stance. She is drawing in a lot of air and raising her imaginary phone to her ear. "Ring, ring! It's the Kettle returning the Pot's call. Kettle says shut the fuck up before I bury yo black ass!".

"Ring fuckin' ring!" Tanker's voice has joined in. It appears to be a conference call.

"It's Tanker and she's wonderin' if the sorry-assed coaches are in the house today and if they are..." and she never gets to finish because one of the afore mentioned coaches blows a whistle and throws a yellow flag. Little Toni, who has been standing mute at wide receiver, screams and points at the flag.

"The Got-dam flag is the same color as Carol's pants!" Whistles are blowing from all three coaches.

"Ladies, you can't behave like this if you are going to play pro ball! You'd get called for unsportsmanlike conduct. Twice. One on you" and he points to Big Dot "and one on you!" and he points to Tanker. "We would be penalized thirty yards and we'd be lucky if he didn't include another for cursing!"

"If I were reff-ing, I'd call the game!" another coach yells. "If you ladies can't behave, a good ref will call the whole game!" Now he's made me mad. I know for a fact that players in the NFL use language that would embarrass Satan, yet he feels we 'ladies' need to 'behave?' That our expressions of frustration should be monitored and curbed to please his programmed views of how women should behave?

"They can't just 'call the game' for disruptive behavior," I say and I am heated up. "And watch who you're calling a 'lady!'" I spit the word 'lady' at him as though the very meaning of it is pure insult and he should apologize to us for such derogatory speech. In truth, I don't know what I'd like to be called. 'Girl' is not correct. We are adults. 'Woman' is harsh and sounds like a putdown. But 'lady?' Sounds so old as well as old-fashioned. What is our word? Where is our place? I wonder.

I walk several yards behind where he is spotting the ball to huddle us up. I want to call a play and have him "accidentally" get caught in the middle. I want to throw a "bad" pass and "oops"— watch him have to stop the game to pick leather out of his teeth. Instead, I call the huddle and try to settle everyone down.

How will this group of seemingly hostile New Yorkers pull it off? To be victorious, we will have to unite and believe in each other. There is no power of belief in the air. Instead, there are the remains of an underlying struggle and the inevitable defeat that all of us as women have experienced. I know this because those feelings take up space in my head as well.

We have defended the essence of who we are and fought to be ourselves. We are the masons of the walls we have raised, and the artisans of the masks we display should our walls tumble. Our love of football can break down the walls, but our masks remain barriers to each other. We all have strikes against us just for showing up. To be born into this world a curious and zestful female, is one strike. Two strikes if you are black. Three if you are gay. Our team has all of the above, plus other odd concoctions of humanity.

I reflect on my best friend, back when I was around seven, an African American girl named Taylah Abernathy. For some reason when I was in elementary school I referred to my friends by their first and last names together. So whenever I mentioned her to my mom it was always Taylah Abernathy. One day my mom picked me and Taylah Abernathy up at school. She often did this because Taylah Abernathy lived across the field from us and could easily walk to her house from ours. There were some other kids waiting for a mom to pick them up. They were going to swimming lessons. Taylah Abernathy didn't know how to swim. She was very curious about going to a pool and taking lessons and said that she wanted to go, too, but when the mom arrived and heard that Taylah Abernathy wanted to join, she was clearly not comfortable. The mom was attempting a lame excuse when my mother, noticing what was going on, told Taylah Abernathy that she had someone teaching swimming lessons at our pool and that she could come to our swimming lessons which were, just like the other kids' lessons, going on that same afternoon.

When we got home, Mom told Taylah Abernathy to go get her bathing suit and come back for the swimming lesson. Then she called Eric, Annie and Jan's good friend who was a lifeguard at the pool, and hired him to come up and give Taylah Abernathy swimming lessons. He did, for two weeks, until Taylah Abernathy learned to swim. After that, we spent so much time in that pool, me and Taylah Abernathy, that my blonde hair turned green from the chlorine and hers turned into a spool of wire. I can still see my mom coming to the glass door every few minutes to check on us. Every now and then, she would get in and float around with us.

"You girls can swim like fish!" she would say and I would do a poor imitation of Flipper squeaking and bouncing on the surface of the water and Taylah Abernathy would paddle into the deep end and tread water and grin at my mom like she had just won an Olympic swimming medal. My mother always understood there was no need for disparate threads in society. This knowledge just came naturally to her. This way of bringing us all into the same pool.

The Sharks, however, are diving into our journey not as a band of conquering heroes, but more as a group of confused warriors encouraged by few to better ourselves or to fight for the chance to play. And not just tackle football, but to play this competitive game called life. And if you do choose to play, make sure you don't win. It isn't lady-like.

CHAPTER 22

1010 WINS

"That's Christine Davis, quarterback of the New York Sharks of the WPFA getting ready for the opening game against the Louisiana Vixens this Saturday."

The big day is coming closer and for some reason, I am chosen to do the sound bite for 1010 WINS news radio, a very popular New York City AM news channel. The radio reporters come to my job in Manhattan. I follow them to the lobby of the building where I work to record the piece because they want me to shout the cadence as if I am on the field calling the play. And I do albeit in a very self-conscious way: "White 220! White 220! Set. HUT! HUT!" It is to air the next morning, so I get up early and pull out my tape recorder and await 1010 WINS news and soon I hear the announcer begin talking about us:

"Some Long Island football players have something to prove in the battle of the sexes."

Then I hear my voice: "White 220! White 220! Set. HUT! HUT!"

"That's Christine Davis, quarterback of the New York Sharks of the WPFA getting ready for the opening game against the Louisiana Vixens this Saturday. For Davis, it's something she's dreamed about since she was a little girl. Do you ever remember scoring a touchdown against the boys and thinking 'Hey! I can do this?" he asks me.

"All the time!" is my answer, and I let out a little a laugh that can be heard all over New York City. He finishes the spot.

"The Sharks aren't making NFL money, but they are making history. Sean Montone. 1010 WINS News.

My parents have no idea what is brewing in NYC, or that I have been attending practices for nearly two months for this one upcoming event. Somehow I felt they would disapprove, I don't know why. But after the announcement hits the news on 1010 WINS, it feels real. Almost important. I can't wait to call them after work to tell them about it and play them the cassette. My heart beats fast as I dial their number and I ask my Mom and Dad both to get on the phone. I choke back tears, as I explain to them about the upcoming football game. It is such a proud moment for me, yet I am terrified that they will be critical.

"It's a REAL game!" I say and my voice cracks, but I try to sound like it is simple fun and nothing more. "They want to start a league…a pro football league and I am one of the quarterbacks for the New York Sharks. Listen to this! I was on 1010 WINS this morning. EVERYONE in New York City listens to 1010 WINS!" I am emphatic as I beg them to feel my excitement. "Listen, Mom and Dad! Listen!" And I play the recording into the phone receiver. There is my name, my voice on a major NYC radio station. Me. The REAL me being a real QB for a PRO team in a PRO league with pads, helmets and all. This is really going to happen and I am going to play. I am finally going to get to play! I am so excited that I don't need a radio station for all of New York City to hear me!

Listen, Mom and Dad! Listen! Hear me. Please.

The lump in my throat is hard to overcome and I can barely speak after the recording ends and I put the receiver back to my ear.

They try to sound excited, but what I hear is less than enthusiastic. Or maybe it is what I don't hear. Then that little baptism of sadness washes over me and I am hollow, even soulless. I feel so embarrassed, so silly. I know they don't mean to make me feel that way, but I am overcome and overrun with the insecurities of being female and the shame of loving a forbidden sport.

My voice quivers and I pause to rebuild a wall of words. A wall that allows the three of us to dismiss the event as insignificant, juvenile fun and then move on to other topics. This feels 'every day' familiar and I wonder if it will always be like this? Will anyone ever look deep? Or are all events supposed to skip like stones, one, two, three times over the surface of the water before they sink into the abyss of self, never to be exhumed, and too often, unremembered? I should let this stone sink but I can't. My teammates and I are skipping like school children through a mined playground, but we can't turn back now. We won't turn back. Maybe after the game, the stone will sink. Battered, but safe on the other side of our journey, maybe then the run will be over and it will be time to rest. But not now.

CHAPTER 23

OUR FIRST TACKLE GAME

Win or lose, each woman on the field belongs to the same team.
We are challenging societal norms and expectations
to make our dreams come true.

The day of the big game, December 11th, 1999, is undoubtedly the coldest day earth has ever produced. I am "hypothermia" cold, and we can hear each other's shoulder pads rattling as we shake within. It is three quarters into the game and I have not gotten to play. Not surprising because I am told early on that I am too small to be effective and the coaches have never given me much attention after that. Another quarterback, Juana, is out of the game after breaking her arm and QB, Eve Edwards, isn't moving the team. The score is 6 to 6.

I never thought I would say this, but I am so miserably cold, it begins not to matter if I get into the game. My lips are blue, my teeth are chattering and I want to go back inside and stand; as we all had at halftime, in front of the warm air from the blow-dryers in the locker room. It is a frozen tundra out there, wind howling through the black night, temperatures dropping to way below freezing, and despite Ellen and three of her friends sitting swaddled in blankets, up in the stands, I am numb and unwilling to move. How will I throw? Even the plays I have practiced for weeks are iced over in the caverns of my frozen brain. I am a replica of a body undiscovered from the ice age. Our three coaches will have to pull out ice picks and "chink" me loose from the gelid sideline to get me on the field.

But as we approach the end of the third quarter, the three of them are getting desperate for something to happen. Poor Eve is producing nothing but three and out. And though the coaches have not bothered to learn many of our names, I know they are coming my way when I hear one say through the howl of the wind "Look. There's another one over there. Number seven."

A human! (pick, pick, chink, chink) My GOD! It's been frozen for over forty million quarters!

I hear a deafening thump of a fist on my helmet and feel a force shoving me onto the field. "Put her in. See if she can get somethin' started."

Who MEEE? Aw, shit.

I run, stiff as a forty-one year old tin man, onto the field, limbs aching with each movement.

"Huddle up!" I yell into the wind. "We're going to run Jet left" which is a screen pass to Jade Max. I hate to break the huddle, as it is a small source of warmth, but we break and assume our positions. I am in shotgun and looking across at the other team. I have never seen them from this perspective before and can't help noticing that they are huge! All of them over there, roving around, a galaxy of planets, each large enough to have their own climate! A warm one, no doubt. I try to visualize the heat of the upcoming hot shower, as I call for the snap. Then I see the icy, little brown football leave the ground between the center's legs and go rocketing over my head. Piper has snapped the ball too high and when I reach up to try to stop it, my arm cracks off! I am certain of it because I hear a horrid noise fly out of the left sleeve of my jersey, then I don't feel my arm anymore. I look behind to see the wind blowing the ball away from me. My arm must be somewhere back there, too. I turn to go after it. Everyone thinks I am chasing the ball, but the truth is, I want my arm back!

I catch up to the ball and fall on it, which really hurts! That ball is a petrified rock! I lay there waiting for the other team to slam into me, wrestling for possession. And they do. One after another, until a crushing mound forms on top of me. But something happens during the pile-up that makes the unpleasantness worthwhile. As I lay there waiting for the layers to unpeel, my facemask is no more than six inches away from the facemask of one of the Vixens. We stare at each other momentarily. Her eyes, replete with eyeliner, blink several times.

Due to our society infused guilt, women, when remotely close to being an inconvenience to another person will say, "Sorry!" The Vixen, feeling she has terribly inconvenienced me, says this right into my helmet as she extricates herself from the pile of players. "Sorry!" she says loudly. This triggers my own ingrained issues and I courteously reply, "Sorry!" thus triggering reflex cries of "Sorry's" from nearly all the players on both teams, regardless of what has happened on the play. "Sorry's" reverberate across the field and outward to the far shores of Long Island. Yes, I am over forty, yes, I am frozen, but I pause after I get up to look at all the women on this field who display the courage to challenge society's definition of what a female may or may not do.

It is Tanker who picks me off the turf with one hand and sets me on my feet. She is now standing like a sentry beside me, hands on hips and huffing winter air. Sarah is helping a slow-to-get-up Vixen off the ground with genuine concern. She is smiling confidently, clearly loving everything that is happening and not missing one detail of the experience. Jessie is repositioning her arm pads, which extend like a suit of armor from finger tips to biceps and Jade Max is complaining to the ref to watch for holding! How can she run the pattern if she has to drag the Vixen secondary down the field? She wants to know!

The Vixens are somewhat celebratory in their sack. They seem unsure; like they want to celebrate, but perhaps it is inappropriate. It was a bad snap, so maybe they don't deserve credit, plus they are still on our side of the line which will make celebration all the more tacky. They give several sans confidence high fives while rumbling back to their side of the line of scrimmage. Piper shakes her head as they pass her. She looks at me with an apologetic plea, and I put my hands out to communicate that, "It's ok." And it is ok. Win or lose, right then each woman on the field belongs to the same team. We are challenging societal norms and expectations to make our dreams come true. To hell with the obstacles! It is the warmest feeling I have had all night. And I'm not sorry at all.

I get yanked the next play and Eve goes back in, but it doesn't matter. And later that frigid December night, the swagger and confidence of simply being New Yorkers triumphs over all else, and the New York Sharks beat the Louisiana Vixens 12-6. Eve Edwards emerges as the amazing athlete she is and throws, on the run, a perfect forty-four yard pass to Jade Max. Twisting and juking, Jade Max turns the final sixteen yards to our end zone into a dance of magic. The eight Brooklyn tribes, who bickered and bashed each other far more than our opponent, perform a beautiful, though ungraceful merging and the celebrations afterward consist only of talk about a real 'pro' team, a real league. We are high on victory and want another fix at any cost.

Not long after they drove the yellow cheese bus full of Vixens back to Louisiana, the suspect trio, despite low attendance during their "Barnstorming Tour," announced the formation of the Women's Professional Football Association. In hindsight, which is always 20/20, I can tell you exactly what they did. They realized the public was not going to give the support they had hoped, but they saw our reaction at getting to play. All of us, Sharks, Vixens, women, and girls in the stands that night, gushed with thanks for making dreams come true, for all they had done for us. For Christ's sake, I thanked them myself, profusely and without shame, and they never knew my name! Sarah, our star linebacker told a news reporter that suiting up and playing tackle football was the coolest thing she had ever done in her life. "I can die now" were her exact words. I have the interview tape.

We all felt that way. Thousands of females who heard about the Women's Professional Football Association wanted a hit of the football drug, and we made it clear that we would do anything, pay any price, cross any line, do whatever it took to suit up and get onto the field. We were desperate for a fix. This was the message we sent to the suspect trio and being the suspect trio; they sold us the drug.

CHAPTER 24

THE ORANGE BOWL OF
THE MIAMI DOLPHINS

How rare are the moments, when I do not feel gossamer thin,
but instead a solidness of self.

Kendall Covington, Joey Minor and Trent Rankin announce an All-Star game to take place in January in Miami. In the Orange Bowl! It isn't really an All-Star game. It is whoever can pay the three of them $500 and get to Miami to play. Nonetheless, I can't write the check fast enough. The Orange Bowl was the home of my beloved 1972 Miami Dolphins, still, the only team in the NFL to ever go undefeated through the Super Bowl! I would play in the same stadium. I am going, no question. Eve, Jade Max and Sarah send their checks in, too and we are granted a room in the roach motel provided by the WPFA. Many years ago, the hotel might have been up to the minute, but now it consists of two headboard-less queen beds, one chair, a rickety table with an outdated TV on it, and an off-centered 40 watt light bulb hanging noose-like, at the end of a brown cord. We are standing in the back of the room looking through a smudged plate-glass window at the Orange Bowl squatting in the distance. Eve offers candy, and we silently take a handful from a white paper bag.

"This hotel is a dump." I offer to no one in particular.

"A real dive," Jade Max adds. The sheets won't stay tucked in, and I warn Jade Max to keep her socks on as she patters towards the bathroom. Eve rolls a joint while staring out the window.

"There's no organization, no schedule or professionalism, but we don't care. This is all we have ever wanted to do," smiles Sarah and we continue staring out, each in our inner football sanctum with Miami's own Orange Bowl against its skyline. I finally finish staring, but say nothing. The others say the same.

We locate our practice field the following morning, with no help from the league representatives. We find a parking spot for our rented car and make our way towards the most logical location, a lined football field amidst many open areas. After a while, Kendall Covington gathers up the 50+ players who are milling around the bleachers and introduces himself and the coaches for the All-Star game. He says the group will be divided into the East coast and West coast according to where we are from. Our team, the East coast, will be coached by Trent Rankin, a former Kansas City Chief player who steps forward. He is tall and bald, a very muscular man, who has a way of putting us right at ease. We are instantly in awe. Trent is not one of self-importance or one of those somber men thickly coated in others' ideas of who he is supposed to be. He's having a good run of things and there is no shortage of happiness to spread around. His chuckle rises up through his chest, bubbles with joy, and spills across us. We are drawn in. To us, his words are biblical.

Trent and his assistant coaches get us fitted in pads first, and then helmets. Some have never put a helmet on, and I watch as they struggle to get into it and when they do, their eyes are large behind the facemasks, and they speak in a mixture of excitement and discomfort.

"It's too tight!" says one.

"It's supposed to be tight, girlie." says Trent with a big grin and grabs her facemask to look into her face. Her eyes are bugged out like a snail, and her cheeks are turning bright red.

"Mmm," remarks Trent and reaches for a larger size. It takes two assistants to remove it without popping her head off with it. I briefly reminisce about my sisters' Barbie dolls and the many unfortunate days of their headless lives.

"Just remember girls" Mom would say when she discovered a Barbie head between couch cushions or under a chair. "It does no one any good to lose your head." She would hold Barbie high to be claimed by one of my sisters. "And it's not very attractive either!"

We break into groups and begin to warm up. As a quarterback, I am on the field throwing and running basic hand-offs, when Trent comes over to me. "I'm going to tell you a secret," he says. "You'll have three reads as a QB. You got one when you're walking up to the huddle. Two when you're calling the cadence. Three as you're dropping back." He says "See, I'm a defensive player and I like to do all kinds of shit on the field when the offense is lining up for a play. I call it shit—lots of moving around. It messes with the quarterback. So what you see walking up and what is there when you're dropping back is gonna be different. Here's what you do." He is demonstrating the call and the drop. "For one, you look down too much when getting situated. You need to be looking around." As he does, his hand is flat while he "feels" the width of the field with his palm. "Your key is the free safety. If he's, I mean if SHE's alone dropping back, it's cover 3. Your split and flanker are one on one and you can hit the seams. If you see a cover two, the outs should be open. You have to read as you drop.

Your read is the safety." I try to absorb it all, and as confused as I am, it's the most fascinating thing anyone has ever said to me in my whole life.

Back at the hotel that night, Eve has gone to Miami Subs and brought back an abnormal supply of chicken wings. She says she can't eat them all, but we know she can. Jade Max and Sarah and I order pizza.

"Trent was showing us some great moves today!" says Sarah. She loves to learn, and this particular experience is appetizing to all of us.

"Yes!" I reply, "He was hitting the high ribs on me." They all look at me quizzically and wait for the explanation. "It's this thing my dad and I used to say when we got a kick out of something." I don't tell them the story but I go there in my mind.

When I was around eight, my dad would count my ribs. It was part torturous, but an exhilarating ritual and it always left me breathless with delight.

"I think we need to count your ribs!" He would announce without provocation. I would freeze and a grin would invade my face and I would shake my head 'no' but the smile overrode to 'yes.'

"Lay down on the floor and let's see how many you have today." As if I had perhaps grown a new one or two since the last inspection. I would stretch out on the floor and began laughing before he even got his long rib-counting finger near me.

"One!" he would declare as he pressed and wiggled his finger on the first rib at the bottom of my rib cage. "Two!" he'd say moving slowly up the side of my twig of a torso. I would try to refrain from laughing but was never successful. Taking his time, he would move to number three rib and by the time he arrived at seven or eight I was squealing and squirming and laughing hysterically. The higher the rib, the louder the squeals until I could not stand the delirium and had to wriggle free and bounce about the room in utter euphoria.

Learning football from Trent, an NFL player, made me jubilant. Each rib of information he shared made me more delirious with glee. This game tickled me, it loved me and I felt at home.

After Eve finishes her wings, she eliminates any sign of pizza in our room as well. She throws the empty boxes into the corner of the room. "The maids won't even notice, this place is such a dump." She turns on the antique TV sitting on the wobbly, scarred table against the wall. She finds an old re-run of the Honeymooners. We all wear protective socks as we go to sleep that night.

Day two, first practice. 10 AM, Flamingo Park again. We stretch and divide into offense and defense. Trent tells me to take a few warm-up snaps from CK, our center. The snaps are taken up under, not shotgun and we are to go over the passing tree. The ball we are using is youth size instead of the familiar and slightly smaller junior ball and I find it hard to get my hands around its fat body. I overthrow the receiver the first few times and CK decides she should tutor me on how to throw a football.

"Lead her," she says. "You want to hit her on the run." I shake my head to blow her off. "Shut up..." I say to myself, then I overthrow the receiver again.

"I hate these fat fucking balls!" I say out loud. "Why can't we use a junior? This youth size ball is killing me!" CK offers up additional advice. "You have to squeeze tighter."

"Shut up...." I say again softly as if I don't know how to hold and throw a ball.

"Hit 'em right in the numbers." She is still talking, as I put my hand between her fat thighs to receive the snap. She snaps it hard and I knuckle up knowing it's going to stab her where it counts. In Eve's language, 'It's going to hurt her box.' After that, she remains quiet until another QB moves in for a few snaps.

We are on the ground stretching for the second practice of the day. Five rows of us, seven players deep. In row three, player 5, I am on my back looking out through my facemask—nothing but blue sky, warm weather, and a bright gleam off of its bars from the Florida sun and the perfect sky. I am so happy and I feel the tears coming.

Seldom have I felt this solidness of self. How rare are moments in my life when I do not feel gossamer-thin in value, anticipating someone finding grievous faults with most moves I make. Even in our strengths, as women we are more often judged to be half-good, but here on this field amongst like souls, I am less of a stranger to myself, not a holograph image, fading and finding form, fading and finding form.

My teammates are counting in response to the drill leaders in front of each line. They yell ONE, we answer TWO, they yell THREE, we yell FOUR, all the way to TEN. There is nowhere in the world, *nothing* that I would rather be doing than this. We get up to start practicing plays.

And then it happens. Jade Max throws one of her signature fits. Trent is calling our names to go to positions and today; he has the audacity to replace her with another receiver. Even before he is finished calling the imposter's name, Jade Max has worked her gut into a small tsunami. Her hands are dancing, and she is trying to speak the words conjured by her fingertips. Then, suddenly, like a wanton champagne cork, it pops out.

"I just want to play football! I came here to play football. I need to be thrown some balls!" She begins to cry, and Trent tries to calm her down.

"Talk to me...tell me. What is it?"

"You don't understand Trent. You're a guy! You don't get it! I spent a lot of dollars and I missed classes to get here. I want to play!" Jade Max bleats. "And Bullet..." she gasps to reload, "goes out and gets drunk and still gets all the passes and all the attention!" Trent isn't sure what to do, but says he understands. He doesn't. There's no way he can. He says he knows she's upset because she loves the game, and he is right about that. He just doesn't know the feeling of loving the game and never being allowed to play. To us, it's the pain of unrequited love. To him, it's the drama of a long-term relationship.

"I wanted to play football so bad when I was little, that my dad finally bought me a football and I used to sleep with it!" Jade Max tells him. "When Dad and I went to sign up for the Peewee league that fall they told me I couldn't play because I was a girl, so my dad sued them and you wouldn't believe what we went through because of the lawsuit!" We are all listening intently now. "People in our town turned against my family and some people withdrew their business from my father's law firm. Some of the boys at school and even some teachers wouldn't even speak to me."

"What happened?" asks Trent.

"We won and I got to play but it wasn't easy being on the team. Only a few of the guys supported me. It really sucked because I was as good as them." Jade Max is really worked up and we are nodding at the familiarity of her story. We try to console, as women do, and Sarah tries to calm her down.

"We know you love the game. That's why we're all here Jade Max. We're all doing the best we can and you're going to get the play." We all nod in unison at Sarah's soothing words. She is a lesson in kindness. Nothing could be simpler, nothing could be harder than kindness and I wonder how someone so young can possess such insight so easily. Eve walks over to her bag laying on the sideline, pulls out a large can of deodorant and brings it back to the group.

"Alright, I'm passin' this around. Spray it on your boxes. Hooooooeeee!" She waves her hand in front of her nose. She has delivered the perfect icebreaker and even though it hurts to laugh because we are so sore, no one can stop. Trent is bent over and his eyes are squeezed shut he is laughing so hard and Jade Max is wiping her tears and laughing at the same time. And I love it! Everyone is blissful once again and one more tear streaks down my face for so many untold reasons.

CHAPTER 25

SARAH STEPS UP

Three days ago, we didn't know each other's names, yet at this moment, there isn't much I wouldn't do for this group.

First practice, third day. We lay in the sun waiting to begin. We are tired, stiff, but conversations are flying. Sarah suggests that we "Rise up and leave two by two, until we are all gone and there will be no more practice today." We all laugh. Just two days ago we couldn't wait for this to begin. Sarah gets up to stretch and walk around and accidentally steps on Bullet's hand as she lies in the sun. Bullet rolls over in pain.

"You are a walking calamity!" says Jade Max to Sarah.

"I'm so sorry," she quips to Bullet. "I killed four of your fingers. I owe you four beers!"

"Hey sis!" yells Tara, the defensive back from Atlanta. "Come step on my hand. Anything for a beer!"

"Sarah," clucks Eve. "I told not to waste your money coming down here. You can't play football!"

"Shut up Eve and let's get some fans in the stands," teases Sarah wearing her smile ear-to-ear as she walks over to a handsome guy who has paused his morning run to see what the deal is. She decants her smile over him and shows that special something about her which is magnetic while she tells him all about women's football. We know her magic has taken effect when we see him make a call on his cell phone.

"Yeah, there's a Women's Professional Football team practicing over here. They play in the Orange Bowl tomorrow night," he says. "Yeah, tackle football—the real deal! Pads, helmets, and all. I'm right here with them! Alton and 12th." he pauses. Sarah is excited about this enthusiasm. "Not at all, well a few, yeah," he says. Then he turns his head away from us and mutters something into the phone. All I hear is 'fat' and 'dyke,' but Sarah hears all of his words; cold, hard little rocks. Sharp-edged, and cruel.

Sarah's expression flames to anger and we hear her deliver a sharp "Go to hell!" as she turns and walks back towards us. We are looking at her for information, an explanation of her abrupt departure.

"We don't need fans like that, teammates." She says. "And don't ask me what he said. I refuse to repeat ignorant words."

So we don't. But for a minute, the sky looks miffed and bruised, a heavy blanket pressing down on us. Even Eve is quiet, as the familiarity of ugly images and remarks from the past fill our heads and our hearts and later, when I tell Sarah what I figured he said, she tells me I was spot on.

Today's practice is special teams. "Who can kick?" yells Trent to the team. I can kick so I try some PAT's---point-after-touchdown---and field goals. CK is centering but doesn't say much. Eve has inserted herself as the holder. The first of five or so go either through the uprights or very close. Then I kick one low and the ball hits CK square in the ass. She lunges forward as if she has been put into gear, but still has her foot on the brake, then falls over facedown into the soft grass. Everyone is howling! I fall on top of her, laughing uncontrollably and apologizing.

"CK!" I say "You have to admit, it was right down the center!"

"I see your foot can't get a hold of the ball either!" she says but she is grinning. The magic of football is happening. Three days ago, we didn't know each other's names, yet at this moment, there isn't much I wouldn't do for this group.

I'm standing in our roach hotel room again, looking across the city lights and over to the Orange Bowl. It is 8:30 PM. Tomorrow night, it will be lit up. For us. Because women's pro football has come to Miami and I am a part of it.

There is no practice tomorrow. Walk-through only. Today was our final practice. We had gathered around after our final drills and stood in the Miami heat as Trent spoke. "You are not women football players, you are not trying to be football players, you are football players! From the bottom of my heart, I am proud of you. I love each and every one of you and remember, it's your fault we're all playing tomorrow night in the Orange Bowl." He emphasizes "fault" and then poked at several of us — "YOUR fault! And YOURS!...and YOURS!" Sarah was grinning proudly. Jade Max and a handful of others were crying. Eve tells us we are all fuckin' crybabies.

The four of us get into bed that night lost in our own images, separate dreams about the same passion, the same magic. Living a passion is a carpet ride that flies you to that elusive elsewhere. Passion is a door. You fly through and do you return? Either way, you are never the same.

Only after the room is dark and quiet do we have one final utterance from Eve. "Any of you crybabies got candy?"

CHAPTER 26

THE MAGIC OF MIAMI'S ORANGE BOWL

"You are in the Orange Bowl.
You are the first women's team ever to be here and it's happening now!"

I am inside the Orange Bowl trying to be suave and nonchalant. I always try to be that way, mostly because I'm not sure what to do with drawn attention. Plus, it's embarrassing to be star-struck as are so many of the other players. It's difficult nowadays to be an individual instead of a collection of personality traits selected from the character automat. Seems we all work from the same dog-eared script. I don't want to be the one who is most star-struck at being in this locker room, so I'm cool, but always slipping my glances here and there, absorbing a place I never thought I'd be.

Players are suiting up, wrapping hands, ankles, knees. They are stealing looks, too, and we start stealing looks at each other stealing looks. It's a wonderland to us, a pinch-me feeling. Trent's pre-game speech confirms this.

"I can't psych you up any more than you should already be. You are in the Orange Bowl. You are the first women's team ever to be here and it's happening now! If that doesn't work for you, I can't do it. You know the time is now!"

Many of the players get choked up. And I, of course, do too. So much for being an individual. I am sure they feel like I do; real, authentic. Sometimes I feel like we have lived in the echo of our own lives. This time, we are the voice.

My heart is twirling like a kaleidoscope, as we walk through the tunnel and onto the field of the Miami Orange Bowl. My desire to play has been so pruned through the years that I am not sure if I will erupt into unchanneled joy or break down into a boneless, babbling pile of ectoplasm. Again, I find myself bottling my emotions---more containers to add to my belly basement of emotional stash: doubt, indignation, inadequacy and now, mouth-gaping joy and awe!

'THE CITY OF MIAMI WELCOME'S YOU TO THE ORANGE BOWL' is the sign stretched across the second tier of the stadium whose bright orange seats nearly glow. The east end is open and palm trees bend and beckon behind the tall, metal scoreboard. This stadium was home to Super Bowls ll, lll, V, X and Xlll. I am time-traveling, imagining crowds, names of players I followed who have walked out of this same tunnel, stepped into this same arena and hoped for nothing more than I do right now. To play and play well.

"I'm not really here, right?" It's Jade Max. She is laughing in disbelief.

"We are.... on...another planet....." I say, still standing with arms slack and jaw barely moving. My face is slowly scanning the stadium like an oscillating fan. Back and forth, back and forth. Eve and Sarah come up to us and Sarah's gratitude emanates like a heat source. She has her arms up and is reaching at the sky, silently jubilant. Eve is more expressive. "This is the most fuckin' great feeling I've ever had. This was worth every penny." I believe it to be Eve's first experience with reverence.

Trent is trying to corner his players and pull us back to the ground. It's time to play ball! Our innocence is pervasive. Some are waving at families in the stands. We are nervous, forgetting where and how to stand for the anthem.

"Helmets off and in your left hand." Trent bellows as Poodle, our fullback, trots over to the mic to sing the national anthem. It is the worst rendition anyone has ever imagined. Her voice cracks early on and, with the echo in the stadium, she slows down so much the music outruns her. The small but sympathetic crowd seated cozily behind the 50-yard line, chimes in to pick up her pace. There are no sides to be taken today. No one is screaming against the other team. Only a smattering of friends and family are here to usher our dream into reality. The impossible high note in the song comes and goes with all the players and the entire audience trying to hit it with her. We had christened the Orange Bowl with the most horrendous version of the national anthem in history, but it didn't prevent chills and butterflies and grins as wide as rivers.

The West wins the toss and teams line up for kick-off. I hear my name spoken over the Orange Bowl mic. 'Number 7, Christine Davis kicking off for the East.' There it is. That million-dollar feeling. The real me has materialized on the 35-yard line. Small and transparent before, but now, solid proof that I, too, am part of today.

When I was 13, my mom, astutely noting that I was different from the rest, indulged me in things that I was interested in. I loved photography so my mom and my Uncle Will set me up with a beautiful 35mm camera and all the attachments to go with it. Flowers, butterflies, scenes from the ranch—anything that didn't have people cluttering up the lens—were my favorite subjects. When I decided I wanted to try to develop the pictures myself, my mom called Dooley, our ranch hand in to build a dark room under the stairs in our basement. My Uncle Will, who had invested in a camera store, sent over everything I would need to furnish it and I spent hours poring through books on how to use the dark room. Then I put up a sign on the door: 'Do not enter without knocking!' and I disappeared, like a Hobbit, into a new world. I loved being under the stairs where images would appear from nowhere as I sloshed the paper back and forth in the shallow pans. It was magic.

One day I decided to enlarge a photo of me on my motorcycle. Alvin took it with my camera as I was coming over a jump at the track we had built. It captured the bike and me way up in the air and all the determination it took to get there. If I closed my eyes, I could still feel the bike in the air, but as I pushed the paper around the pan, the bike and I, transparent at first, became real. Solid. Proof that I was part of that day.

I am solid and high in the air again today as I deliver a pretty good boot and the game begins. Eve, playing corner is talking smack on the field.

"Hey, you're too slow to be a receiver. Heard you ran the 40 in four-EVER!" she pronounces it "for-EH-VAH!"

Sarah at linebacker is joining in and having a great time. The two of them 'shazam' knuckles after each good play, beautiful smiles bouncing off of happy hearts.

"Did you see that?" Eve is on tiptoes and in Sarah's face. "I hit that big number 78 full on! It was like two coke machines hitting each other! BAM! I snotted her!" She is pleased.

When we get the ball after three and out, I go in at QB. I try to read the defense, but there's so much about the complexity of the game that I am just learning. Thirty years too late, I might add. I see the corners playing tight on my receivers and know we should be able to beat them deep. I recall the chalk drawing in the locker room, defensive X's across from offensive O's. I look at the middle linebacker position now and see not just an X, but a big, live X, with eyeballs rolling back-and-forth over my front line and finally rolling to a stop on me. I want to call something—something that will outfox her but the defense is staggered and I am at a loss. So I stare back at her hoping she'll think I thought of something and get nervous. I stare and she stares and I figure I better call the play before time runs out. I guess neither of us will ever know if the intimidation worked.

I make so many mistakes, but I've never had so much fun in all my life. Once, I run the play without my full line.

"Christine," Trent says as I leave the field after 3rd down and we have to punt "You have to wait for all your line to get on the field and get set."

"Oh, details!" I say and he throws his head back and laughs. He is having fun, too. Everyone is making mistakes in their 'authentic' glory. The ball is hiked over my head several times. One of the opponents' players runs to the wrong huddle after a play. Both teams, twice, line up on the same end of the field for a kickoff.

But things go well for the Sharks players. Eve gets two interceptions, which is not unusual. I throw a pass to Jade Max which is complete, but we both get hit hard at the same time---me as I release the ball and her as she catches it. Upon return to the huddle, we are picking a fair portion of the Orange Bowl from our facemasks and laughing at being "concussed" simultaneously. For some reason, we are thrilled to say we got knocked loopy!

It's nearing the end of the game, and I am on the sideline when Trent starts yelling for "Kenny Stabler." My heart jumps because that's me! He calls me that because I'm a lefty like Stabler was. He pulls me over, calls a long pass to a very tall, leggy player from Alabama, slaps my helmet and shoves me onto the field with the play. I run to the huddle, shaking with excitement because, though I throw with accuracy, I am small and can't throw as far as some of the other quarterbacks. Trent has called this play just for me and I can hardly believe he has that kind of faith in my pipe cleaner of an arm.

"Guys," I say and I try to hide the shake in my voice. "I'm 40 years old. This may be the last time I ever get to play like this. I just want to say thank you for making this dream come true! Pro right, 34, bootleg left. Flanker, run a split. End run a six route and I'll meet you there." The ball is snapped and I bootleg out and I don't even see that leggy woman, but I know she's there. I throw the ball as far as I can in that Orange Bowl and step back to watch as she appears from nowhere and runs under it on a dead out sprint and into the end zone. Touchdown! Touchdown on my pass! Touchdown on my pass in the Orange Bowl! I have never been higher on life than this very moment! I sprint to the end zone and pick her up, legs flailing and I say "Thank you, thank you, thank you for catching that pass! That was so beautiful and I will never be able to thank you enough for catching that pass!" Trent is jumping up and down on the sideline as I come off the field.

"I've never seen a prettier pass!" He's yelling, his big grin stretched wide. "You need to call the office on Monday and get the film of that. I've never seen anything like it." I am bigger than life, bigger than the full moon, a huge lunar eye that just witnessed one of my greatest days. If I could put a stem on it, it would deserve a Tiffany vase.

Everything about that night is surreal. Even our mistakes are cherished. Poodle, our anthem singer and fullback, scores the TD because I gave the handoff to the wrong player. It was supposed to go to Paula, the second back. After the game, I am in line at the phone booth to call Ellen and my mom and dad. Poodle is making a phone call to her husband in California.

"He's my husband," she says to me in broken English while pointing at the phone in her ear. When he answers, she talks without taking a breath. "I scored touchdown!" Her round, happy face is a second bright moon over Miami.

My call is happy, too, but with reservations. I have learned that expressing my passion to play football is not the quickest way to gain approval from anyone close to me. Ellen doesn't pick up, but my parents are home.

"It was a perfect night!" I tell them. Mom is on the phone in their bedroom and Dad is on the phone in the den. "Dad, I threw a touchdown—she caught it on a dead run as she entered the end zone! You should have seen it!"

"You did! Well that's great Toady!"

"Yeah, it was a lot of fun. Our coach, Trent Rankin played for the Kansas City Chiefs! He said it was the prettiest pass he'd ever seen! I'm going to get a copy of it so you can see."

"Alright. I'd like that." He says and Mom says to "have fun and be careful and to call when I get back to the city." I say I will and we hang up and the empty feeling is there, but I'm not sad. I would like it if they had come to Miami to watch me play, but, to be fair, I didn't extend a formal invite. I knew Ellen would be impatient and not want to be around all the events of the weekend. I felt she disapproved of the tackle stuff. And if Mom or Dad came, I'd be worried about things: the dirty hotel, the roughshod players and their salty language, and what would they do when I was busy? It's work to monitor and worry. I squirm because I try to do and be whatever they want on the outside, but on the inside I have built another self, one that few can see. The football environment is for that self and it's easy. What is hard is constantly shifting from the outer shell to the meat of me. Sometimes I feel like a refugee in my own life.

CHAPTER 27

BACK TO NEW YORK CITY

Each play we run breaks a link in the shackles
and allows us to melt sweetly into a freedom we have never known.

The next day, I fly back to New York. All I can think of on the rainy cab ride to the airport is my name being called over the loudspeaker at the Orange Bowl. Three times I heard it! My name wafting across Miami's Orange Bowl. I can't stop the tears and they stream down my face like the raindrops trickling down the windows of the taxi. I have found and lost, bought and sold myself all in the capsule of a few days. The time in Miami was so much bigger than time in Miami.

I think of my dad and the two of us fishing for largemouth bass. We call the huge fish that everyone dreams of catching 'Old Josh' because that's what my dad called him when he was a boy. I am 10 again and we are riding in his big Impala across waves of pasture towards Weavers Pond. It is our favorite place to fish because we think 'it just looks fishy.' The bottom is white and sandy for about 15 feet off the shore, and though the water is clear, it gets dark when silt and brown, acidic leaves take over. Large round lily pads float under low hanging loblolly bay branches. You can see stumps and logs peering up while offering shadows in the under-bellies of their soggy torsos—all good places for Old Josh to rest.

I am envisioning our boat silently gliding towards the floating tussock that has run amuck on the east end of the lake. Appearing to be an island rising out of the water, it is actually a drifting mass of peat, mud, and plants. This one is about the size of my dad's Impala, scooched and stranded like some big, pot-bellied fish hung up on the lake floor. "It's a very 'fishy' place," my dad says and I agree.

The windows are down and I watch as hundreds of acres pass by. Sometimes the vastness of pastureland is comforting. Other times it makes me feel lonely. Big white clouds cast globes of shade into the Florida heat, but nothing squelches the crickets as they complain to the blades of grass they cling to. I am listening to them and wondering if that noise really comes from them rubbing their legs together, like my friend Karen told me. I ask my dad and he smiles, but doesn't answer.

"If we could catch us some of those crickets, I bet Old Josh might like them for supper."

"Too small, Dad. It'd be like having a parakeet for Thanksgiving instead of the turkey we're gonna shoot." We ride on towards the lake, prep our poles and are soon paddling towards the tussock. My dad fishes with a top water lure because he can work it through the lily pads like a pro and loves to see the bass hit it with a big splash. I prefer to fish with a 'springtail' worm because I like to be surprised when I pull on the line and find a fish on the end. I am sitting in the front of the boat decked in cowboy attire and sunglasses and I calmly throw my worm close to the tussock and let it begin to sink. Dad works the open water spots from the back of the boat with his lure. I have reeled the worm in and am about to throw to another spot when my dad leans across the boat and pokes me in the ribs with his long bird finger.

"Put yours down and take this." He whispers and hands his pole to me. "One just swirled at it and it was a biiiig one. Just jerk it a little," he says and when I get situated just right, I do. Seconds later, a huge splash wets the tussock, and the lure disappears under the roll of a large, spiked fin.

"Hold the pole up Toady!" Dad says and he is grinning. My eyes are big and I'm turning the handle on the reel as fast as I can to take up the slack. It is clearly a large bass and he is headed for deep water. The line goes taut and the drag on the reel sounds, and I am holding on as the nose of the boat slowly turns toward the tussock where the fish is headed. I am keeping the pole up as my dad has taught me, and turning the handle, when suddenly the fish comes up and out of the water. It is Old Josh! He is three feet out of water and shaking violently trying to throw the hook from his mouth.

"Pull it tight Toady!" says my dad and he is laughing out loud and I am so excited I can hardly hold on. Then the fish goes back into the water and straight down into the strong, wiry anchors of the lily pads. The line is still taut but I don't feel Old Josh pulling. "Keep it tight," my dad says as he paddles the boat towards the line descending deep into the lily pads. He carefully reaches down into the water and tugs at the line to see if the bass is still there. He is not. Old Josh has escaped. Dad holds up the lure and we see one of the hooks has been straightened out.

"Well look at that. Old Josh was so big and strong he straightened the hook and swam away." He is shaking his head as he looks at the lure in disbelief. "You did everything right, Toady. You played him just perfect, but sometimes they still get away." When he looks up at me, all he sees is a red face with tears streaming down from under my 'cool' sunglasses. Catching Old Josh was so much bigger than catching a fish. I knew this.

"We would've stuffed him and hung him on the wall," I say in a small, wounded voice as I wipe a runny nose on the snapped cuff of my cowboy shirt.

"Yes, Toady. We surely would've stuffed him. I bet he weighed fifteen pounds. I got a good look at him when he came out of the water. Never seen a fish be able to straighten a hook like that." We continue fishing into the evening, lost in Old Josh thoughts and the fine company we provide one another.

And now I can't stop the tears, because I know everything I did the past weekend is so much bigger than football. Women are being set free. We are flying. After years of being clipped, our wings are unfurling into colors and patterns that only God's eyes could've created. Each touchdown, each play we run, breaks a link in the shackles and allows us to melt sweetly into freedom we have never known. We bond. We grow. We fly. No more paper wings. As we splay our true feathers, they make an elegant, dry, rustling; the sound of antique taffeta in motion across a dance floor. And all eyes are on us and our splendor might finally be seen.

When I land back in my wonderful New York City I, for some reason, zero in on Midtown saying "Come through, New York, come through!" I feel I have won a round in our sparring game. My city has ceded me this one small feat. Just lately I've been pointing my chant uptown instead of towards Wall Street and the southern tip, and the tide seems to be turning. Maybe I've been yelling at the wrong end.

CHAPTER 28

NO ONE WANTS THE SHARKS

We keep on practicing my friends and me.
It is our dream and we know we have a shot at being really good.

Eleven initial franchises are offered for sale in the Women's Professional Football Association, the New York Sharks being one of them. Football fame and fortune are only two of the promises made to potential buyers. Sponsors are allegedly lined up, inclusive of Nike, Bike, Wilson and all the big names in sports. Televised games are 'in the works' and endorsements will follow along with merchandise, brochures, schedules, stadiums, coaches, doctors, business cards, contracts, trademarked logos, bank accounts, and insurance. Whatever you want, the trio promises it.

As a team of proud New Yorkers hailing from mythical, magical Manhattan, we are certain someone will pay the suspect trio the meager franchise cost of fifty thousand dollars. Having no doubt about this, we practice diligently and await our owner and coaching staff.

I am at practice on a Saturday morning in late July and as one of the quarterbacks and because we have not found an owner or a coach, I am trying to control the offensive practice and make it an effective one. Jessie offers coaching suggestions. We exercise Shark trademark by not listening. But still we work hard at it and manage to keep our spirits high. We keep on practicing, my friends and I. Coach or no coach. It is our dream and we know we have a shot at being really good.

The deadline looms closer and still no one wants the hot-shot NYC team despite our defeat of the Vixens, our formidable flag record, our big mouths and cocky swaggers. Without an owner, we can't play in the crooks' league.

I go home after practice one Saturday morning. Ellen, my life-partner of ten years now, is out with a friend again. I am listening to Vivaldi while observing the unfolding of a cloudy day from my window. It is customary that I listen to Vivaldi's 'Winter' from Four Seasons while warming up before a game or during a run, but sometimes I like to just turn it up loud and stare. So I do.

It is August of 2000, and another summer is falling like one more domino in a line tipping its way through life. An "owner" for the Sharks is not going to show up. It has been a silly mistake to get excited about this league. Soon the whole idea will fade into another disappointment. In a matter of months, the holidays will return and I look forward to going home to the family who always welcomes me back to the nest. I wonder what I will do when I don't have "home" to go to. Or what the feeling will be like when I am elderly and mine is the home to which others travel? Will I sit and reminisce about the times when I was the one arriving from life's journeys? And fifty years from now, those whom I watch while reminiscing will be sitting in their homes reminiscing. Like the domino days of summer, each falls away leaving only a part of themselves touching the next in line.

I am thinking uplifting thoughts like this when I decide to clean the house. As a ritual, I fuel my house-cleaning adventure with coffee strong enough to knock the hairs off a sweater. Like installing a fresh set of batteries, I become so full of energy I can glow in the dark and somehow this beverage makes life good. Who needs Mr. Right when you've got Mr. Coffee? I change the CD to Clint Black and turn it up really loud. Not one for domestic activity, I vacuum my bed and am loading socks and underwear into the top part of the dishwasher, when Clint's words from "No Time to Kill" hit me hard. My God, he is so right. I push repeat and listen to the song again.

"There's no time to kill between the cradle and the grave

Father time still takes his toll on every minute that you save

Legal tender's never gonna change the number on your days

The highest cost of livin's dyin'.

That's one everybody pays.

So have it spent before you get the bill.

There's no time to kill.

If you don't look ahead, nobody will.

There's no time to kill."

Dina has her pretty, feathered head cocked, looking at me, and I cock my head and look back. I am fortunate to have a passion... and a good job. My God! Was fulfilling my dreams that easy? Was I like Dorothy in the Wizard of Oz? All she wanted to do was go home and had she at any time, clicked the heels of her shoes three times; she could have gone.

"Think, Dorothy!" I said to myself. "If I were to purchase the team, all of my friends and I would have a team and get to live our dream. I don't have fifty thousand dollars, but still, there must be a way. I cock my ear to the stereo, as Clint's second verse proves even more inspiring.

> "If we'd known ten years ago
>
> today would be ten years from now
>
> Would we spend tomorrow's yesterdays
>
> and make it last somehow.
>
> Lead the cheers in someone else's game
>
> and never learn to play
>
> And see the rules of thumb are all the same
>
> that measure every day.
>
> The grass is green on both sides of the hill.
>
> There's no time to kill.
>
> If you don't look ahead, nobody will.
>
> There's no time to kill."

I dial up the suspect trio right then. I tell them "I might be able to pull off buying the team, but not for fifty thousand dollars." Also, I ask them if I can keep it anonymous. All I want to do is play the game, not be in charge of the entire operation.

"Make me a deal," I tell them. "I'll give you the money for the franchise, but just let us play without making a big thing over my purchase. If anyone asks, tell them it was an anonymous donation."

Realizing that there are eight million New Yorkers and I am the only one to step up, they do cut me a deal. For me: Twenty thousand. But Covington and Minor are adamant about having a point person and anonymity is out of the question. I reluctantly agree, but I am uncomfortable announcing myself as the owner. This will catapult me into a status I do not desire. These are my friends and I have a hard enough time fitting in, a ranching Floridian with a bunch of hard-core Brooklynites. Will they thank me or resent me? Will the coaches play me because I own the team, or because I deserve the position?

But I buy us. I buy the team, because no one else does. I don't do it to be a hero or savior. I buy the team because I want to play. And my friends want to play. And our dream is about to get away. Again! But it doesn't. Like one of those hokey dream catchers, I net the mother. All for the crooks' low, "insider" price of 20k which comes straight out of Christine's Bank of Football Follies, otherwise known as my Time Warner 401k. Seems like I have been paying the price to participate in sports all my life. I can still feel the very muddled emotions of being a 'girl jock' at my high school—comfortable because it was my authentic self, shamed because of the negative stigmas attached. I was strong and alert, not soft and delicate. I preferred strenuous, aggressive, competitive team sports, instead of individual, aesthetically pleasing activities that girls are commonly steered toward. As a kid, I paid with tears and humility. Today it was cold cash and high hopes.

CHAPTER 29

THE REDBIRD

*Still, people step up. In particular, Turpie, my dependable
wide receiver from our flag football team.*

I have purchased a business and want to run it like one, but there are several obstacles. One being my increasingly distant partner, Ellen. I can feel the change in the way she dismisses things I say. The way she looks at me no longer makes me feel seen.

My friends are becoming my employees and my employees are strictly volunteer. We have no money. And no one, anywhere, has any idea of how to run a women's pro football team.

Still, people step up. In particular, Turpie, my dependable friend from our flag football team. She very much wants to be the General Manager. Turpie is a good looking black woman, dapper always, and slicing the world wide open with her scythe-shaped smile. She is not adept on the computer, can not perform public speaking, can not compose professional letters of communication, but collecting hearts comes without effort.

"I saw the redbird today, buddy." She says to me as she turns the curve in the stairs leading up to my kitchen. A cardinal, according to Turpie, delivers deeply significant messages to us. She believes the cardinal she has been spotting is bringing messages from her mother who recently and unexpectedly passed away while sitting at a slot machine in Atlantic City.

"Really?" I ask. "Where?"

"He came to the window this morning. Looked in like he had something to say. I know it was from her buddy. I know it was." I nod in agreement and offer her some coffee. She shakes her head 'no.'

"I can't play tackle buddy. It's not my game, but I want to be the GM," she says, no doubt in her voice. "I know my mother wants me to do this." Turpie takes solace knowing her mother had been doing something she loved. In her mom's world, she was doing her own spinning, being her own little round of life, and she died a happy woman. Turpie is insistent that being GM is her answer, her own spinning, and that we would make a perfect duo with perfect alchemy. I offer her a place to belong; she offers me companionship in the foreign place of owning a sports team. Together, we are many edges; the same seeking, the same love.

"I can do this buddy," she is wielding that grin.

"I know you can. The job is yours." The void Turpie felt is now being filled with a new substance, a fresh purpose and belonging. To me, life seems a narrow path between freedom and belonging. I have rarely felt either and often longed for both. She leaves our meeting with a freshness in her step. She has a new bounce, a new spin; she's a new planet in a new galaxy. She is a new little round of life.

CHAPTER 30

NO SUPPORT FROM THE LEAGUE OR HOME

*Not suspecting what lies ahead, I sit on my roof deck and open
what is usually a cheery letter from my mother*

Everyone involved with the Sharks is optimistic, even when our tasks are agonizing. As my home life begins to lose form, the team agonizingly does the opposite. It isn't apparent at first, because we are all so excited, but the truth is, from the first minute, it was never easy. None of it goes down like the league promises. There are many late-night phone calls with the other owners, players, league administration and staff. Schedules are constantly changing, promises from the WPFA are nearly always broken and player's expectations of a "pro" league are unrealistic. They are looking for endorsements, advertising, television coverage and attention equal to the NFL players. It is hard to disappoint them, and hard not to show them my own disappointment. It is harder to get the basics together such as a website, publicity, communication, game day organization and so many things that you would never think about. Who will sell merchandise, food, tickets...who will create and pay for the merchandise, go get the food, print the tickets...details that people who aren't trained in such logistics would never think of until the moment they are needed.

Turpie and I spend most of our time scrambling to make things happen. The WPFA has not helped at all. Where were the marketing materials, the sponsors, the field and bus contracts? Where were the coaches they were supposed to send? Only one man applied for the coaching position, so I guess we had "decided" on Mr. Jack Oliver. Big Dot's brother Walnut will help, and our flag coach Hayden will show up when he can. We have a cow pasture to practice on, not the promised stadium, and no uniforms or equipment. It is only weeks before kick-off and the schedule is not even out yet.

At least we have gotten a doctor assigned to us who is a great help. Dr. Samuel Enriquez sets up physicals to be given at the clinic on Long Island and today is the day. When I pull up, the parking lot is infested with Sharks.

"Did I miss 'girl's night out?'" I ask the group in an attempt to be light.

"Yeah, by about twenty years! Oh!" says Eve. I laugh, as I usually do when she utters her quick-witted comebacks.

The lobby has been taken over as well. Sharks are filling out forms, signing in and being general nuisances as they wait their turn at stations: heart, eyes, ears, nose, throat, knees, weight, etc.

Always complaining, Wendy wants to leave because it's taking too long.

Kim walks past in front of me just close enough to utter remarks, which she thinks will be unheard. She leans in: "They told Tanker to lose some weight. HellOOOOO!" She still has another comment to let out so she circles around to the back of me, and grunts from the other side of her mouth into my shoulder. "She's hired a crane to take her home. How can she be any good at that size?"

"She was a size 6 when she came in," says Wendy, loudly letting Kim know she has been heard.

Kim ignores Wendy and leans her head in what she believes to be a subtle way in my direction. "YOU talk to her!" According to Kim, everything falls to me as the owner and now, even the player's weight. I go into one of the examination rooms and sit down. Eve boldly pushes into the room and closes the door. She is as football-obsessed as I am and we constantly talk about the game.

"Christine, I am so pumped! I am working out, I'm eating right, I'm in great shape! We're gonna kill some teams. KILL THEM!"

The door swings open and we expect to see Dr. Enriquez. Instead, Dulce leans against the frame, eating candy that Wendy has dispensed.

"Oh, it's you," Eve says. Unfortunately, Dulce can't argue that.

"I have it," she says and steps into the room.

"Take penicillin for God's sake!" Eve offers.

"I'm referring to the colors of our team."

"That's a done deal," I say. "Hopefully we will get the uniforms soon." I know Dulce's idea of uniforms would not make us look like football players. She would more than likely "upholster" us like an eclectic team of easy chairs in an Ethan Allen showroom.

"Whatever you're thinking, absolutely not!" Eve says.

"You didn't even listen to what I had to say!" and Dulce stomps her heel. "I know we're stuck with blue jerseys, but I thought if we picked a muted kind of blue. Like a robin's egg with a little bit of texture in it...."

Eve is disgusted. "Our jerseys don't come from a fabric bolt, Dulce. They are pre-made, blue mesh and we pick out numbers and names, then a nice color for those numbers and names, and the jersey man prints them onto the blue, mesh FOOTBALL jersey's!"

"Well, can we have the numbers in a complimentary color like..."

"The numbers are black." I cut her short to answer the phone. Ironically, it's the guy from our local sportswear company. Turpie made a list of names of players and jersey numbers and faxed it to the league weeks ago, but the league is just now passing the info to them.

"I know it's late," he says in a thick Brooklyn accent "but I want to confirm 'dis ordeh. You see, I'm reading dis ordeh and it goes like dis: Tootsie, Gentle Lady, Flagmeister, Chief, and I'm sayin' to myself—is dis a FOOTBALL team or am I reading a list of horses from the Belmont Stakes?! So I just wanna make sure I got de right list, ok?"

"Oh, GAWD," I say, "I need to call you back. No nicknames allowed!"

"Yeah, yeah and let me tell you something. Dis 'Gentle Lady'... I ain't makin no judgments, ok? But I'm tellin ya, she would have trouble walkin' onto a football field with dat on her back."

"I know." I say again. "I'll call you back, ok?"

As days pass, I become more and more skeptical of my decision to purchase the team. The first months in women's pro football have been a rollercoaster of highs and lows. Not suspecting what lies ahead, I sit calmly on my roof deck amidst potted plants and the sounds of Vivaldi and open what is usually a cheery letter from my mother, but it is not her normal update of things at home. Instead, it outlines her distaste for my decision to buy the team. She doesn't "think women should be playing tackle football," and she is sorry for saying so, but that is what she feels. It is money "not well spent" and, in so many words, a "bad business decision."

For an instant, I am 12 again, trading football cards with Walter and Alvin and the neighborhood boys. I need Billy Lothridge, number 7, on the Miami Dolphins to complete my set. Alvin has the card but doesn't want to trade it, because they are hard to find.

"I'll bet you for it," I say. "Whatever team I'm on will beat yours." He says "There's not enough people for football," but bets me a game of 'Horse.' "If I win, I get your signed Pete Rose card." The Cincinnati Reds trained in Tampa every spring, and we would badger one of our parents to take us down to get autographs on our trading cards. Walter's mom finally agreed, and when Pete Rose came out of the locker room one afternoon, we were there waiting. For some reason, he only signed a few things, and my trading card was one of them. He had passed Alvin by. That card was coveted by the whole neighborhood, but I put it on the betting block knowing basketball wasn't my game. When I lost the Horse game and my special card, I mourned for weeks. It had been a very bad business decision.

Approval of a parent is utmost in human longing, and this scolding for the road I have chosen is devastating. I put down the letter and, living my life in the manner to which I have recently become accustomed—I cry. Not long after, my phone rings and I hear the voice of my oldest sister Annie sending alarming disapproval through the wires as well.

"I just don't understand why you need to be doing this. It must be a bunch of angry women who want to go out and put on those funny suits and hit each other like rams. There is something WRONG with them! I'll pray for you, and you should do the same!"

My sister Jan is quiet in the background. She is usually the one in the family to support me, but her silence tells me this is not the case. I am furious. I am hurt, and for the first time in my life, I tell them to go to hell and with shaking hands, I slam the phone down. I am shocked at myself, but somehow, it feels good. I pick up Dina and kiss her little beak. She is an ardent Packer fan, and just now her green and yellow feathers ruffle. Her head is perfectly helmeted in gray and her little shoulders have pads of yellow peeking out of brilliant green. She had always believed in me from the first time we met at that pet store in Stamford when she walked up to me and crawled onto my hand and up to my shoulder. And here we sit today, still in the same position.

CHAPTER 31

THE ANTI-CHRIST OF
WOMEN'S FOOTBALL

I don't doubt that the unruly Sharks need some handling, but I never
expected methods consisting of bullying, belittling and badgering.

The purchase of the Sharks was meant to be a good thing, but I am getting no support. My father has summed his reaction up with his signature "Hmmmph!" and Ellen has not been her blue-ribbon best lately. I stare at a geranium and wonder if this was not going to be the journey for which I'd hoped. A sinister speculation flashes through my mind that, when it comes down to it, this Sharks saga might be something of a pill. This thought's lightning entrance and exit has taken at least forty percent off the entertainment value of the blue Manhattan sky and blossoming flowers when Ellen's "cheery" countenance blows through the French doors.

"Oh, am I happy to see you," I say to her while stroking Dina's beak with vitamin E oil. Since my familial support has not been arriving by the bushel-full, I am in need of a shot of pick-me-up and I tell her so. She tells me she agrees with my family and that she is going to one of our friend's houses in the Hampton's. She spins to leave.

"Can't you even say 'goodbye' to Dina and me?"

"Eack! Birds...on a plate or in a tree! That's where they belong!" She leaves after these words and only a slight residue of her perfume remains.

This is one more display of discontent shown by Ellen and I realize I can't endure anymore. I call the suspect trio and tell them that this has, perhaps, been a mistake and I would like to reconsider my decision. The trio is empathetic. They cannot, of course, return my money but they can offer assistance and, shortly after this heart-to-heart, they do so by sending to me the Anti-Christ of women's football.

"She'll help you out," says Number One of the suspect trio and hurries me off the phone by hanging up. Several days later, help arrives. One Milly Pamplon from New Hampshire. Or, as Eve quickly dubs her, Messy Tampon. We don't suspect anything at first, since we are still high on the football drug and she presents herself as our savior who has driven from New Hampshire to New York to help with "several things":

1. announce my purchase of the franchise and...

2. run the first official Shark tryout and...

3. "handle the team like they need to be handled."

I don't doubt that the unruly Sharks need some handling, but I never expected methods consisting of bullying, belittling and badgering. With great purpose, she parallel parks in front of the hydrant directly outside of my brownstone and I go out to meet her. The second she gets out of her car, she hands me her business card and stands firmly planted on short, tree-stump legs while I read it. Her chubby arms are crossed and the look in her round, beady-eyed face radiates self-importance. The card lists several titles:

Owner/New Hampshire Cobras Women's Professional Football Team

And in even bigger and bolder type:

East Coast Director/Women's Professional Football Association

Within minutes of meeting her, she volunteers to tell me that she holds a paid position in the league, that her team is far more advanced than any other team and that she, because the media is already insisting on following her and only her; will put women's football on the map. Those of us who wisely choose to follow her will be indebted to her for offering such brilliance to the fledgling sport in which without her, none of us are capable of success. She stops just before suggesting I swath her feet with cheesecloth and rare oils. Clearly, Messy Tampon of the WPFA sees herself as our omnipotent leader, the anointed one, the veritable pope of women's football. And if for some reason people aren't aligned with this belief, she is an officer of the law.

She sums me up, an obviously unworthy subject, and in her all-important manner tells me that if there is anything she can ever do to help, just let her know. Then she pulls out a New York Sharks tee-shirt from the trunk of her pope-mobile and tosses it to me.

"You can have it. I won't charge you. I'll see you in the morning at tryouts." She winks and speeds away, all super-hero-ey. The only thing she lacks is the cape. I put her business card in my wallet and go back inside.

The Sharks team is founded on passion, which is part of it's magic. We are in love. With the game. With our team. And who can account for love? Look at Rapunzel who lived upstairs in a castle with her long hair. Late at night, her knight in shining armor stands under her window and says "Rapunzel, Rapunzel, let down your hair." She does. It works. Point is, they could have taken the stairs but they were in love. We should have known then. But we were in love.

CHAPTER 32

ULTERIOR MOTIVES

Sheldon says I am free to go if I will sleep with him, and when I realize
what he has said, I want to throw straight up.

Also in love were the other ten franchise owners who are mostly women and mostly women who have always dreamed of playing football. Los Angeles Launch, Texas Bandits, Miami Waves, Montreal Mountains, Rochester Goldrush, Oklahoma City Coyotes, Tampa Tide and the New York Sharks. These are the woman-owned teams. The Denver Mile Highs, Louisiana Vixens and the Pensacola Stingrays are owned by men who try marketing their teams with the tired shtick of "sex sells." Posters are made of "Vixens"-- players in just shoulder pads, hot pants and seven-inch heels. They have long flowing hair, thick make-up and the figures of runway models. I finally complain to Kendall Covington at the league when one of the men's teams gets a sponsor from Dickens Cider.

"That's disgusting. The league should not allow that. It's degrading!"

"You should be flattered" he says defensively "that someone wants to sponsor a team!"

"I don't understand what is flattering about getting sponsored by some Troglodyte who is marketing a drink with lewd allusions to copulation," I retort.

He laughs. "At least they have a sponsor." I think of my latest attempt to garner sponsorship from a New York City insurance millionaire who also owns a men's semi-pro team in upstate New York. Somehow I get to present a partnership package so his men's team and my Sharks can cross promote our seasons. I am optimistic and excited at this prospect.

I am on time to our meeting at his impressive building overlooking Central Park, sponsorship package in hand. I am escorted by a woman named Louise into a large office replete with a fabulous view of New York City, furnishings from overpaid designers and, last but not least; the overweight owner of the men's team. His name is Sheldon. I try not to be disarmed by his initial slow head-to-toe survey of me. I focus, instead on the potential of sponsorship. We exchange minor pleasantries; he about the mid-west and his team, me about growing up in Florida and my team.

He tells me of his interest in women's football, and how he might want to "invest" in a team and possibly the entire league. "Great!" I say innocently, and reposition myself on his well-appointed leather couch. He is a well-dressed man in his late sixties, a man I see as very pleased with his life and perhaps wanting to add color to his broad palette of successes. His interest in women's football and the possible infusion of capital would certainly give the WPFA a leg-up to a higher shelf.

He watches me with beady eyes, that are so close together it looks like they both come out of the same hole. I'm getting skeeved while he commandeers the conversation with descriptive talk of his accomplishments starting with his "beautiful wife" and "fine family," who tell him all the time "what a great guy he is." He was a college football player, "in his youth," —a defensive back. A superstar. His success in business came "naturally to him," and I am concerned that he is just peeling back the first few layers of this life-onion, when the voice of Louise fills the room telling him his 1:45 is here. He tells Louise not to interrupt his goddam meeting and proceeds. My ears have begun to curl in and I am taking little out-of-body trips to other places to keep from falling asleep. I have no idea what he is talking about, but occasionally I say "Really?" and he says "Absolutely!" and he continues until Louise comes on the air again.

"Sheldon, your 2:30 is here," and he instructs Louise to tell the 2:30 to "go fuck himself and the goat he rode in on." The word "goat" triggers stories of his days as a big game hunter when he would sneak about thick forests in search of unsuspecting, large, horned animals. He points to the head of an unfortunate elk, which is now staring blankly through a plate glass window at the New York skyline.

"There isn't much I haven't done and even though I'm older, there isn't much I can't still do."

Can you shutup!?!?

"I've put on a few pounds through the years but am still fairly svelte." I marvel at the image he carries of himself. Though perhaps svelte in his youth, the years have brought with them a certain solidity and any twig trodden on by him today would go off like the explosion of a gas main.

"And then there's the business side of me." I pack a mental carry-on for another short adventure and he rambles incessantly until nature takes its toll and forces him to take in air. I return just in time to see my opening.

"I'm going to be late if I don't go!" Late to what, I know not and care not, and then Sheldon says I am free to go if I will sleep with him, and when I realize what he has said, I want to throw straight up. I am gathering my un-presented presentation while giving him a confused, but horrified look. He correctly translates the look into an offer turned down.

"Must be frigid," he grunts while I gather. "Or you're just a real bitch," he adds as I flee for the door, still so stunned I have no voice. This man is older than Europe and I don't understand why, just because I am female, he feels entitled to my attention.

"You're just another fuckin' dyke aren't you?" he is standing now and walking towards me. I stop and look him right in the hole where his two beady eyes are fighting with each other to look out. "Are you the alternative?" I say softly and wish I could raise my voice, but I am close to tears. I hold them until I get outside on the street and then I put my head into shaking hands and sob.

I want to call my mom and dad but I'm too embarrassed. Embarrassed that I worked so hard at the presentation and he never intended to listen. Embarrassed that he didn't take me seriously and I thought he would. Embarrassed that his reaction seems to be the norm for women trying to be heard instead of the exception. I won't call. No. It's easier to fold it up, crease after crease tighter than an origami shirt and place it into one of my figmental storage boxes; the 'embarrassment' box next to the 'I'm sorry's' stored on top of my many 'unpolished ideas.' There's the big box of 'thoughts-never-expressed,' 'tomorrow's dreams' and the one in the back full of 'past experiences.' Some that should be thrown out and forever forgotten but they seldom are. That's why they're still in the box behind all the "I told you so's."

CHAPTER 33

CONSTANT BOBBING AND WEAVING

If the league is truly full of crooks,
we will find another way to survive.

"Pope Millie" is not the first person in the WPFA who gives me the inclination that I have made a mistake. Some of the people encountered thus far in women's football are really hard to take. Including the ones running the league. I ask other owners if they have received any promised information or assistance.

"No," replies Ruby from Texas. "They haven't acknowledged that I'm in the league yet. Ever since they got my check for the franchise, they forgot my name."

"Those guys couldn't stick a finger up their ass with a funnel," is Mia's only remark. Messy Tampon is too busy wearing her big "S" (as in Savior) cape and wreaking havoc in New Hampshire to be concerned with the rest of us who have every right to worry. Our kick-off is not far away and the franchise documents for owners to sign finally arrive after we are well into the formation of our teams. My brother-in-law, William, is a lawyer and he agrees to look over the documents. He confirms what I suspect. The documents give us a percentage of nothing. He eyes me with an "I-told-you-so" look and, though he does not outwardly criticize, the shake of his head speaks volumes and echoes the sentiments of Ellen and my entire family.

This does not deter me or the other owners. We have our teams, and though we are all flying by the seats of our football pants, we will be ready for kick off. If the league is truly full of crooks, we will find another way to survive. Once you let Jeannie out of her bottle, she's not going back to that little round couch.

CHAPTER 34

OFFICIAL PRACTICE BEGINS

Eve and Wendy are best friends, inseparable and, because of their caustic mouths, the most hated duo to play the game.

On September 2, 2000, Eve Edwards and Wendy Wayne stop at the 7-11 in Baldwin, Long Island. They buy eight packs of Twizzlers, four rolls of Sweetarts, 22 Fireballs, a bag of hard candy and a dozen Tootsie pops. They are now ready to make the drive to Cow Meadow Park, in Freeport, Long Island for practice. The first official football practice for the NY Sharks Women's Pro Football team with a head coach!

Quarterback Eve is 5'4" and 135 pounds. Linebacker Wendy is 5'5" and 140 pounds. Both of them are record setters in women's flag football. They are best friends, inseparable and, because of their caustic mouths, the most hated duo to play the game. Not by their teammates, but by other flag players across the country. They are so jacked on sugar by the time they arrive; they can hardly concentrate on the tasks at hand.

From the other direction, Mr. Jack Oliver, the only coach to apply for the position of Head Coach of the New York Sharks, shifts his family van into gear and motors towards the first official practice of his career as a "professional" football coach. He is singing loudly because that's the only volume with which Jack is equipped. Somewhere in his youth, someone told Jack to speak up and he had never forgotten it. As he sings along to the song "Music," by Madonna, the windows shudder from the volume of his baritone voice.

In Brooklyn, Sarah gets into her RAV 4 to go pick up Jessie and Kim for practice. She has been to the gym twice today. Her students at PS 257 in the infamous section of Bensonhurst, Brooklyn are in awe of her. "Miss Parham" is the favorite of favorites. The prettiest, the smartest, the most energetic. She promises to take them to the first Shark game to watch her play. Sometimes her dad, Thomas, has come to a flag game, with several of Sarah's students in tow. They bring homemade signs with hand-drawn pictures of Sarah: flowing yellow hair, a happily bowed smile and–always–pink clothes and shoes. Sometimes she is holding a football. Other times, she holds the hands of the stick figure students on each side of her. One day, the drawing has Sarah and her teammates all featuring heads shaped like footballs. The laced strings are bent into smiles that stretch across our oddly shaped faces. Sarah is wearing pink. The rest of us wear brown.

"How come I'm in pink, and my teammates are wearing brown?" Sarah asked the artist.

"Because you are the only one that glows," the child says, and smiles.

At 92 Bank Street, Ellen is on the phone. She is making plans to go out with that friend tonight for dinner. She is telling our friend, her friend, in particular, something I am not supposed to hear.

"It's something I just can't understand," she says with disgust. "It's aberrant behavior, and I don't like having a girlfriend who wants to put on that stuff and get out there and do that!" As if I was affixing myself to a bomb and going to Times Square to explode amidst hundreds.

I pretend to not hear, but when I duck into the bathroom and shut the door, my heart aches from a place untold. After many years of being in each other's lives, she is planning her exit. I feel it in places foreign to me, even throughout the brownstone where we live, the home I worked hard to manifest for us. I am a great manifester, but Ellen wants nothing of me. She is blaming the Sharks for her unhappiness, but it has nothing to do with the Sharks. I have felt she has wanted to leave for years. Her bad moods, like birthing pangs, have become closer and closer together and soon she will birth her departure.

I begin to sink into the abyss of depression. To abandon my football passion would be so easy at this point. The seduction of instant approval is intense. Instant approval from my family, my friends, and most importantly, from my Ellen. It is hard to resist just giving the team back to the shoddy league, knowing my persistence with the team will create further estrangement from those I love most.

"You just straighten up and fly right up there," says my mom one day at the end of a phone call. I'm not sure if this is in reference to my being gay or to my bad business decision but approval seldom accompanies my inner decisions. In fact, quite the contrary. My players and I endure senseless ridicule, just for wanting to play. Society's judgmental head has a way of shrieking "What? You're thinking for yourself? You are applying your own yardsticks, using your own judgments, your own values? Who do you think you are?" I hear it clearly and it is a good question. Who was I? The phone was ringing and I picked it up.

"Who is this?" says Turpie's voice.

"I was just asking myself the very same thing."

"Oh, it's you. Sorry buddy. I forgot who I called. We have a little situation here. You on your way?"

"I'm on my way." I hang up and head for the door knowing I am late for practice.

Most of the Sharks are there when I arrive. Miraculously, practice uniforms from the league arrived at Turpie's house in Brooklyn and we can finally give them out. "They are 'donated' by Nike," the suspect trio boast. When I go through the box, I discover they are all large enough to be car covers. No wonder Nike donated them.

"So was this the situation you mentioned?" I ask her as we stare at the tarp-sized practice apparel in the box. She nods. We decide there is not much we can do about it at this point and hand them out.

Regardless of sizes, the Sharks are excited and put them on. Real practice uniforms! Black mesh pants, white jerseys for offense and black ones for defense and both the shorts and the jerseys have the WPFA logo silkscreened on them. We put them on and feel important, even though some players have taped the pants up behind the knees and most are held up by an odd assortment of belts, namely duct tape. Nike didn't send us one small! All are XL, XXL, XXXL and even 4XL. Sharks swim in them, oddly happy because Nike gave them to us. Tanker looks at my shorts and belly laughs. "You gonna run three yards before you even hit fabric on them shorts!"

"We're gonna have to live in the gym to grow into these!" says Sarah who is modeling a fully taped up version of shorts and jersey.

"Sharks!" I call them together before we begin. "I don't know if Turpie told you, but your last names must go on the backs of your jerseys. No nicknames." Groans from some, others are happy.

"Good!" says Wendy. She points at Big Dot. "That jack ass there wanted 'Hi Mom' on the back of hers," Wendy utters and mutters, even during games and constant insults fly from her mouth without warning. She is a live broadcast of random neural firings.

"She better put it on the bottom of her shoes, since she's gonna be on her back after every play," chimes in sidekick Eve. I suppress a laugh. It is funny and very fitting of Big Dot, who thinks highly of her ability, but rarely backs it up.

"Heh-heh!" they both cackle and dip for another handful of candy.

Wendy and Eve criticize and make cracks at fellow players, staff and coaches. Some laugh, knowing they are mental. Others ignore them, but most of us have a soft spot for them. I find them amusing. Kim and her minions constantly try to discredit their abilities and character, but the problem is, we know too much about each other.

CHAPTER 35

THE SEASON LOOMS CLOSER

Pay for the game uniforms ourselves? Not No, but Hell No!!!

We await the real uniforms with eager pride, but nothing shows up. Later that week, I call Mia in Los Angeles to see if hers have arrived. She tells me the suspect trio has asked her to fund the game uniforms, because they haven't gotten all the money in that they expected and would she loan them uniform money until the sponsor and ticket money comes in. Mia gives them $25,000 and believes she will see it again. They call me and ask to help pay and I think back to a late fall afternoon at the hunting camp when my dad introduces himself and me to a new guy at the hunting camp. I don't like meeting people and I don't want to go over but my dad says it's being polite to newcomers so we head towards the Adirondack chairs circling the campfire. The man stands up as we approach. My dad extends his hand.

"I'm Henry Davis and this is my youngest daughter, Toady." He says to a man dressed in camouflage, but it doesn't camouflage his huge belly.

"Glad to meetcha,' Henry," and he looks down at me and winks. "No boys?" says Mr. Camo-Belly to my dad.

"Nope. Three girls, but this is my huntin' n' fishin' partner right here." My dad says proudly. And then that stupid, fat man leans into my dad and says "I bet you'd trade all three of 'em for just one boy!" He 'heh-heh-hehs' and from my view lower towards the ground, I watch his voluminous stomach wobble up and down until it comes to a stop and droops over his belt. I am about to tell him that I may not count for much but my ears function as well as anyone's when I hear my dads' loud reply.

"Trade even one of them—not no, but HELL no!" Now I am the proud one, even though I really want to take my pocket knife out and prick this guy's belly…watch him swirl and spiral out over the swamps like a punctured balloon. I use my dad's line today as I answer the crooks request.

"Not no, but HELL no!" It is a good business decision.

To the few following the debut of the WPFA, the league looks organized and well planned. The website is finally unveiled and surprisingly, it is in fact, informative. The New York Sharks are members of the inaugural season of the Women's Professional

Football Association. The WPFA consists of 11 teams divided into two conferences, the American and the National. The National Conference is divided into two divisions, the East and South. The American Conference is also divided into two divisions, the Central and West. The Sharks are in the East Division of the National Conference. League play will begin on October 14th with each team scheduled to play 10 games. The season will culminate with the WPFA Championship Game, on February 3, 2001, in Daytona Beach, Florida.

The Sharks are to play home games at Mitchell Field in Uniondale, New York. We are to open our season on the road in New Hampshire against the New Hampshire Cobras on October 14th.

After many weeks of squabbling, practice, experimenting, rearranging, herding, talking, yelling, heavy sighing, more squabbling, several downright fights, and hours of driving to and from meetings, practices, sponsor leads and contract signing, October 14th, 2000 arrives. It is time for the Sharks to play their first game.

I wake up at 4 a.m. that Saturday. The Sharks are to meet at Mitchell Sports Complex. From there we will take a bus to New Hampshire. I am the first to arrive and Turpie follows soon after.

"Oh! You're here!" she says, while settling into my front seat.

"Some of the time," is my dry answer. We sit sipping hot coffee in my Jeep. It is a quiet time and we are congratulating each other on assembling the team. We worked hard when we played flag together and though this has been a different kind of hard work, it seems like a natural transition.

"Remember when we went to the first practice of our new team and we were the only ones there?" she asks.

"Yes, I do." I answer, as I stare out the windshield. "I don't know how you rounded up so many people after that for our team, but we had a great group!"

"Yes, buddy, and we do today, too. We did it! We got us a good team!" She has a genuineness about her and a very caring nature. I am not surprised at all that she can assemble groups of people for just about any undertaking. Some kids end up just like one or the other of their parents, and Turpie is very much like her mother; joyful, fair-minded and proud. Maybe it happened before she was even born—a little rump roast of a fetus marinating in her mother's personality.

I look at her and smile and we high five. We are happy for each other and confident more than nervous about the game ahead. We are discussing the many attributes our team has and the probability of winning today in New Hampshire while the assemblage of players is taking shape right outside of our windows. First comes Sarah and Jessie. Sarah, wearing a pink Junior Seau jersey, is jubilant and she hops towards us and hugs Turpie tightly through the open window, then bounces around to my side for a tight wrap around the neck.

"I couldn't sleep last night! I stared at my alarm clock all night until it went off." she says.

"Me too. Did you play powderpuff in high school?" I ask, remembering similar excitement when I was a senior.

"Yes!" she answers. "I was the wide receiver—as usual, buddy."

"Naturally! I was the QB, as usual. God, that was fun." I drift off.

"Sure was." She drifts for a minute, also. "I stared at the clock the night before that game, too!"

"Hell, I stared at the calendar! Counted the days, hours and minutes until I could get on that football field and play with a real high school football jersey on!" We are both buoyant with past memories and present potential.

Jessie, never as enthusiastic, swaggers over, leans against the car and chews contentedly on a 6" cinnamon stick.

"You ready Jess?" I ask.

She removes the stick momentarily to allow a huge smile to cross her face. "Oh yeah. Oh yeah," then she reinserts the stick and silently chews.

A car arrives, jammed so tight with Sharks, it rises six inches off the ground when they finally pile out. Drop-offs are made, each player unable to contain the thrill of what today means. Then a tire squeals and a car horn breaks the morning stillness. I see Big Dot erupting from the sun-roof of Kim's car, as she and Kim's tight-knit group pull into the parking lot. Big Dot's large frame is writhing to Emimen's "Slim Shady," while Kim, careening through chatting groups of players, wins the "parking lot Preakness." Players are scattering for safe havens.

It's not easy to bolt upright from deep in a car seat, but I manage the feat. I leap from the car and try flagging down Captain Earnhardt and the pit crew with my jersey.

"What are you doing!?" I shriek. Nothing good could come from this. If someone got hurt, our season and the entire team would be over. She finally parks the car without dismembering anyone and is walking to the group, as if every parking lot was consistently being entered in the same manner. Turpie's face is worked up and searching for the right phrase when Jack's enormous voice arrives. It precedes Jack and we all pause to search for its origin. We hear it again, a call like a jungle animal with dyspepsia, but still no Jack. It's shouting for Kim, its' noise level somewhere between jackhammer and tornado.

"Kim! Kim! I need you to help me on this team, not kill players off with your car!" I couldn't agree more with Jack's voice. There was no room for slinging Sharks from sun-roofs or squashing them under squealing tires.

"They act like a group of witches, Christine. Always brewin' up trouble. They a Coven of witches is all." I don't disagree. "Always causing drama. A Coven!" she adds as a matter-of-fact finality.

But the real drama, our first game, looms ahead.

CHAPTER 36

THE FIRST GAME

Dreams are becoming reality as one by one,
we step off the bus and into the world of tackle football.

Hours later, Turpie and I shoehorn the Sharks onto the bus. The October morning is crisp and fall leaves flare like rising birds in the spits of wind. I sit in the front seat looking out of the large bus windshield, not because I am the owner, but because I might horck if I sit in the back. Some people think I sit there to be a big shot. I never correct them. Let people think what they want. At least they are thinking.

As we drive North, the rising sun plays hide and seek as it makes its way to the bluing sky. The Sharks are chatty, even in the early hours. Sarah, sitting four rows from the front is leading a Q & A as she crunches on carrots. She holds one up, a faux mic, and interviews Big Dot, who has been playing defensive end.

"Where did you see yourself playing when you first joined the team?" Big Dot pauses and tosses a cornucopia of dreadlocks behind her left shoulder.

"Aw man, I dunno. I mean— I just wanted to play." Big Dot is leaning over the back of the bus seat in the third row.

"See! These will be the stories that go national when the league gets big," says Sarah in a loud announcement. Her Brooklyn accent is apparent. She is scrunched down in her seat with her feet on Big Dot's back. She is waving the carrot around in the air for others to answer the question. Most of the players are grinning and listening as she continues. It is no surprise that she has taken the stage and the entire team is participating.

"What'd ya mutha say when you told her you were gonna try out?" the carrot waves above her slouched, but comfortable pose. She is wearing her signature ear-to-ear grin, and her eyes are sparkling to match the rising sun. "No! No!" she corrects "Whatdya GRANDmutha say when you told her you were gonna play tackle football?"

Big Dot takes the cue again. "My mother and my grandmother weren't surprised," she says. "I've been doing strange things all my life, so tackle football was nothing to them. One time, when I was little..."

"Sit down Rosa Parks!" yells Eve from the back of the bus. "No one wants to hear your sob stories!"

"Amen!" shouts Wendy.

"She can talk the back legs off a donkey!" Eve continues and the players laugh and shake their heads in disbelief at her candor.

"My brothuhs and my fathuh refuse to come watch me play," injects Janet. "They say women shouldn't be playing football. But my fiancé is gonna come to the home games. Fuck my brothuhs!" She laughs and repositions herself from across the aisle to listen better. Janet is a large, attractive woman. Her long blonde hair, always squeaky clean, frames a thin face of impeccable skin and light green eyes, all of which are made up to perfection. Her matching velour sweat suit, Shark blue, matches her shoes, headband, and accessories, one of which is a Shark blue purse.

I am in the front seat with Turpie and we are adding stickers to our silver helmets when Kim comes to the front of the bus under the guise of throwing out a Coke can. She does her typical drive-by and leans towards the top of my head while bending down towards the garbage bag hanging on the rail leading down the steps of the bus.

"I can't believe she is starting," whispers Kim into the back of my head. "She sucks." Kim's eternal lament. She is referring to Piper who will be our starting center. I ignore her and ask Turpie for another sticker. Kim stands for a minute looking out the big bus windows as we roll down I-95N, then bends down. "I don't want to start anything but, all the blacks are in the back of the bus. Don't you think we should mix everyone up?"

"I'm here, Kim. Don't I count?" says Turpie

"You're management. No, you don't."

Fortunately, Coach Jack makes his way to the front of the bus and has something to say, so Kim's ever-astute observation is put on hold. "Ladies, ladies, ladies. Let me have your attention!" The man is alarmingly loud. Then he sneezes, which sounds like he detonated himself. The Sharks, after diving for cover, emerge and in unison say, "Bless you!" Only on a bus full of women, I think to myself.

"Thank you," says Jack, still abnormally loud and he grabs the back of the bus drivers' seat for balance. "Now listen, listen, listen. Today is going to be very different than practices. We are not playing at home," he pauses to consider his next words. "It's gonna feel different because it's in a different stadium." He pauses again and I look up from my helmet stickering. Surely, he must have something inspiring to boom out. "And it's gonna feel different than a practice. It's not the same as a practice." I see the bus driver's shoulder twitch to ward off the invasive sound next to him. "So, I just need you to relax and play ball," he goes to sit back down in his seat three rows behind my own. That's his pep talk? Is he really finished?

"Isn't he supposed to motivate the team?" I say to Turpie.

"He's motivating me to want to kick his ass," she replies.

I pause to select for utterance one of three devastating remarks, which have entered my head simultaneously when our destination hoves into sight. Honestly, it takes my breath away, which was fortunate for Coach Jack because the breath about to be expelled was peppered with unflattering observations regarding his speech. Instead, I stand and stare out of the front windows onto one of the most memorable views I have yet to witness. It is a candy corn day of orange and yellow. The stadium is old, rounded, shaped like the days of gladiators and is steeped in the feel of Packer-esque football. The ghost of Knute Rockne might easily be hovering if Jack's loud mouth hasn't scared it away. But there is no glitz other than the shine of our new silver helmets and there isn't the glamour of a typical NFL game day. No media, not many fans, yet I can feel magic tipping from Shark to Shark and sparks leaping around the heels of our cleated feet. We are silent as we approach. Reverent, for a change. Dreams are becoming reality as we step off the bus, one by one, and into the world of tackle football.

Messy Tampon, puffed with importance, approaches our team like a ship in full sail. Without precursors, she says, "Do all your players know who I am?" "Yes, you are an Olympic class ass." is what I want to tell her, but I say "Of course they do," and it seems to calm her Olympic size ego for the moment. "Follow me," she grunts and beckons the Sharks towards the locker room. She stands in her New Hampshire Cobras coaches shirt at the entrance, stern and direct, occasionally pointing at the door as if my players might not know to follow each other into the locker room. While looking like a toad who has been peering into the darker side of life since a tadpole, she tells me that my players, staff and coaches will have to comply with all rules of the WPFA. She informs me that she has been the one to finalize said rulebook for all of women's football. She turns her energy now to an unsuspecting guard, leaning against the wall in the sun. "You aren't being paid to lean on the walls!!" are the words I hear as I escape into the locker room, and head towards the bathroom.

Every stall is filled with nervous players. Every mirror reflects black smears under their eyes, and a few are adding eyeliner...just in case. In case of what, I am not sure. Eve and Wendy are handing out Halloween candy.

"Uppers, downers, candy corns?"

I get in the bathroom line behind Cooper, who has stretched herself tall and is looking very alert and birdlike. She stands on one leg, then the other, her head moving around the locker room as her gaze alights on different objects, angles, a mockingbird looking to line her nest. She is clearly nervous, but I suspect it is due to being in a locker room atmosphere. Some of the Sharks have not played team sports and pulling clothes on and off in front of strangers can be unnerving. Embarrassing.

"You shave your pussy!" It is Tanker, arms crossed, leaning back and uttering tasteless remarks. I don't know who she is talking about, but I see Cooper squirm. Tanker often burps up such inappropriate thoughts at inopportune times. Mental gas, out of control. Stereotypical towel snapping and posturing ensue by some of the players. Others are quiet, shy, folding themselves inward as I have done so many times. I notice it is Sarah who blends with both. She can snap the towels and be an asshole, but still make the Coopers of the team feel comfortable.

Moments before we are to take the field we gather to say the usual prayer before each game. A big huddle is formed. One arm from each player reaches upwards towards a center point forming a teepee of sorts. Where our hands meet, we extend our index fingers, a number one sign pointing into the heavens. This is a serious moment and we remain quiet, heads bowed or resting on our closest teammates shoulder. We listen intently as Tanker, our team reverend, turns a simple prayer into a Broadway production.

"Lawd, we know that you are in the house today. Me and my teammates ask that even if our backs is painful or if our knees are hardly strong enough to hold us up—or if we get busted lips, or if our arms get bent in wrong directions, Lawd we know that you will still let us play this game and give us the power of a win. I can feeeel it Lawd, and we ask that you..."

"Is that Old Spice you're wearing?" asks Eve of Turpie as she leans further in to her underarm.

"and we ask that, please Lawd," Tanker speaks loudly and tries to drill Eve with a cold look, but can't turn her big neck that far.

"...we ask that you keep us all from hurt, harm and danger and give us the power of a win today. We ask this in your precious name, Lawd, Amen." She always finishes this way—about the hurt, harm and danger and I try every time to decipher the difference between each word.

Tanker is always the first one to run to a downed player.

"Are you hurt or are you injured?" she asks. "'Cause if you're injured, I'll call the doc. If you hurt, ya better get up and play." I never can figure the difference between that line either, but somehow the Sharks always know how to answer. Today, we all answer "Amen" and disperse to our bags for last minute prep.

Tanker disappears to call her mom—something she has always done before and after every game of whatever sport she is playing.

"Nobody better hurt my baby!" her mom tells her. "You're my big baby and no one better hurt you! But I am so proud of all you girls because you are playing tackle football— something girls are not supposed to be doing."

"Mama, you are my queen." Tanker always replies.

The game starts at 1:30 p.m. Finally, after the long hours of practice, the hot summer days and cold fall nights, kickoff is about to happen. To look out and see the New Hampshire team at the other end of the field is exciting. It sends chills across my neck and launches butterflies in my stomach. In fact, every vital organ slides into my cleats as I try to place the opening kick-off away from their speedy threat, number 21. I hear Jessie say "Shit" when it goes directly to her. We are off and running.

Rarely do things happen as expected. After feeling confident in our strategies and abilities, we are shocked when Ava, our safety, gets beat long on the 3rd play of the game. Touchdown, New Hampshire. Two-point conversion, good. 8-0, New Hampshire Cobras.

When we get the ball, we drive downfield on running plays until Dulce, our speedy halfback, takes it in on a dive three. Two-point conversion also good. Score is tied.

"Confidence is born from demonstrated ability." My father's words ring in my ear as I guide our next drive down the field. I can hear him telling me that passing requires finesse as much as a good arm. "You know," he says and pauses before he throws the ball back to me, "Ol' Bart Starr they say couldn't run and couldn't pass. All he knew how to do was beat you." Then he grinned and tossed it back. "You have to know when to throw with finesse or drill it."

Sarah catches my finessed left end middle screen and walks into the end zone behind nearly a thousand pounds of front line.

Sarah and Tanker chest-butt with confident grins.

Tanker takes a turn at kicking off, and the ball sails deep into New Hampshire's territory. Return of ten. Their quarterback is sharp enough to see our secondary flailing and strikes with another long pass. Complete. She does it again and again but time runs out, as she is eight yards from scoring. We are still tied at half-time: 8-8.

In the locker room, we await Jack's sage advice. He does not disappoint. "Ladies, ladies, ladies! You have to HIT those women! HIT them!" The plaster on the back wall is going to crack and fall from the decibels he is emitting. I am tallying the cost to repair in my head, when Wendy's remarks begin.

"How about some useful information Coach. I'm freezing my dick off out there! Tell me something I don't already know! Something to make this worthwhile" Tanker breaks into laughter and opens a plastic container of soup. A halftime snack. Our five vegetarian front linesmen whose weight combined, is no less than a thousand pounds, graze constantly.

"What is that?" asks Sarah, peering onto the container.

"Gazpacho."

"Does anyone have any real food here?" Eve asks while high-fiving Little Toni who is riding to the bathroom on a razor scooter. She is as slender as a sapling and her equipment is so large and ill-fitting, you can hear it rattling as she passes.

"LADIES!" Jack explodes and we take cover for the second time today. "You need to sit here and think about what you have to do to win this game! And then get ready to go out there and show this team that you can play football!"

"I thought that's why we had you," says Wendy and she laughs loudly and shrugs her shoulders. I am not sure what to do and neither is Turpie. I don't know enough about the game to talk and I can't throw Jack out because we have no one else. Luckily, Coach Walnut steps up. He looks at me for permission and I enthusiastically shake my head in favor. Kim rolls her eyes.

"They know we are weak in the secondary," says Walnut. "We're going to put Eve in at free safety to try to keep them guessing. Meanwhile, let's keep running it up their asses. Use time—all you can."

The Sharks respond to this. "OK" they say and heads nod and look to one another like Walnut just imparted the secret code to obtaining the Super Bowl ring. Dulce lets us know that it's in God's hands and Kim says she hopes God hands can catch and for the remaining five minutes of halftime, Tanker slurps, Little Toni rides and Kim funnels negativity into the ears of those close by.

The second half is plagued with bad snaps over Eve's head by Piper, our center. And several times, she gives me the ball crooked from up under center and it slams into the ground. We punt. New Hampshire strikes with their usual long bomb. Connects. Damn. But Sarah, at middle linebacker, intercepts and Sharks take over.

Time passes until there is 1:42 left in the game.

"There's enough time to run the ball," Jack is telling me. "Keep pounding it out." Dive three. Tanker makes her block. Seven yards.

Dive four. Three yards.

Chains come out. Measure.

First down. We are in their territory. We have three time outs and we use one now. I run to the sideline to get the play.

"Slot right, slot flat and go. I'm putting Eve in as a decoy." I nod and run back to the huddle. Eager blue, green and brown eyes on black, brown and white faces await. Except for the blue and black of our uniforms, however, no color is noticed.

"Slot right, slot flat and go. They are playing a free safety so look over your outside shoulder. Everyone clear? On one, ready?" We clap in unison and run to the line.

"Ladies, clock starts on the whistle," says the ref. He blows it and I take my stance.

"Down. Set. One." Piper fires the ball and Sarah squares out from the slot. I fake pump and she turns up field but someone misses the block on the line and a defender is coming at me. I release the ball to a spot as the defender grabs my jersey. Sarah makes a perfect over-the-outside shoulder catch and we are on the fifteen-yard line. Time out. One left.

"Do what you are confident with," says Walnut and as we run back onto the field to line up, I can't help but think of my dad and his line when he gets excited; "If the boys at the feed store could see me now!"

"Wendy," I say, trying to stay calm "Do that V-out again. Sarah, post. BE LOOKING!" I stress "On set, ready?" We clap and line up.

The ball is snapped. I drop back in the pocket. I see Wendy fake in and begin the out and I unleash the pass to the corner. One step ahead of her defender, she gathers it in. Score! We go wild. Extra point play calls for Kim as my primary but she gets covered so I fire to Wendy, my secondary, who has done a button-hook just across the goal line. Wendy catches the bullet in the gut. Extra point for two is GOOD. Sharks ahead 16-8 with 32 seconds left. Our defense must last for 32 seconds.

First play is off. Incomplete pass. 28 seconds.

Another incomplete pass—overthrown. 22 seconds.

Long pass right on the money. They are 25 yards away from our end zone. 10 seconds.

Play begins. The New Hampshire QB wants to pass, but sees no one open. She scrambles. Jessie, at defensive end, has taken the inside route AGAIN, allowing New Hampshire's QB to run around her and turn the corner. She is running. 7 seconds. Running, running. Sharks are chasing her. She is by the sidelines. 5 seconds. Little Toni sees her step out of bounds and showing abnormal behavior, stops pursuing her. But the whistle doesn't blow. New Hampshire is still running. The ref on the sideline is counting audibly.

"Four, three, two, one—no more time ladies," but she is still alive, twisting, and turning her way towards our end zone. Inches before the end zone, Eve appears, just like a Shark in deep water and slams her to the turf. Pop! We all hear the hit and we know the game is won. Shark teammates flood the field.

"That's it ladies. The game is over." I hear the finality of it and wish out loud that he would stop calling us 'ladies.'

Tanker, in her Hollywood, histrionic way, becomes a mock preacher. She draws in a full breath which makes her even larger than she already is. Her expressive face points upwards and she skips like a pleased kindergarten child around in a circle.

"Ring! Ring!" She is holding the now infamous imaginary phone to her ear. "It's the Lawd." she says "Lawd wants to know if the defense is in the house?" and this time we laugh. We have won our first ever game in the WPFA!

CHAPTER 37

LAST PRACTICE
BEFORE THE HOME GAME

Not that I always listen to classical music, but life had rolled
up its sleeves and given my nerves a work-out lately.

When I drive up Eve, Wendy, Cooper and Jessie are encased in Wendy's smoke-filled truck listening to a rap song. I hear it before I turn the engine off, thus discontinuing my nerve-soothing "Air on the G String." Not that I always listen to classical music, but life had rolled up its sleeves and given my nerves a work-out lately. Bach is doing his blue-ribbon best to unfurl the frayed ends, but his work is eradicated upon hearing the disembodied voice of their music. The "singer" is proposing to do something of a crudely surgical nature to his topic of interest. Many of his plans seem difficult to put into practice. His threat, for instance to pull off someone's head and make them swallow it.

My sisters, only two and a half years apart, were sibling rivals. Frequent disagreements led to 'stereo wars' that could be heard all over the house. By the time I was ten, I had songs permanently embedded in my head;

> "I've got sunshine on a cloudy day
>
> When it's cold outside I've got the month of May
>
> Well I guess you'd say
>
> What can make me feel this way?
>
> My girl, my girl, my girl."

Now, we have this;

> "I'll take you to the candy shop
>
> I'll let you lick the lollipop
>
> Go 'head girl don't you stop
>
> Keep going 'til you hit the spot, whoa"

When I was ten;

"I'm picking up good vibrations

She's giving me excitations (Oom bop bop)"

Now;

"The way you move it, you make my pee-pee go

Doing, doing, doing"

Then;

"She loves you, yeah, yeah, yeah

She loves you, yeah, yeah, yeah

She loves you, yeah, yeah, yeah"

Now;

"Bitch I'm wild! (Hold up), do the Stanky Legg (ayyyy!)

Do the Stanky Legg (ayyyy!), do the Stanky Legg (ayyyy!)

When I hit da dance flo', (I be) do the Stanky Legg (ayyyy!)

Do the Stanky Legg (ayyyy!), do the Stanky Legg (ayyyy!)"

I can't actually see the Sharks in the car through the pot smoke, but I know they travel together in its alpine cloud wherever they go. An occasional body part presses against the glass, which confirms the car contains human substance. I am parked next to them, but don't get out. I am finishing a call with Mia in Los Angeles, when Turpie opens the car door and sits down in the passenger seat.

"Hey buddy."

"Hey buddy." We sit and listen to the words pumping out of the car.

"I don't get it." I finally say.

"Noise diarrhea." She says, knowing exactly what I'm talking about.

"Audio pile of animal droppings." I add and we are quiet.

Sarah arrives and walks past the pot mobile. She doesn't ask to get in.

"Come on!" she knocks on the hood with her fist. "Let's get going before we freeze!"

Kim and Big Dot are next to arrive and now a group is forming around Wendy's small, yellow truck. Dulce joins. Little Toni gets out of her car and saunters over, her T-shirt begging the question "Is that fear I smell or is it just your normal hygiene?" Tanker eyes the shirt and approves with a belly laugh. Conversations between people of different sizes and hues can be heard.

"Piper, you better not have your period tonight," says Kim. "You gotta fill those gaps better." I don't know who appointed her coach but ours hasn't shown up yet so why not?

Piper puffs on her cigarette and says nothing.

"New Hampshire thinks we're a bunch of pussies because we didn't hit the gaps on defense," Kim croaks to the group. She sounds like Harvey Fierstein.

"I don't appreciate the vaginal references," says Dulce the turbo-charged Christian who appears to be serious. "In my church, we try not to use words like that. Hey, they asked me to write an article for the Pews News. Maybe I should write on the Sharks." Moments later Dulce is instructed to "Shut the holy fuck up," by someone I can't identify.

Coach Jack finally shows up and loudly begins telling Sharks what position to fill.

"I hope you don't pay a phone company Coach!" Eve tells him. "Just open the door and aim at whoever you're calling." He points to Cooper who reeks of pot smoke.

"You!" he bellows. "I can never remember your name but you look like Shelley Winters times two. You're our tackle tonight." This doesn't seem to bother anyone. Neither does the reference to Shelley Winters times two, nor that Cooper is playing tackle. Women's football celebrates the big girls and Cooper glides into the position with a stoned, but pleased look. Next, Coach Jack brays at Little Toni, the human celery stick. "Go to guard." Turpie and I look at each other. This undernourished woman will get slurped up like a dinner mint at that position.

"Buddy, that man is dumb," Turpie says dryly.

"He has way too much yardage between his goal posts." I softly answer while watching with my arms crossed. I hear my grandmother and my mom discussing a man in our town who ran for city council.

"I just don't think I can vote for him, Mom," says my mother. "I don't think he is sharp enough for the job."

"I agree. They had to burn the school down to get him out of sixth grade." I tell Turpie and we chuckle shaking our heads.

At 10:20 pm, Jack wakes up a 6-mile radius of sleeping humans with his announcement that practice is over. We have all survived another cold night of practice under a black sky drilled with stars and full of Sharks.

CHAPTER 38

FIRST HOME GAME

Piper takes a long draw on her Marlboro before she answers.
She looks away, flicks her ash. "Nope. No balls."

Another sleepless night has produced Saturday and I go to the field for a home game.

I suit up, but, due to the stress of home life and Shark life, I have become too thin to even think of getting on the field. Tanker is right. I need to eat. I am now 5'8" and 112 pounds.

We had gotten a call from an old flag player asking if she can promote her book for children at one of our games. "Sure, whatever. Join the circus. Bring your own table, flyers and fans." She does. And she brings Mabel, her publicist. Mabel Outzen.

"Do you know why I am the best person to help promote your team?" she asks when I meet her about two hours before kick-off.

"No," I tell her. "Nobody tells me anything."

"Because I'm part *Fin*nish." I think I am supposed to laugh, but I can't. I am too busy talking with Andrea, another former flag player who wanted to help, about the speaker system.

"You checked to make sure it all works?"

"Yes," she says. "All good to go."

"And you're sure the music we are playing doesn't tell women they are bitches and ho's and basically useless?"

"Clean as a fuckin' whistle." Is her droll answer.

"Awesome." I say and walk briskly away to hand out jerseys, put air in the game balls, make sure the ambulance is here, and the trainer, and the refs, find a room for the refs…wonder if I brought enough checks to pay the refs, and the ambulance, and the field crew, and the coaches, can I trust who is handling the money, will the other team show up, will we sell enough tickets to pay our bills, why is my linebacker throwing up in the hall, who smells and why is Sarah putting on make-up? With her helmet on? What other job must I tackle? Stick a broom up my ass and I'll sweep the locker room before we kick-off.

Piper arrives. Forty-ish Jan Piper who is an original Shark from the flag days and is our starting center as well as our appointed Director of Football Operation. Since we have realized that the league does nothing, Piper orders equipment for the team, tries to find fields, and does other odds and ends that come along. She is in her pre-game attire: sleeveless, black Underarmour shirt, black Shark football pants replete with all hip, knee and thigh pads, and black cleats with "peds" crawling just out of the top of each cleat. Tall, stoic, manly Piper, a Police Detective of few words and strong conviction. She is smoking a cigarette and has acid rock thumping from her early eighties black Jeep Cherokee. A North Shore of Long Island native, Piper never misses a Shark practice or event. As a homicide inspector, she takes in more than we know, but rarely shows her cards.

"Hey Boss." she says in a low manly voice as I walk up.

"Hello Piper." I reply. "Do you have the balls?" The Sharks, like most of the women's teams, rent practice facilities for a few hours on game day so we have no storage for any of our equipment. Players keep their pads and helmets in the trunks of their cars and we delegate to those who have additional room to carry certain items to games and practices. It's hard to keep track. Piper takes a long draw on her Marlboro, before she answers. She looks away, flicks her ash. "Nope. No balls."

"Shitballs!" I say. A word that has become my word du jour. I really didn't used to use the foul language that comes piping out of me now as easy as 'hello.' "How about the cones? Do you have those?"

Another drag. A short one. "Nope. Nope. No cones."

"Good God. Tell me you brought the water coolers."

"Nope. Couldn't fit 'im in, Boss. Had to bring players." Her mullet cut capping her finely chiseled face turns away for one last puff, then she drops the butt and grinds the last spark from it with the heel of her cleat.

Fortunately, Turpie arrives with a few game balls.

We have on our new home jerseys. They look nice. Crisp blue mesh with big black numbers, outlined in silver. We are excited. There is only a small cacophony of displeasure from Kim and her Coven because the blue is "baby" blue. But it doesn't take long before the love of the game has all of us giddy.

I want so badly to walk out with the team, in uniform, like a regular player, not an owner. I just want to play, not own this team. I have few precious plays left in me at this age and I feel I am beyond my shelf life as it is.

Turpie is sporting that wide grin when she walks up to me in the locker room. "Good to be alive isn't buddy?"

"I wouldn't know." I glumly reply, knowing I will end up doing some inane bit of Shark shit that will prevent me from walking out, two-by-two, with the team.

"Come on buddy, things could be worse. Suppose you were gettin' shot at sunrise!"

"Impossible. I'm never up that early."

Then Jack blows out the locker room doors by demanding that we "Line up at the door in pairs. In pairs. Hats on. Hats on." Cooper looks perplexed about the "hats."

"Helmets, Cooper. He means helmets," says Sarah compassionately and Cooper is relieved. Pleased that I am getting to walk out with the team after all, I line up next to Jessie. We walk down the hall and out through double swinging doors. The click of cleats on cement is no less soothing than Bach to me. My own private Air on the G String. Our names are being called out on the loudspeaker: "...No. 51, Sarah Parham...No. 63, Jan Piper...No. 19, Gemma Torres...No. 58, Jessie Norval...No. 22, Caitlin Delmore and our owner, No. 7, Christine Davis!" I freeze when I hear the word "owner." The moment turns from uncut joy to mortification. I don't want anyone knowing that I own us! Oh God...... I run onto the field following Jessie and give a little wave to the stands. I will be talking with my GM very soon.

We are smaller, but look better than Rochester and our swagger is intimidating. So is number 94 on their team. In fact, they look like a family portrait of a multitude of well-fed relatives.

"Hey!" shouts Eve towards the Rochester sideline. "Is that a football team or a Jenny Craig meeting? OH!"

Someone laughs, but Cooper is immune to Eve's comments by now. "They're going to convert us to snacks," she says in her clipped boarding school deliverance. Piper agrees with a somber nod. Piper is a reasonable woman. She knows that you cannot have everything just so in this world. Nevertheless, as she lines up at center moments later, she wishes the nose guard across from her was a shade less formidable. Her opponent has a massive girth and a jungle of curly hair protruding from all regions of her helmet. A jet-black uni-brow is accented by unfriendly bulging eyes that shoot hate-beams out of the faceguard directly onto her. "Bring it on! Bring it on! Bring it on!" is number 94's popular phrase of the moment. Eve, playing QB, does just that.

"Ready.....set....have another hamburger number 94!...Hut...Hut!" Piper snaps the ball and prepares to lose her liver as number 94 steamrolls into the Sharks front line. Eve releases the ball as several of the D-line close in. "Nice try Starsky and Butch!" she taunts as the fallen bodies of the O-line and D-line upright themselves.

"Eve!" snaps Piper, though a snap for Piper is just an octave louder voice. "They have to hit me first, before they get to you. Stop making it worse for your front line."

Cooper nods, first up and down in agreement, then back and forth in disbelief. Jessie is silent as she readjusts her arm pads, a determined warrior serving silently on the front line of action.

The next play, Sarah, in an unusual act of poor coordination, drops an Eve pass and our offense has to exit stage left. Led by Wendy's rasping howl, the defense takes the field and is no less charming. Eve's incessant offensive rantings have evoked a veritable spring of eloquence from Wendy.

"Are you gonna run a play or not? Don't you have any idea how to play this game? Hey! Is there a ref who can count the seconds on the delay-of-game clock? I should have brought a sandwich. Could have had a picnic. Let's FUCKIN GO!!!" she prepares herself for action by tugging on her own facemask and squatting ever so slightly in anticipation of delivering her pounce of death.

By late in the fourth quarter, The Sharks are shredding the Goldrush in spite of Coach Jack. It is third and one and Rochester is clearly trying to draw us off sides but so far, it is not working. I hold my breath because at any moment, one of the Sharks will detonate, exploding over the line of scrimmage, giving them a first down. This will keep their drive going with plenty of time left to score. Not that it matters but, to remain in the spirit of the game, those of us on the sideline can only pray the Sharks defense will remain intact until after the ball has been snapped. They do and Janet, on the verge of being offsides, gets a half second start on the tackle and throws her down like an air-filled punching dummy. Sack number nine takes place and Janet chews the remains of her kill while Wendy rushes up to deliver the final blow.

"Here's a quartah, call your muther." She flicks an imaginary coin to the flattened Goldrush QB. "Fuckin' crybaby. HEH!" is her parting grunt and, chest puffed, she struts away. After they punt, we run out the clock and the game ends. The final score is a lot to nothing and we do our obligatory hand-slapping-good-game lineup. Coach Jack gloats, as if his coaching is the reason we have won. Unfortunately, some rookies and other players without as much talent as our starters, see no action at all. Nevertheless, the sideline is mad with excitement, but I am mad at Coach for not getting all of my players into the game. He even gloats aloud and I glare at him, wondering what I should say to him and how to say it. All of this, while I freeze in the night air.

"Turpie, could you bring me something very hot to drink, please?"

"Sure, buddy. You want some tea?"

"Anything hot. I don't care if you have to boil Gatorade in a helmet." She disappears to get it. Turpie, though she played flag football, never wanted to play tackle.

Everyone who is around the Sharks and not playing wants to play, but can't due to age, injury, schedule or family, but Turpie's reasons were less tangible. After her mother died, she called me to design the program for the funeral. I did. It was pink paper and had a redbird I had drawn on the front and the inside had her moms face smiling out at us with some bible quotes that were her favorite. There was a poem in a calligraphic font that Turpie liked which explained to everyone that "You end up like you start out." Turpie said her mom felt that was the way of all things, not just life and death but relationships, jobs, friends. She was not only grateful but expressed it so in many ways. It felt wonderful to be so appreciated and needed.

I am piling into Turpie's cup of hot tea while counting the exiting fans. Eighty-nine, ninety, ninety-one...looks like we have a few hundred today...when I catch the rather large image of Scarlette Xavier, the owner of the Rochester team rapidly stepping off yards in my direction while saying, "You!"

Her eyes are effectively boring holes, even from the fifty yards that separate us and in seconds, they are less than a foot from my own. "You!" she says again. There are really no good answers to the word "You!" so I do not attempt one. "You have got to do something about that team of yours! They are THE most classless bunch of poor sports that I have ever seen! I am going to file a grievance to the league!" I beg her not to say that. A foolish request seeing that she has just said it.

"What happened?" I ask.

"What happened?" she says.

"Yes, what happened?" I say.

"What HAPPENED?" she repeats and I wonder does she have a hearing problem.

"One of them...ONE...of your...goddam Sharks...tore down our banner, THAT'S what happened!" she has mouth froth flying she is so worked into a lather. "THEN!" and I brace myself for the second course.

"Then?" I say.

"Then!" she says and she pauses, her hands trembling. She points to the end zone and when I turn my head, I see six to eight of my Sharks hunkered over said banner like lions sharing a fresh gazelle.

"They are tearing it up!" She is horrified!

"Tearing it up?" I am horrified.

"Into little bits!" We are both horrified and we stand, mouths gaping and eyes bulging like two crazed carp.

"I'm so sorry..." I offer and she asks what the hell was the good of being sorry and for the life of me, I can't tell her. "I will go get it back for you." and I begin to walk towards the carnivorous herd in the end zone.

"I don't want it back! What am I going to do with shreds of a sheet, build a giant nest?"

The fins of the guilty Sharks droop immediately upon my arrival. Everyone present is a true rookie, not part of the warring flag tribe, and they know they have blundered. "It was a bet," one offers. "We didn't mean any harm." Another, like a gorging lion, still has sheet strings hanging from her mouth where she nipped at it to make it rip. "They said they'd give the person who tore it off the bleachers twenty bucks!"

"And another twenty to shred it," chimes in lion number three.

"Who?" I ask. "Who said that?" They are silent. Neither Wendy nor Eve are in sight, but they have to be behind it. Turpie and I go to the locker room where a group of Sharks are discussing the various events of the game with much emotion and glee.

"Buddy," says Turpie in a bold voice. "I'm the GM. I should handle this." I am surprised at her offer but thrilled and say, "Go right ahead."

"Sharks!" she yells and the smelly room goes quiet. Then she swells up like a piece of bubble gum and pushes off. "You have the nerve, the.... the..." I see she needs help-ing out. "Audacity" I say, throwing her the line. "The audacity to embarrass us in our own house! Why would you do such a....an...."

"Inhospitable." I again offer assistance "Asshole thing and be so mean to a team we like? You guys have the...." and she struggles again. "Crust?" I lend. "The fuckin balls..." She amends and I admit it was stronger... "To rip up a banner of a team who we just beat the shit out of, and who we now have to go and apologize to for being assholes! I don't even want to claim you! For the love of God!" She adds, driving her point home. "Now get up and go apologize!"

The Rochester Goldrush later drives away with many apologies offered, but they are happy to put a whole lot of "gone" between themselves and the NY Sharks.

It made me think of 'pack mentality' that usually afflicts groups of teenage boys and young men. Can it affect women in a similar way? I wonder.

CHAPTER 39

THE SEASON CONTINUES

*"We are paving the way for all the little girls in the future who
want to play, and isn't no one gonna tell them no!"*

My team is a huge pain in the ass. The suspect trio at the league level are liars and the players are naive, making things difficult at best. Sponsorships are impossible as is an acknowledgement from newspapers and television. Since the month I bought the team, I have tried to get ESPN to televise a season of the Sharks. Even one game would be nice. Acknowledging we exist would be a starting place! I have left countless unanswered messages. But that idea is not to see daylight either. And difficulties abound.

As the season wears on, it quickly becomes apparent that the WPFA is having financial difficulties. Surprise. By the end of November, the operations are largely taken over by Mia in Los Angeles and the rest of the regular season is cut very short. The sudden changes made in efforts to salvage the season result in a bizarre chain of events where the Sharks have to play 2 games in 2 consecutive days. The league wants the Sharks to go to New Hampshire to play the New Hampshire Cobras, but we have already scheduled an exhibition home game against a start-up team called the New York Skyscraper and it's too late to cancel. So we trounce the Skyscrapers 50-12, and the next day, we go to New Hampshire to play Messy Tampon and the New Hampshire Cobras. Coach Jack decides that this game does not affect the outcome of the standings for the Sharks and leaves the starters, as well as himself, in New York to rest. Lacking so many players, we are overwhelmed and lose 48-12.

The next Saturday, the Sharks and Cobras are to meet again for the National Conference Playoff Game.

The week leading up to the game is no different than others. A usual Tuesday night practice at Cow Meadow finds Cooper, Eve and Wendy stuck in traffic on the L.I.E. They have been driving for two hours when Wendy, always the one to break, speaks first. "That's it! I'm playing for another team next year if we keep practicing in Bumfuck!"

"Let's turn around. I've got a migraine and I don't feel like going tonight," whines Cooper.

Eve is trying to ignore them. "Only five more days until playoff number one! I am so psyched! I am so pumped." Finally, the car pulls into the parking lot where other Sharks are gathering and putting on gear. Turpie's phone is ringing. She answers, cups her hand over the phone and rolls her eyes "Its Tanker," she whispers. I smile and wonder what her excuse to miss practice will be this time.

"I have to go get checked out at the hospital. I'm gonna be late," she tells Turpie.

"You had all day to go to the hospital. Why you wanna go now when it's time to practice? WHY you going to the hospital anyway?"

"My knee is swollen really big, and I may need them to drain it and I can't wait! It won't take long, then I'll be there."

"Well see you Thursday Tanker," Turpie calls her on her excuse.

"I'm telling you, I'll be there!"

"I gotta go." Turpie hangs up and breaks into her big smile. "She can't help herself, buddy. Think what kind of a player she could be if she would practice. Man!"

Thursday does produce a better turnout. It usually does since the game is only two days away.

"Ladies, ladies, ladies." Jack blares at the players at the end of the night. "Saturday morning is it! It's win or go home. I want you to get rest Friday night. No partying and, and, and....all of that. You need to be on time to the bus Saturday morning. We are leaving at....what time are we leaving Christine?"

"Eleven sharp." I answer. "From right here."

"Eleven sharp! Alright Sharks? Eleven. Right here. Eleven o'clock sharp! Be on time!"

"What time we leavin' Coach?" says Eve. "OH!" and laughs at her display of mockery. Coach Jack doesn't catch on.

"Eleven sharp!" he says in an irritated and even louder voice. "Does everyone understand? Come eleven o'clock, we are leaving! You better be here!" Surely this man was dragged screaming from the MENSA society when the calling to be coach entered his atmosphere. Einstein must be looking down on us now, scratching his brilliant head and saying "What a waste that ol' Jack is coaching football and not quantum leaping towards world peace and eradicating diseases."

Like every Saturday, eleven arrives. The on-time Sharks are zipping around the parking lot in good spirits. Coach Jack is late. When he shows up, he has his three-year-old in tow.

"He's no problem. No problem. He'll sit with me." *He certainly will*, I say to myself and I wonder if the NFL ever encounters these problems.

On the bus, we watch a movie. "Remember the Titans." At the end, Sharks weep like finned babies and Sarah takes a packet of Kleenex out of her backpack and passes them out. Tanker takes one and wipes tears from her face. Physically, it's hard to imagine her as the Special Education teacher that she is. She is bold in speech and stature, but her desire to make connections with people is apparent. She is always the last one to leave on the rare occasion that kids want autographs. She is the one who will go over to a dejected looking stranger to make him or her laugh. Tanker is the one to bend down and put her helmet on a child who stands mesmerized while look-ing up at her. And she will pick up a kid, too, and put them on her shoulders---but never before employing the courtesy of asking the parent. Today, when she stands to make a point, we all listen.

"You see that movie? They made history. We are makin' history, too! We are pav-ing the way for all the little girls in the future who want to play and isn't no one gonna tell them no. That's gonna be because of us! You better hear me 'cause I'm speaking a language no one else speaks. I'm speaking SHARK language. You mutha-fuckers are my team-mates and I love you! Now let's go win us a football game!" She tousles Little Toni's hair as she makes her way back to her seat. Little Toni grabs her arm. "I love you, Tanker" The NFL must not see much of this either.

Moments later the Sharks are happily slapping hands and sharing individual methods on how they will delve inside of the New Hampshire players and extract vital organs through small orifices when Coach Jack gets up to inspire us.

"Ladies! Ladies, listen up!" He sounds like a leaf-blower. Nothing but annoying noise, propelling dirty air over everything. "In minutes, we will have the chance to win the first ever WPFA playoff game."

Actually, there are two playoff games today; the National and the American but he's just a coach. Why would he know who plays today?

"Hey Coach, ya got spinach in your teeth!" says Eve with raised hand. Jack ignores her, but Little Toni and Dulce roar with laughter.

"You can either win it......or......"

Wait, wait!....don't tell me! ....LOSE IT? My sarcasm is functioning on all eight cylinders.

"....or you can lose it. It's up to you. All up to you," he blows. "So go out there and put to use all the... stuff we have been learning these past months. And win!" A rowdy school of Sharks swarms off of the bus. Messy is there to 'professionally' escort us to our lockers again. She must assume everybody now knows who she is because I don't hear her asking. It begins to snow, and I tell the Sharks to put on all the layers they brought. Odd, I think. I don't really like kids, yet I feel I have a whole bus full and, odder still, I care greatly about each one.

CHAPTER 40

COACHING WORRIES

*"It's time we went out there and played our kinda football
'cause we are going to win this game or my name
ain't LEAH-TANKER-WOODS!"*

The kick is off and Dulce catches the ball and returns it for about seven yards. On our first possession, she finds a huge hole and runs 40 yards down the field for a long gain. Eve is calling a lot of the plays herself, because all Coach Jack can do when she looks to the sideline for a play is act out a sweeping-the-floor motion. As if no one will de-code that we are running a sweep. Our defense, led by Sarah and Tanker, is holding New Hampshire pretty well. But at halftime, we are down 7-0.

In the locker room, we wait for Coach Jack to appear with adjustments for the second half. We have another thirty minutes of football and we know in our Shark hearts that we can pull this out! Halftime is nearly over when he comes in. He stands in front of us, but says nothing for an awkwardly long time. Then a thought strikes him. It strikes him very slowly. We watch it coming like a long wave on a sandy beach and he leans forward, screwing up his face like he's going to say something extraordinary. Then his mouth turns into an exhaust pipe expelling useless, gaseous words.

"This is the worst football I have ever seen!" awkward pause. "I can't believe that you can play this way after all the time we have put into learning this game!"

The Sharks, expecting some direction and advice, look stunned. His remarks appall me and while they are appalling me, he moves backward towards the door intending to be gone. Then he is. As a team, we are reeling. Even Kim looks speechless. I stand up to say something...anything, but Tanker recovers and takes the floor.

"I don't care what that crazy man says, we are the NEW YORK SHARKS, and we didn't come here to lose this game! Now I know you all for a long time and we been through lotsa shit and good times and bad times. It's time we went out there and played our kinda football and show this team who we are! 'Cause we are going to win this game or my name ain't LEAH-TANKER-WOODS!" We rally ourselves and Walnut calls us together for a cheer, but I know Coach Jack's words hurt us. And I hurt for my Sharks.

We play good football when we get back on the field. We seem to have overcome the shock of being berated and abandoned and we rely on each other to keep the game in check. Sarah catches a one-handed pass from Eve to tie the score until Cobras player Willow Blake kicks a perfect field goal and pushes New Hampshire ahead with a score of 10-7. We are driving the ball with a minute and three seconds left, down by 3 points, and Eve is looking to the sideline for Coach Jack's play taken straight from his MENSA playbook. It is fourth and four yards to go.

Then I see her scanning the sideline somewhat perplexed, like she's five years old and lost her mother at the airport. I begin to scan the sideline, too. So do the other Sharks and we realize the sideline is fresh out of head coaches. Walnut, the next in line, though not an offensive guy at all, steps out to call a play. With seconds ticking off and forty stunned Sharks staring at him for some golden words, Walnut sends in the play: "Run one that works! We are short on time!" It's fourth and four and Eve calls a play to Sarah to gain a first down. Eve scrambles a bit but delivers the ball, which bounces off the tips of Sarah's frostbitten fingers and into the benches where the Sharks are watching. Sarah begins to cry. With seconds left on the clock, we know we will not get the ball back.

As the seconds tick off the clock, I know what is about to happen. The Sharks are going to lose the game. I feel at peace with it, though I hurt for my players. I look around at their faces. Long eyelashes peering hopefully through the facemasks. They glance from the clock to the field, pleading for another chance to score. But it is not in the cards for the Sharks this year. I look across the field and I see unparalleled joy in a group of people I do not know. A group of football players who have accomplished a goal and are proud and elated at a job well done. White jerseys bob up and down on excited toes and I can feel the grins of anticipation from across the field. When the final second expires, many Sharks are in tears. Even with all of our starters playing in this game, the Sharks tough play does not get the victory against the Cobras. New York loses to Messy Tampon's team on a snow-covered field in New Hampshire, by the score of 10-7.

I am still looking for Coach Jack and minutes later, I see him nonchalantly getting off the bus with his 3-year-old walking back towards the stadium. He had gone to the bus to feed his son. He had left, in the middle of the fourth quarter... of the play-off game.....to feed his son.

CHAPTER 41

FOOD FIGHT

Some have forgotten the loss, some are still trying to forget it, but
all are hungry and emitting noises that sound like feeding time at the zoo.

No one feels like showering after the game—we just want to go home. Most players are quiet as we gather near the bus. We sit under the raw, pewter skies and try to find solace from each other. We know Coach Jack is mostly to blame for the loss, but we feel cheated, not angry. Like we drank the potion from the wrong vial. He diminished us. Erased us.

We sit on the snowy ground, bonded by the betrayal of our coach until Sarah asks that we get up and do our chant. Her voice is sad, but encouraging somehow. Like a hymn for the oppressed. We rise and lift one arm skyward, coming together to form the teepee. I position my nose away from the least offensive armpit, close my eyes and listen for Sarah to speak. I can hear sniffles from a few, sobbing from Eve and Sarah's calm voice takes over. Even Big Dot is huddled close. "Let us be winners in our hearts," she says, and I open my eyes to see the collection of arms and hands of the players. Smooth, hairy, freckled, polished, cut, bandaged, splinted. My New York Sharks.

"Here he comes, Christine," says Tanker, before Sarah can say more. Coach Jack walks by us and gets on the bus.

"Aren't you going to say something?" shrieks Kim and I hear my grandma's words telling me that silence is sometimes the loudest statement.

"No. I'm just going to fire him when we get home," I answer, and slowly herd the players onto the bus.

The first stop we make is to a liquor store. I purchase several bottles of cabernet and the players opt mainly for beer and vodka. Many empty bottles later, the bus is a veritable dance club. Some have forgotten the loss, some are still trying to forget it, but all are hungry and emitting noises that sound like feeding time at the zoo. I tap the driver on the shoulder and slur words asking him to find food. He does. A McDonalds off of I-95, somewhere in Rhode Island. The Sharks spill into the restaurant like a bin of fish onto a dock. We are sitting at tables, standing in food lines, crowding bathrooms, and I am not sure what goes through my very inebriated mind, but I pick up a french fry and wing it at Eve who is seated across the room.

"Settle down Numbah 7," she yells across the room and then wings one back. Wendy joins, but chooses a hamburger bun from her artillery. It spins like a ketchup laden frisbee and smacks against Jessie's shoulder.

"Fwoogh!" says Jessie—the only time I've ever heard the word. "Look at 'dis shit you got on my sweatshirt!" and she hurls an apple pie in defense. Cooper brings me another installment of fries, seeing that I could run low on ammo, and the air is pretty well congested with food items when I hear a shout from behind the counter.

"You people need to get outta here! Now!" so I grab a ketchup pack and drill her upside the head. She lets out a screech not unlike the Orient Express going through a junction. Turpie decides it might be time to go and shouts for everyone to "Get on the bus!"

"Now!" crows Coach Jack astutely. I am standing in my seat armed with Cooper's fresh pack of fries, when I see Piper talking to a man and pointing at me. Piper, somewhat Eeyore-ish by nature, has taught her anger to have manners. It is contained in her detective shell, which keeps her just the right size for her world. Humor is important for her balance and I know she gets amused at Shark antics, yet says nothing. So, I don't know what she is telling the man, but I'm sure it is sparse enough to supercharge the situation. The man arrives just as I am wiping mustard off my wishbone. He asks if I am in charge and I say "Yes" and he asks me what organization we are with and I tell him we are not very organized at all. He says we are going to be in trouble if he doesn't get some answers soon so I sit back down and take out my wallet. I thumb through it and extract a business card to give to him and when I look back up, there are three of him. I hand the business card to the one on the left, because he looks a little more solid than the other two. In the end though, the one in the middle takes it. He stares.

"Millie Pamplon? That's you?"

"Yes."

"And this is your....football team?...the New Hampshire Cobras?"

"Yes."

"Miss Pamplon, your group needs to leave and not come back. You've made a huge mess and if there are any damages, we will be contacting you for compensation." Turpie and Jack have been shoveling Sharks onto the bus, but are now standing next to me listening to the conversation.

"Sir, we understand and we will be happy to pay you if we did any damages," Turpie says. "We'll be on our way back to New Hampshire now. Thank you so much..." she takes my arm as I stand up, but my legs are not interested in moving.

"I got her," says Jack and throws me over his shoulder and hurries outside. He deposits me into my seat on the bus. I sleep.

The next day, I am hung over. The ring of the phone that afternoon is most unwelcome, but I pick it up anyway since it is Turpie. She starts the conversation with a laugh, then a long pause and finally "How you feelin' buddy?" More laughter.

"Later today, I'm going to try to stand up. If that goes well, tomorrow, I'll try to make it across the room to a chair."

"Buddy...." she is laughing. "Whhhooooooeeee! I never seen you like that, but that was some kinda funny! You gave him that card and I nearly died! I could hardly keep a straight face."

"What's really going to be funny is when I tell Millie they have her info and they think our team is hers!"

"When you gonna do it?"

"As soon as I can make it to the phone" I am laughing a little, but it hurts my head.

CHAPTER 42

THE AGONY OF DEFEAT

*I think of all the young women who will now be able to fulfill their dream
of playing football that couldn't before.*

Around 4 that afternoon, I feel well enough to compose an e-mail to the team.

Dear Sharks,

*I am so very proud of you! Each and every one of you! We overcame some tough
obstacles this season and we ALL have much to be proud of. New Hampshire is
a very healthy organization (physically that is, not mentally because we are all
nuts for doing this!) and it took every bit of them to squeak by us! Our team is
like no other. You don't always have to win to feel Shark magic and I felt it yesterday from a wonderful, talented group of football players: THE NEW YORK
SHARKS! My love and gratitude for giving it your all, making me proud to own
such an incredible franchise. And more important: to have you all in my life as
friends. Long live the finned ones!*

Christine

I read the responses, as I administer ice and aspirin for my head. Sarah's seems to
sum up what most felt. She was always finding the upside to a situation. Maybe that's
why we all respected her even though many of us were much older. She wasn't even
near turning 30, yet she always found the 'glow' in other things, that same glow that
her student had seen around her. And she always had the courage to speak up.

Christine,

*Thank you for your beautiful email. I awoke today with a bit of a pit in my stom-
ach, and I keep replaying the dropped passes, the turnovers, and their aggressive
defense in my mind. However, I don't feel any regrets. For all the injuries, bickering, lost coaches, etc., we did pretty damn well! We were sort of a rag-tag group,
but a good one at that. I walked away yesterday with a tremendous feeling of
pride for being involved with such a gritty bunch of women. Also, I got to thinking that this league isn't going to be like the Women's Pro Baseball League, and
fold. Women's football will live on way past us, and we were a part of it in the*

early years. That's pretty special! I think of all the young women who will now be able to fulfill their dream of playing football that couldn't before. We're a rare breed, but we exist and are growing. What we did yesterday is about far more than winning or losing. It was about inspiring people, ourselves, and others.

Sarah

Yes. Regardless of any situation, Sarah always had the courage to glow.

Then I call Messy. She "goddam sharks" me throughout my story of the Mickey-D food fight, until I get to the place where I give the man her card, then she begins to rumble like a volcano just before it starts to set about the villagers. She is panicking and short of breath and just before hanging up to call the league, she promises to sue me. I guess I should be concerned, but I just don't have the energy to care.

The season ends with the loss in the playoffs, but the drama and strife continue. I have to replace Coach Jack, but feel bad about it even if he does make me irritable, short-tempered and mean. Plus, Dulce and a few others still truly believe in him and will be devastated when he is canned.

So I call a meeting and decide to approach the subject with caution. I will ease into the firing of Coach Jack and treat it like a "catch and release" program of sorts. But Kim stands up while I prepare papers to hand out and derails my plan.

"We know Christine's gonna fire Coach Jack and we all know we need a real coach." There goes my approach and I glare at her.

"And the league isn't doing well either."

Dammit Kim, nobody needs to know that.

"Anything else in the box, PANDORA?" I say loudly and point to the bleachers for her to go sit.

"We need a real coach...." she mutters on her way to an empty seat on the front row.

We all want to win the next championship. The question is how? Most understand we can't possibly get there without a much better coach. Dulce keeps insisting that we're underestimating Jack. Others wonder out loud if I'm dismissing him because he's black. I am incredulous, but try to reason with them. "This team has tremendous talent and not enough focus or leadership to win the championship," I say trying to remain both calm and strong.

Growing up in the south, I have seen the cruelty of racism. I know it's uneasiness and I feel it creeping into this conversation directed towards me. Words sting. It feels as if each letter were a small needle piercing my psyche, and I feel my body go limp. I revisit the exclusion I felt from my childhood when all I wanted was to play football with the boys. The game gave me a feeling of camaraderie, a hope of finding my identity and feasting on the shavings of glory that had been denied to me for being a girl. I had felt isolated and banished from mainstream childhood for so long. This same rejection is pelting me like a cold rain now, and I try, like I often did as a child, to become clear-colored and invisible.

"If you don't believe in this team, why don't you just leave it?" one player calls out to another. That, along with other hurtful and destructive challenges are thrown around the room until Dulce starts crying. "Is this how it's going to end?" she wails. The room becomes unusually quiet and still, and then Big Dot gets up and walks away. We all stare, as Big Dot becomes a little dot on the horizon.

CHAPTER 43

MUCH NEEDED WISDOM

You must first know who you really are
in order to have what you really want.

Several of my Significant Others have been the ones to take off. Two of them found Jesus, and felt I would be a bad influence. At least those two were perceptive. Another was schizoid. Had at least eight personalities. Word between them must have spread quickly because one afternoon, all eight of them packed up and took off. Only one lingered long enough to string up my stuffed duck over the bed. The noose was so tight the button eyes bulged. I cut that duck down quick as I could, but to this day her long neck flops over.

I don't remember what happened to the others. All I know is I'm like LaGuardia airport: Someone is always taking off. Now my twelve-year love is at the end of the relationship runway, listening for the towers' clearance for departure! After hanging out with that "friend" of ours in the Hamptons, Ellen has decided I am no longer an asset and she should, like a good bra, 'lift and separate.' So she does. Just fires up the burners and zips off, while I stand helplessly on the top floor of our Greenwich Village brownstone with Dina on my left shoulder. We watch her shoot down the proverbial runway. At one point, she makes a 180-degree turn and heads back. A faint smile appears on my face, until I notice she is flying low and straight at me. To further use the airplane metaphor, she is buzzin' the tower! Everyone hit the dirt!

The first flyby comes with this message: "I can't stand that fucking bird of yours!" How could anyone hate this parrot, I wonder? "Plug your ear holes." I softly say to Dina. "She doesn't mean it." Little human trapped in a green-feathered body. She just wants to be scratched and....Oooo! Look out! She's headed back for fly-by number two.

150

"And that SHITTY COUNTRY MUSIC you listen to!" she bellows and begins a third circle. They say the third one's a charm and indeed it is round three, which delivers the most venomous sentiment, and the one she proceeds to tell every bi-pedal carbon based creature on the planet.

"And.." she begins and then inhales all the air that will fit into her lungs to unleash the finishing touch. "...I...HATE...those...GODDAM SHARKS!!!!!" Then she maxes out the burners and is out of sight, my "serious" twelve-year human investment fizzing away like a bottle rocket.

Silence. Earsplitting silence. But after twelve years, I guess I'm not surprised. Knowing someone so well can become a curse. Every fake laugh...you know. Every forced interest...you feel. The low level, snide comments...you hear. Even so, this split is not my choice so, like most broken-hearted humans, I immediately begin to manifest death.

Back when marriage was invented, people only lived to be thirty or so. By the time a couple began to really know each other, one of them had the courtesy to drop dead. I would gladly do her a favor, but in the months to follow, I can only muster malnutrition and over-all poor health.

It is February of 2001, in New York City. It is freezing out. I hate cold and I'm a bit of a homebody, so I light a fire, turn up Vivaldi and peruse my bookshelf for some answers. This is what I find. A book called 'Simple Abundance—A Daybook of Comfort and Joy.' It had been a gift from my oldest sister Annie, who inscribed these words to Ellen and me.

This looked interesting, so I bought one for each of us! I love you dearly. Merry Christmas! Annie, 1996.

'*Each of us.*' That is so like Annie. Although claiming to be acquainted with a "rough life," Annie and "rough life" have never met. Married to a man who allows her to indulge, Annie is the star of excess. If Annie were to write the same book, it would not be 'Simple Abundance—A Daybook of Comfort and Joy.' It would be 'Over' Abundance—A Daybook of 'Too Much' but 'Who's Counting?' Buying one for 'each of us' means she emptied the shelf, ordered more and began dispersing them to everyone she knows and many she has yet to meet on the streets.

But how fortuitous that one such 'Simple Abundance' book has found its way into my hands, if for no other reason than to replace the revolver. I look at it: 'A Daybook of Comfort and Joy.' I weigh the odds:

A. Suicide

B. Comfort and Joy.

151

...Suicide

...Comfort and Joy

...S

...C&J.

I open the book. C&J is set up logically. It begins with January, and no year or day of the week is mentioned, so one can experience C&J, year after year, without it becoming dated. January 1st begins with a quote from Margaret Young who, clearly not a recent dumpee, has this to say: *"Often people live their lives backwards. They try to have more things, or more money, in order to do more of what they want so that they will be happier. The way it actually works is the reverse. You must first be who you really are, thus, do what you need to do, in order to have what you want."*

It takes a minute for the words to penetrate my pervasive numbness, then it sinks in. My response is succinct. I make the noise one makes when one sticks ones' tongue out between ones' lips and expels air with great force, thus indicating that I think Marge's theory is a load of shit. But somewhere inside myself, her words ring true. *"You must first be who you really are, then do what you need to do, in order to have what you want."* I ask myself again, for the second time in a short span: Who am I? What the hell do I want? I sit in front of the fire looking like I've been sent for, and can't make it. Personal hygiene went out the front door with my ex. My hair, protruding and matted, looks like someone faxed it to me from an unidentified quadrant of the galaxy. In my attempt at procuring death, I have proudly manifested a huge lump of disease on my lower lip, which affects the surrounding glands, swelling the lower left side of my head. My attire which I have not changed in days, is a collection of simultaneously worn socks, a pair of twenty-four-year old sweatpants emblazoned with a Florida State Seminole insignia and my cut-off sweatshirt bearing the name of my women's 'pro' football team, the New York 'Goddam' Sharks which I acquired only six months prior to her departure. I don't think I smell, but I know by the time you start smelling yourself, your friends have been smelling you for days.

I repeat Marge's wisdom again. *'You must first be who you really are, thus, do what you need to do, in order to have what you want.'* Who am I 'really'? What do I need to do? And after I do what I need to do, what do I want? I am unable to summon answers. Since Ellen left and I set my sights on expiring, I have simply lost interest. I have friends, but the one I titled "best" is in full-throttle towards Ellen's side of life and I am not sure who I can trust. My family, all living in Florida, are an odd mix of stability and lately, I can never tell what shoot any of them will be coming out of.

I know they love me, but their disapproval of my team and earlier, my relationship with a woman, causes me to keep a safe distance. Pained and wary, I am penurious with information and petrified to ask for support. Rejection, to me, can be one word spoken or one action never taken.

Again. Who am I...really? The answer; I am a suicide-in-progress who has nothing left in life but a women's tackle football team.

What do I need to do? The answer; I need to open another bottle of wine.

What do I want? I cock my head and say out loud, "I want off of this disgusting little planet. That's what I want. There, Margaret Young. That wasn't so hard to figure out!" I pad over to the wine rack, one set of socks having slid partially off, makes my feet look sixteen inches long. I pause then pluck a bottle of "Fat Bastard" from the remains of our collection. Ellen took all the good wine we were saving for special occasions. Even the bottles we dragged home from the duty-free stores in Italy. Getting rid of me must be very special to her. She is undoubtedly, at this moment, littering the Hampton's with celebratory corks.

There's that damn phone ringing. It does this with alarming frequency and is, I'm sure, another of the countless items that spooked Ellen into flight. I pick it up because I always hope for her return. It is Tanker. Her demeanor can be aptly described as "jolly." Mine is not. So there we are, the antithesis of each other. Black-white. Small-large. Jolly-depressed. Optimistic-defeated.

"How's my favorite owner?"

"Above sod and foggin' mirrors," I utter with no emotion because it has poured out with my tears, leaving its rusty sediment on my pillow, during sleepless hours of the previous night.

"I just want you to know that we are gonna kick everybody's ASS this year! I don't want you to worry about things, because it's all good. It's all good!" It was fitting of Tanker to try to protect me from any worry about the team. She was like a mother bear and would shred anything that threatened anyone or anything she loved though, in truth, she would prefer that everyone just got along. She was all about loving others. Except when she played football and even then, when she stepped off of the field, she was back in 'love' mode. She carries a picture of herself teaching school. It shows her in front of her classroom with about eight kids hanging off her like a big tree and another five or six trying to find a place to grab.

"I tell them if they need some love energy to come hang onto me 'cause I am the love. They're always trying to hang on me for some energy. They think I give it to them. Ha! Them kids believe everything I say, but it's them giving me the energy so I can finish the day!"

I first met Tanker when I quarterbacked her flag team. All of the members were African-American except me. They said I was white chocolate and called me Alpine. Once, in a flag game, she dove for the flag and when she hit the ground, a rock peeled the skin on her shin up about 6 inches. I got to her just as she sat up to examine the skin rolled up her shin like the top of a sardine can. I was taken aback by the sight of the pink flesh and the bright white of her bone. She grimaced at first, then flashed a big grin at me. "See, Christine! Underneath, we all white."

"Thanks Tank," I say to her now.

"Ok, favorite owner? It's all good! Now you go eat something cause you gonna disappear if you don't. Those new shorts you had on at practice were the size of a Ziploc bag! You need to eat, ok, favorite owner?" she has a soul of goodness that we suspect she gets from 'her mama.' She never speaks of siblings or her father, good or bad, but her mom is a gentle person who babies 'her Leah' every chance she gets. And Tanker passes it on. Tanker is, as she claims, "the love! I am the LOVE!"

"Thank you, Leah." On occasion, I slip and call her by her real name. She usually complains, but today she ignores the slip.

"I'll talk to you tomorrow at the meeting. We gonna KICK SOME ASS THIS YEAR!" I grin in spite of myself. "They irk my nerves," as Turpie says, but these "goddam Sharks" are always able to produce a smile in one fashion or another.

CHAPTER 44

WOMEN'S PRO
PHFFFFFT-BALL TEAM

"Let them come after me!" I say to Turpie as well as to the woman
interviewing me from the Village Voice

As best as I can, I prepare for the 2001 season. There remain disagreements between the WPFA and the Sharks on what is expected from each party. Namely, they expect us to send them money for doing and offering nothing and we expect a league that is not full of crooks. Virtually everything the WPFA tells us turns out not to be true, almost immediately. The only exception to this is when we are told something will happen immediately, in which case, it turns out to be not true over an extended period of time.

Messy Tampon is suing the WPFA because Mia's team, the Los Angeles Launch beat the New Hampshire Cobras in the Championship. She is also suing the other team owners...because...Mia's team, the Los Angeles Launch beat the New Hampshire Cobras in the Championship. I have had enough of Messy Tampon's claims, rants, fits and lawsuits and refuse all conference calls with the league concerning her bogus and juvenile threats. She needn't ask her infamous question anymore—I definitely know who she is! I want nothing to do with her.

I take my team and jettison the WPFA. "Let them come after me!" I say to Turpie as well as to the woman interviewing me from the Village Voice, the newspaper of Greenwich Village, which is miraculously following us. I declare the New York Sharks independent and it goes to press.

"I'm with you wherever you go buddy," Turpie says. "And, without the rules of the league, we can choose our own coach and I think I know just who to talk to," she has that charming grin on her face.

CHAPTER 45

HAYDEN AND REASONS

She found the courage to finally stand up for herself
and play regardless of people telling her no.
She says it's the best thing she has ever done for herself.

"Why didn't I think of that? Of course Hayden will do it!" I hug Turpie's neck and shortly after that, I hire Hayden, our flag football coach who has some playing experience and a good flag record. We also find a guy from Maine who has fled from Millie's team and wants to coach us. There are a few others, namely brothers or friends who want to become involved with the Sharks and slowly, a staff is formed.

Players like Tanker, Dulce and Sarah are very excited about the new season but since the last meeting, when Big Dot rumbled off, and players were crying and fighting, we aren't sure who is coming back. Turpie and I have been on the phone to all the players.

"Buddy, I heard some things on those calls." I look at her and nod my head in agreement. "Janet said she wasn't going to come back, but her cousin accused her of not being able to handle the physical aspect of the game. It pissed her off. A lot! So she's coming back to prove him wrong. Plus she loves us."

"I like Caitlin's story," I say. "She says she started playing as an honor to her mom, who always encouraged her to do anything she wanted. Her mom said that women were strong, but we had to change the way the world perceives us. After her mom passed away from cancer, Caitlin said that she was still scared of what people would think, but her mom's words challenged her."

"Watching her on the field, you'd never know she had any fear of anything!"

"She told me she was never going to quit. Plus she loves us, too."

We take turns revealing the underlying motives some of the players have for being a Shark.

"Paige said it was a blessing in disguise because when she lost her dad last year, we were the only family she had left. She told me there were more Sharks at his funeral than anyone," I tell her "And the Sharks didn't even know him. They went for her and that meant the world..."

"Gemma said that a few years ago her parents refused to let her play on a college team. She's regretted it ever since, so when this came along, she said she found the courage to finally stand up for herself and play regardless of people telling her no. She says it's the best thing she has ever done."

"And Jade Max. Jade said that after she got cancer, the only thing that got her through was her determination to get better so she could get on the field again. We do a lot of good for people, buddy. We really do."

"I know. It's true." We don't tell our own stories out loud but we know we both share space in that group and are silently grateful.

Most say they are returning, but you never know until practice starts. That day is scheduled for late in February, which is about to bloom. It will most likely be an icy cold morning when the sun is reluctant to peer into the new day. Sharks will appear from nowhere, giving hugs, checking to see who shows up, and who got fat in the off-season.

"Looks like she stuck an air hose up her ass," Eve says about Kim. "And look, it looks like she combed her hair with a pack of firecrackers." I didn't notice that Kim had gained weight, but the firecracker-hair comment made me laugh. Kim's hair looked exactly like that.

I am hoping our season can have a 10-game schedule against teams from the WPFA, like the Tampa Tide, the New York Goldrush, newly formed teams like the Arizona Beasts and the North Carolina Lynx. I call the owner of the Lynx first in hopes of setting up a game. Donnie and I chat briefly regarding the direction of women's football and how difficult it is owning a team. He says he "Can't get no press coverage and the only ones in the stands are friends and relations." I tell him I understand.

"I would really like to schedule your team, Donnie. My Sharks would love to come to North Carolina, and we hope you can give us a return game here in New York."

"Well, I have to check our vineyard. I may change it this season, and I'll let you know because if my vineyard changes, then I won't have an answer so quick."

I suspect he means 'venue' and immediately recall our neighbor who entertained my mom and grandma with her constant bloopers. One of her more popular gaffes was the time she announced that she was going into Tampa to see the Royal Lesbian Stallions. Neither of them told her it was the Royal Lipizzaner Stallions. Nor did they correct her when she brought a 'latrine' (tureen) of soup over for dinner one night.

And they joined right in when she said she was off to get her 'tennis' (tetanus) shot saying they had to go get their 'tennis' shots, too.

I try to steer him onto the right path. "Our venue is actually in New Jersey this year, so you won't have the hassle of coming into the city. It's very easy to find, our venue—right off I-95!"

He misses the suggested turn. "Some vineyards are easy to deal with and others are not. You know how that goes."

'Oh, what the hell...' I think and join in. "I would hate that...for you to have to change vineyards. Especially if the one you have is a good one. I haven't been in a good vineyard since Tuscany, 1994."

"Naw, it's not any great piece of real estate, but they got what we need. I'll get back to you."

"Please don't change vineyards on our account." Now I am having some fun. "My motto is---any vineyard is a good vineyard!" Caymus crosses my mind as I hang up the phone and think of the wonderful wines that have graced my lips. I feel I should have some right away, so I do. I open a bottle and begin a session I call "drink and think." I drink and think of ways to earn money for my team. Will it ever happen? And how can I ever pay for all of my players to get to North Carolina if Donnie does find a vineyard for us to play on? How can I afford to go on like this? Finances are tough without Ellen, and this team is steering me towards financial and emotional disaster.

When Ellen and I first got together, I was a typical struggling artist. My heart was set on being a cartoonist and I worked diligently on submissions, namely to The New Yorker magazine. On submission day Ellen would drive me in her Neon to the offices of The New Yorker while I ran in to deliver them by hand. She believed in me.

I also created a cartoon strip called 'Sally the Maladjusted,' and when it came time to put Sally on computer, Ellen withdrew money from her savings to purchase the equipment. She liked my art form and knew that someday I would be successful. She believed in me.

I had some success with Sally starring in a greeting card line; then got the job at Time Warner and left Sally behind. And now Ellen had left me behind. Why had she stopped believing in me? Why did she leave me behind?

CHAPTER 46

LEE AND INDEPENDENCE

The reporter had wanted to "See what it was like to play tackle football." I am trying to remember how much those flowers we sent to the hospital set us back.

Lee Hurd. Lee flutters down from heaven. Lee, like the rest of us, is addicted to women's football. Lee, a friend of Coopers, offers to create a website. I am thrilled and say yes, and so he does.

Lee is convivial. Though extremely polite, he is not shy, and there is a mischievousness to him that comes out in his subtle humor. He lives in Boston. His parents live in Brooklyn, which, lucky for us, encourages him to come down for every Sharks event. Lee is never without his video camera and takes copious notes, which gives our website a supply of ever-changing content.

The website Lee builds isn't just any website. It becomes the heartbeat of the NY Sharks and the most popular, raved about site of all women's football teams; the number now up to over twenty. Our website has content like no other teams' website, and it changes almost daily. It has pages for stats, pics, events, schedules, article links, and team related contests. Lee takes pictures of our apparel and creates what he calls the "Baitshop." He takes pictures of the players and staff and creates individual trading cards. He posts them as postcards we can send to friends and family. He adds personal pages for sponsorship and personal e-mail addresses, just in case we garner a fan or two. Lee attends every game, home and away, and films interviews with Sharks when they receive game balls, something the coaches award after each game.

He films Sharks accolades outside of football, like job promotions or other kinds of recognition. He creates "Shark Player of the Week" and Mabel even persuades Carson Creamery Company to sponsor it. Five hundred dollars! It is the most we have ever received. Because of Lee's website, potential players show up to try out, a few more people are in the stands and the newspapers cover us a little more than before. In addition to that, Lee is fun! And normal! And supportive! Lee rocks!

The team seems happy with the website too, except for "the Coven." They think it should always feature them, since many of them are our best players: Paige, Asha,

Amy, Holly, and several others like Big Dot and Gwen who drift from one side of the fence to the other depending on the benefits.

The day of the meeting and our first practice finally arrives. I have written an agenda, which outlines new policies and changes, and I will gather the players up before the practice starts to tell them:

A. We are independent this season (Why we jumped out of the WPFA)

B. About our new website (Lee rocks!)

C. New fundraising efforts (I can't afford you people)

D. New Coaches/Staff (Let's try again)

E. New rules of the season (Let's rise above troglodyte level in our behavior)

Meanwhile, I sit in my car at August Martin high school in Queens, our new practice and game location, reminiscing about Wendy slamming into a news reporter who suited up at a practice last year. The reporter had wanted to "See what it was like to play tackle football." I am trying to remember how much those flowers we sent to the hospital set us back.

She was a slight, spirited kind of woman, with short, blonde hair bowed in a way on the sides of her head that made it seem like she was wearing parentheses. She was excited to have the uniform on. We were excited to get some press coverage. Overall, it was a win-win. Just before the play began, she said "Don't hit me! I just want to get some footage of me in the Shark uniform with Sharks coming after me. Just don't hit me!" she pleaded. Shark heads bobbed with acknowledgment. I know Wendy heard her too, but hit her anyway on a dead run, turning the reporter into a human missile firing across the field so fast her parentheses stayed behind.

We searched for missing reporter parts until her cameraman said the car was ready and he was taking her to the hospital. She didn't object. We helped her to the car, several Sharks carrying her belongings and all of us apologizing for Wendy's behavior. The flowers we sent were an additional apology for two broken ribs.

Finally, the Sharks begin to arrive. Turpie and I are eager to see if Big Dot is amongst them. The perennials are the first to arrive: Jade Max, Kay, Little Toni, Sarah, Wendy, Caitlin, Dulce, Jessie, Wanda, Asha, Kim, Molly, Piper, Rose, Cindy, Tanker and Azure. Then the annuals begin to trickle in: Joy, the Reynolds twins, Disco ball Carol, Heather, Ava, Tara, Josephine, LaToya, Bendel, Barnyard, Sandy, Jessica and Kellie. And finally, Big Dot arrives looking like a human snapping turtle. I attempt communication.

"What's the matter, Dot? Did you leave the hay a bit early this morning?" She looks at me, but does not respond. Clearly, my words confuse her although they make perfect sense to me. If one 'hits the hay' in the evening, then one 'leaves the hay' come morning. Perhaps this whole 'hay' concept is throwing her off.

"Not in a confetti-scattering mood, eh?" I take another stab at it.

"Do I look like a fuckin' people person?" she asks and slowly walks towards Kim and the Coven. I give thanks that she is not our opponent, but a tiny alarm in my head goes off.

Mabel arrives and immediately invades my air space with important news. She stares up at me through her thick glasses, and I take a step back to regain some lost personal terrain.

"The Hong Kong Dragon Boat Festival is coming up."

Well call Grandma. Wake up the kids.

"And there is a dumpling eating contest. I'd like to send an email out to the team asking if anyone would like to participate in a dumpling eating contest. It is a lot healthier than downing hot dogs!" She is serious. "It will take place next Sunday, at Flushing Meadow Corona Park and there is a first, second and third prize in both men's and women's divisions. There is no charge for the contest or the festival, so if any of the Sharks want to bring their family or friends, it would be a great afternoon at the lake." She pauses for air intake or whatever life-sustaining substance she requires to continue life.

Turpie takes a deep breath. "There must be somethin' in the water out here, buddy. They all crazy." I silently agree.

Dulce bounces over to Little Toni, Sarah and Azure who are standing around watching Jessie don her suit of armor, which has more padding than a Sealy mattress.

"Hello my loves!" she greets them, while swishing her hair. "Everybody come look at the poster my Sweetness made for me." She holds up a 2 x 3-foot poster of herself in full make-up and gear looking out at us, queen of all she surveys. "I look so good here!" she declares, and she is right. "And look at the article the Staten Island Advance wrote on us." She has a huge stack of papers and begins giving them out. Since the Staten Island Advance has agreed to cover us, and Dulce is our only Staten Island resident, she is usually featured. Works for me, but some of the other players are not as impressed. Tanker skims the article and passes it to Sarah who says Dulce should frame it since she is featured in it. Dulce then pulls out a framed version and holds it high for her subjects to see. There is a picture of her running the ball, looking rather "Heisman-ish" and then there's a shot of her without her helmet on, smiling proudly into the camera. As a substance abuse counselor and a devout Christian-gone-spiritual, it is a true dichotomy in the study of human behavior. But none of the Sharks are studying human behavior. They are hahaha-ing and bitch-bitch-bitching about the article all around the parking lot until I call them over.

"2001 New York Sharks!" I say to the A.D.D. riddled group. Little Toni is in helmet, full pads and sunglasses on her razor scooter. She rolls to a stop beside Azure, whose spiked blue hair is thumbing through the breeze. Kim has brought her spider monkey who is sitting on her shoulder fondling an unidentified item the size of a baseball. Janet and Eve clearly have hangovers, but are trying to be polite and listen. Wendy's yellow pick-up, jammed with the gear of several players, slides to a pebbly stop dangerously close to the group. She gets out and trots over.

"Sorry. Heh heh."

Turpie leans in. "Buddy, I think you bought a fixer-upper team."

"...overpaid...." I say and segue into the start of the meeting.

"Sharks! Please listen while I go through a few announcements, so we can get on to the good stuff. First of all, WELCOME to the 2001 New York Sharks!" Applause. Several hoots. One screech from a rookie, that sounds painful. "As you all know, we are no longer part of the WPFA." More hoots. "We have formed our own schedule and will be governed by our own rules until further notice. Our rules have been set by management and our new coaches." Turpie begins passing out copies. "Please read them, sign the bottom and hand them back to Turpie. This is a contract and we expect you to uphold the rules of the New York Sharks and represent the team well at all times! Any questions?" I can hear muttering as they scan the list, but no one says anything. "Good. Now, I'd like a round of applause for Lee, our web master, the man who has created our incredible website!" More loud noises of approval from the group as I try to coax Lee from behind his video camera to the front of the group. He waves me off and continues to film.

I take up where I left off. "So now, I would like to introduce our new Head Coach, Hayden Bellaci!" Wolf whistles, gurgles and primitive noises fill the air followed by a long fear-based yowl from Dulce, which puzzles me until I see that Kim and the monkey have moved closer to the front of the group, putting themselves in close proximity to her.

"Keep that thing away from me!"

"You hear that you monkey?" yells Eve. "Keep Kim away from Dulce!"

Hayden has lumbered before the team. He is heavy set, shorter than Coach Jack and, entirely opposite of Jack's vocal blasts, Hayden's words are garbled like a poorly mixed recipe and served in a low rumble. He mumbles towards us how honored he is to have the position, how he wants to do a good job and how he wants us all as a team to grow together. This is followed by Janet stating to no one in particular, that it looks like he has been growing all on his own. He ignores this slur, garbles some more info that few hear, and we are off to the practice field.

The season begins.

CHAPTER 47

A RAGGEDY BEGINNING

The Sharks have harvested pure, unfiltered asshole energy
and are ready to decant it, without discretion, on a whim.

It starts with a scrimmage in Baltimore, which is a warning signal I do not heed. We have car-pooled early one Saturday morning to arrive at the start time of 11 am. After an hour of scrimmaging, the prognosis is bleak. Our defense looks barely ok. Offense, not even. Our coaches show no leadership qualities and our players behave like assholes. Jessie struts around the field like a gamecock yelling at her teammates. Piper is openly criticizing Kim, and others are feeding off it. Dulce is boasting of her field prowess from her childhood and demanding to play where she wants. The scrimmage ends when Alyssa, our self-proclaimed Christian goody-goody halfback, careens out of control, trying to block for Dulce at running back, and flattens our own QB Eve, who pops back up like a jack-in-the-box and emotes at Alyssa.

"Asshole motherfucker!" she froths. Alyssa declares her innocence stating that she was just trying to block for Dulce. Eve tells her she "couldn't block a doorway" and from there, all Sharks fire non-stop insults at each other thinking it must be just the right thing to do in a situation such as this.

Though the squabble includes only players from our team, players from both teams somehow become riled up and converge into a human pile of flailing appendages. Candi, the Baltimore delegate, a sweet, somewhat bearded woman of solid stature separates herself from the mound and stomps towards me on the sideline.

"Christine, we're done here!" I, who never intended to counter her statement, am moving in her direction from the sideline waving my hand in agreement. Whistles blow. Scrimmage is over. Players, after dusting and preening, and coaches, after striking indignant poses and burping up surly remarks, settle into a line to shake hands. Somehow, I can only think of how hungry I am. I wish I had some of my mom's chicken and rice. I am 'visualizing' it when sweet Candi interrupts with a positive statement.

"Good luck in the season. Beat Sacramento for us!" she says, trying to move her team past the unfortunate incident. After all, the fracas started between two Sharks and had nothing to do with them. They can rise above and not take it personally.

"Not winning shit for you!" says one of my unidentified assholes. Well, there. That brings it around to being personal. Now both teams have been included and we can hate each other with reason.

The whole aura continues to roll downhill and several descriptive words are grunted out between the two lines of players. I know I should be concerned, but I just want to go eat food at the promised after-party.

Minutes later, I stand wolfing down the Baltimore-provided baked ziti, while Candi pours further details of how beastly and rude my players are into my throbbing ears. I am already aware of this and just don't give a shit anymore, but I want to be polite so I shake the noggin up and down in agreement as I chew.

"You know, it just gives a bad impression of your team." I nod again in agreement, but can't take my eyes off of her chin and the tangle of hairs that dance as she speaks. I have not seen a bearded woman before. Not that there's anything wrong with it.... Christ, am I hungry!

"I'm sorry Candi. My team was built on an ancient asshole burying ground. I will speak to them."

It is mid-chew that I spot Dulce on the far sideline. Trouble has erupted. Her strides are long, her arms swing like guillotines. Her gloved hand holds her jersey which has been taken off in a rage. Head down, she bullets towards her car. The rookies eyes bug out in a manner made famous by snails, as they watch her leg it for the parking lot leaving a loud trail of "I'm never coming back."

"Oh God. I know that walk." Candi looks across the field, then back at me. "I'm sorry." I tell her. "I have to go catch my two-year old before she drives out into traffic." I take a last peek at the awesome dancing hairs and begin to cross the field. Turpie meets me on the field, as I begin crossing it. I nod towards Dulce. "Who's the producer of this theatrical event?"

"Big Dot." She says with a fair amount of disgust. "One of the Coven. They evil, that Coven. She was trying to talk to Coach when Dulce walked up. Big Dot said 'I'm talking to him now. You can brown-nose him later,' and then the show began."

"Oh dear. She should know Dulce's gonna react to that."

"I told her that. She asked if she should apologize and I said probably she should."

"Good." Then I stop in mid-stride. I look at Turpie. "I'm not going after her. I can't. I just can't anymore." These 'goddam' Sharks, I think to myself. Last year, they insulted other teams, our fans and families. This year, we have raised the bar to include each other! We are no Disney team overcoming hardships while going for the gold. We don't epitomize some Spielberg spin where the good guys finally win! The Sharks have harvested pure, unfiltered asshole energy and decant it, without discretion, on a whim.

"There's that bottle of red zin in the car," says Turpie. "Let's open it."

"Let's." And we do.

CHAPTER 48

VICTORY, AND A VERY CLOSE CALL

How do you forget 65 loud, uninhibited people?

Our web becomes more famous, as Lee does write-ups after every game. Other teams attempt to model their sites after ours, but the content is never as fresh as the Sharks.' Our array of players provides limitless fodder and Lee doesn't miss a single chance to promote the team. We, in turn, give him a great season to write about. Our first game is July 28, 2001. We play the New Hampshire Cobras in Portsmouth and beat them 20-0. I had stupidly hoped that I would look up and see Ellen in the stands watching the game, waiting for it to be over so she could hold me tight, and tell me how silly she had been. The only thing silly is my imagination. Still, I always scan the stands during every game. Just in case.

An eerily quiet Sunday and Monday follow the first game. No calls. Not one e-mail. Tuesday, about mid-day came Hayden's e-mail to the team.

'Please let us know if you will not be at practice tonight.' Two responded that they would try, but were working late. Then silence again. It began pouring about 4 pm, so Hayden sent another e-mail.

'It's pouring, so we will meet at the rec center in Secaucus at 7 for film session.' Which is exactly what happens, except for the Coven who arrive at 8:45. Until then, it is fairly asshole-free, until Big Dot rises like a phantom and screams some gibberish about segregating offense and defense, but she looks so ridiculous in front of the team that even Wendy tells her she looks bad. We end at 11:50 with about 12 Sharks left. It appears we have gotten through a practice without incident.

But that is because, I realize later, we have saved it for a special episode. It premieres at LaGuardia airport as we are boarding the plane to North Carolina.

The Sharks make it one by one to the airport, with time to spare. As each Shark checks in, the people behind the counter usher them into an area off to the side and tell us to wait until we are called. So we wait. We pass the time with card games. We listen to music with headphones on. Sarah, being Sarah, involves all of us in a Q and A game.

"What your favorite animal?" she asks to a group consisting mainly of linesman.

"A dog." says one.

"Tiger!" says another.

"My favorite animal is a sirloin," says Tanker.

"You're a vegetarian!" declares Sarah.

"Not when I'm liking a sirloin!" Tanker laughs.

"You're such an oxymoron, Tanker," Sarah adds and smiles.

"Leave off the 'oxy' and you got her," this from Jessie.

I am listening and laughing at them. For some reason I rarely join in the festivities. I feel like the universal friend, but very much an outsider. I look at my watch and wonder why they haven't called us so I leave our little cordoned off area, and go to the desk to ask. The woman is visibly startled when she sees me. Apparently, she has forgotten us, and the plane is nearly boarded and ready to go. How do you forget 65 loud, uninhibited people?

"Tell them to come now," she says brusquely, not admitting her error. I motion for the Sharks and lead the large group to the gate. Kim and the Coven are the last ones in line. About 30 of us are on the plane, the rest are close behind when a flight attendant announces that the doors are closing and "unless you are going to North Carolina, you are on the wrong plane."

Tanker has just ducked through the doorway and is standing in the aisle. "We still got a lot of Sharks out there!" she says. "I ain't leaving my teammates!"

"Ma'am please take your seat." Five feet, eleven inches and three-hundred pounds of Leah 'Tanker' Woods carefully inspects flight attendant number one.

"You got about 30 people standing out there. We aren't quite ready for take off. Just saying..." Tanker continues down the aisle looking for her seat. I am about to open a can of tomato juice that flight attendant number two has just handed me, but instead, I get up to see how many are really still out there.

"Ma'am you'll have to sit down now. We are closing the door and will be leaving in one minute." Flight attendant number two then grabs the door, swings it shut and pulls a long lever down to secure it.

"My team is still outside the door." I can hear them. They are laughing, then Jessie says "What the fuck? It's really closed?!"

"Ma'am they are right there," I say. "You have to let them on." I am standing near the entrance and pointing at the door with the top end of my tomato juice can.

"Sorry we are leaving. They should have been here on time."

"We were here in plenty of time!" I say. Oh God, here comes the anger. It feels like four inner walls have been moved inward a few inches. It's very uncomfortable. She ignores me and asks me to take a seat and says they can get the next flight.

"We are a women's football team. We have a game tonight in Greensboro and we have to be on this flight!" My voice is getting louder. "We paid for these tickets, we showed up on time and one of your attendants told us to wait in a separate area until they called us! We did what you asked!" Now I am yelling and am going into blackout mode and then, with no warning, my inner mother bear rears up on her back legs and slams the full tomato juice can against the cabin wall. The top pops, the sides split and it looks like murder on Flight 222 to Greensboro. The entire plane goes dead silent and we all hear Kim rasp on the other side of the door. "I'll be suing this mother-fuck-ing airline." And then she knocks politely like she would to see if someone's already in the restroom she wants to use. "I know you're in there. I can hear you caring." She says in her loud, sarcastic voice. The whole planeload is crouched, holding their breath like we are playing hide and seek and are about to be found. Dulce begins to pray. Flight attendant number one and flight attendant number two are cowering near the restroom. Then the door to the cockpit slowly opens and a hatted captain's head peeps out. My rage has quelled and I stand motionless, framed by the tomato can exhibit on the cabin wall. He looks from me to thing one and thing two.

"Let them on," he says in a low voice, then pulls his head back into the cockpit's shell. Both attendants jump to action, pushing the long lever back up, twisting the door handle and heaving the 737's weighty hatchway against the side of the plane. As the remaining 30+ Sharks board the plane, cheers erupt from the entire passenger base. Sharks bow and grin as they find their seats and I slide in, buckle up, and stare out my window. I feel so sad. I feel so alone.

CHAPTER 49

THE EDGE OF THE END

I am snapping and sure that I'm not going to make it.
Good. I'm done here.

Game Day. Greensboro, N.C., August 4, 2001. The New York Sharks were flying high after a 20-0 defeat of the New Hampshire Cobras, last week. Their next opponent was the Carolina Lynx who were unbeaten and unscored upon. We were unable to reverse that trend and the final score was 10-8; leaving the Sharks record at 1-1. Not so good.

Meanwhile, I am not so good either. The disease I have manifested on my lip and in my jaw has worsened and my team has started to refer to me as the elephant man. I feel sick all the time. Not your "flu" sick, but odd feelings in my stomach, my head. Feverish, yet no fever. I have nothing left to operate on, no life energy inside and my weight has dropped another four pounds. At Turpie's urging, I phone a doctor from my insurance plan to make an appointment. But after repeatedly being put on hold, I give up.

I finally attempt to get up from the cocoon of my bed. I feel like a wounded duck bumping around, trying to take off from a pond. I cling pathetically to an old letter from Ellen I have read so many times, I have read the words off. We had been so in love, split open to each other and now, zippered closed. I cry each time I read it because I still love and miss her so much. The interminable dramas of the Sharks and the league are simply interruptions to my time spent thinking about her. Wishing her home. I clamber back to my cocoon and whorl my body and thoughts into one. I pick up the phone to call home but I begin uncontrollably sobbing as I have never known before and am breathless as I gasp for air. I am snapping and sure that I'm not going to make it. Good. I'm done here. I'm on the edge of the end. No one needs to know that and no one needs to hear the actual snap. Rational thoughts and those of lesser descriptions fight for the use of my vocal chords, but neither prevails. Just the lump in my throat and the pain in my heart.

CHAPTER 50

WINNING BUT LOSING

She first laid down spread eagle, then curled up tight as a cocktail shrimp,
a big, black period at the end of a long, tired sentence.

Game Day. Stony Brook, N.Y. August 11, 2001. The New York Sharks played their home opener against the Syracuse Bees in Stony Brook, Long Island.

The Sharks came out of the gate smoking and scored early and often as an undersized Syracuse team had trouble containing the passing attack of the Sharks. Just before the first quarter ended, the Sharks scored again on a 30-yard pass play to Dulce Rodriguez. New York went for the 2-point conversion and this time they scored to push their lead to 34-6.

The day concluded with the familiar strains of Frank Sinatra's, "New York, New York," over the loudspeakers. The victory gives the Sharks a 2-1 record.

Little Toni, Janet's best friend and the Sharks cornerback and wide receiver, leaves me a message to please call Janet.

Janet, a short, plump athletic schoolteacher from the Bronx, and I have a special bond. She's one of the older players on the team and we find ourselves standing next to each other on the sideline, especially when play on the field is intense. We cling to each other and say Shark prayers and laugh when we finally let go after the play.

"Two old grannies here on the sideline!" She states and I concur. "Gramma A and Gramma J, we are!"

The staff, however, is often amused or frustrated over the list of chronic ailments which prevent Gramma J's participation in some practices as well as her being punctual. There is also an awful lot of complaining that emotes from Janet, but we are mostly immune to it. Her episode at Thursday's practice, however, was well-founded and I am a bit worried.

Janet had thrown a "quit fit" in response to the Covens' reaction to Kim's remarks to the coach who called the play that made her start a fight that caused the ejection that ate the cat who killed the rat that lived in the house of Christine!

Hayden had put Janet at center, which caused Kim to emote into my shoulder pad about Janet's 'inabilities.' Because Kim only thinks she speaks quietly, Little Toni heard what she said and, in defense of Janet, commented on the "inaccuracies" of Kim's vociferous comments. Drama ensued. The members of the Coven, noticing the time, 'suggested' practice be over by walking wordless and en mass off the field and toward their car. Kim followed trying to "persuade" the "fucking ingrates" to stay and listen to her "wise coaching knowledge." The actual coaches were "offended" by Kim's loud, raspy "allusions" to them being "total DICKS!" and began yelling at Kim while Kim yelled at the Coven who slowly (because they do everything slowly) migrated to the huge Cadillac Esplanade anchored in the parking lot and climbed in. Janet took off her helmet to complain about how "over it" she was.

It was misty out, a low fog rolled off New York Harbor and across the field and the image of Janet, all in black from cleats to the black bandana wrapping her head, faded as she lumbered towards the sideline, mouthing off into the thick fog.

When she reached the edge of the field, she first laid down spread eagle, then curled up tight as a cocktail shrimp, a big, black period at the end of a long, tired sentence.

The rest of the Sharks were watching in disbelief at the other portion of our imploding team. Some of our players were so bizarre and obnoxious. The coaches and I didn't know whether to laugh or quit. I owned the team. I should say something. I should yell at someone, but couldn't make up my mind who should be first! I was so tired. And I realized that I did not want this responsibility. I didn't even like the small wad of misbehaving, self-involved humans! What the hell have I done by buying this fucking football team? And to make matters worse, I had paid for this headache! It was meant for us to play out our dream, to do what was never afforded to us before as women and instead, it was being ruined by a small group of amazingly selfish people! Turpie and I stood off to the side and were both silent. Of all we had been through together, this was singular. Then, from out of the fog, Kim appeared next to us.

"I'm going to go talk to her. She annoys me," she said of Janet.

"Of course she does. Christ, Kim leave her alone. Just leave her alone."

"I can't believe she would do this. You should go talk to her," she said. I had put on my glasses to check the time. I lowered my nose and focused on her, but said nothing, which should have said everything. Still, the stare slid right off of lizard-skinned Kim. "I know it's just Janet, but she is making everything worse by acting like this," said Kim while I continued to stare, always amazed at her ability to cause trouble and place blame elsewhere.

"You shouldn't have started it all Kim!" says Turpie, standing solid in a three-piece suit and alligator loafers. She always looks professional and I appreciate that.

Especially since I am usually suited up in practice gear or a uniform and lately, I look nuttier than a squirrel's nest in winter.

"I didn't start it!" she rasped in disbelief.

"You said Janet sucked, Kim," I said.

"I didn't say that!"

"People heard you."

"That's not what I said."

"Kim, half the players heard you say it! It's not like I'm making it up." Kim often denied what clearly just flew straight from her mouth and into multiple ears!

"I'm not even gonna argue with you. You fucked up," says Turpie, as she heads towards the coaches trying to re-assemble the remains of a practice. The now absentee Coven constituted the majority of the defense, which made it hard for the offense to get in a good work-out, but they did what they could. At 11:36, they finally called practice.

We left that night with headaches and no answers as to what to do next. Janet, however, had no doubts. I awoke to an e-mail, her resignation as a player.

> Hey Sharks,
>
> I am only sending this email to the coaches minus Kim who thinks she's a coach, the O-line and a select few. I cannot express in words the frustration and disappointment I feel and have felt since last week's game. Last night was the last straw for me. I cannot believe the arrogance, ignorance and egos that exist on this team, and I no longer want to be a part of it. No one on this team can acknowledge their efforts when they are poor and no one can give another team credit for their efforts. They just want to point fingers. This week, it's the "coaches" fault. So they sat there watching film and questioned every call Hayden made. First of all, there comes a time where you, as a coach, just ASSUME (YES, I KNOW ABOUT ASSUMING AND THE WHOLE ASS THING..) but you assume that after many games, people would AT LEAST know where to stand. How do you not f-ing know where to stand? You learn from your mistakes.
>
> Thanks coaches cuz each and every day I have learned from you...you're awesome!!!
>
> Lastly, G-ma A, love ya. Go Sharks!!
>
> banged up Janet -

Shortly after this came an email from Kim sent directly to me:

> 'I have never seen a bigger bunch of assholes in my life. They all annoy me.'

Seconds later followed Turpie's e-mail:

'Is your headache gone?'

'No.' I replied. *'I just got an e-mail from her.'*

'Lol' she wrote. I didn't think it was so funny, and set the to-do list as follows:

1. Sell team

2. Book one-way flight to Italy

3. Buy more wine

I paused, then added a fourth:

4. Stop hating this team.

I needed to let all the negativity go and focus on the positive. Many of the players were true and good, but the insensitivity and cruelty and the way that some players were treating each other, the coaches and Turpie and me really hurt. Partly because of things they had said and done, and partly because I trusted them with my intentions for the team. Now I'm mad at myself for thinking I had done a good thing. This experience has been an emotional poison. I am appalled at the behavior of people I have encountered. Players have accused me of stealing, being racist and dumb. Friends have shown disloyalty and jealousy. Women have been rude and unwilling to help out fellow women, and men are grossly sexist. Or just gross. After three men, all prominent and married offered sponsorship, only if I slept with them, I quit looking. Another offered a book deal, only if I agreed to become his mistress. So the Sharks remain a very poor football team with a weary, wary and increasingly cynical and bitter owner.

CHAPTER 51

FLORIDA GAME DAY

My family is sitting in the bleachers, holding signs for me,
No. 7, QB of the New York Sharks

My team is headed, all intact, to Tampa, Florida to play. I am so excited that I tell my family we are coming, and, to my surprise, they say they will be at the game. Friends, too are coming—Becky and Ed and Tina from high school, my parents' best friends, Raybelle and Sam, who are like second parents to me. Sambo and Linda, the Fettigs, the Nye's and several of my friends are even driving up from Ft. Lauderdale and Orlando! Tina, Jan's best friend, is coming. My nephew says he is going to be there and Karen, my oldest friend ever—her mother and my mother were pregnant at the same time, so we hung out before we were born—is bringing her two children to watch. Ellen and my sisters will be the only ones missing. It hurts that Ellen is not in my life anymore. I want to slow down and understand her heart like I used to. I want to understand why she is not interested. Why she doesn't show up. I need her to be proud of me, to support my dreams, as I feel I have supported hers, but the football tornado has whisked me from my foundation and I cannot get back to a safe haven. The tempest is in control of me. I can only ride it out and hope it, along with her leaving, doesn't destroy me.

It is surreal, the evening my family and friends come to see me play. So many Friday nights during high school, I had envisioned them sitting in the bleachers at Edward B. Krutchen Field, watching me playing. I'd imagined that I was the one they followed in the 12 page Zephyrhills news, where the Bulldogs football team took up more than a third of the space every fall. I was the one given free burgers for the TD I scored against our rival, the Pendle Eagles. And today, so many years later, and almost after the fact, there they are--here we all are. Sitting in the bleachers, holding signs for Sharks, for number 7; me, and for a time long ago that is still very present to me. At one point, Turpie asks the group to do the 'Fins up' cheer where one's hand, placed on the top of one's head, is pointing upward and proud. The home-made signs are gleaming in the late afternoon Florida light. My parents, though sitting in different places in the bleachers, are luminous with pride. Everyone is smiling.

"Snap" goes Turpie's camera.

The howl exploded from mid-field shortly after the second quarter began. It was primal and made players and fans straighten their backs and prepare for a predator's attack. Another ear-damaging, primitive call was emitted and it was ascertained that it came from the bottom of a large pile-up on the forty-three yard line. 'Mmaawwmm!' went the call—the call of a child in distress calling to her mother. 'Mmaaaaaaaaawwmm!' it went off again louder and prolonged which frightened the other players and startled the refs and the players scattered, leaving the caller curled up in agony and Tanker standing frozen over her with eyes bugged and mouth unhinged, looking like a surprised halibut. The caller was Tampa's running back and what prompted the call was sticking from her leg like the branch of a small but supple tree. I believe it's called the tibia, but regardless, it was causing its' owner uncontrollable pain and fear and her cries were fierce and unnerving. Our cavewoman ancestors must have cried just like this to our cave mom's wielding the club when they were cornered by the sabretooth tiger. 'Mmmmmmmaaaaaaaaaaawwmm!'

Shortly following, the call was answered. Mmmaaaawwmm came leaping out of the stands like the sabretooth itself. Paramedics gathered their nerves and trotted towards the wailing player. Tanker stood petrified and stared down at her. I ran out with Turpie. Several players from both teams were retching off to the side.

"Tanker, come on. Let's go to our sideline." I said. She stared downward.

"Tanker, let's go buddy." Turpie tried to budge the giant from her fixed pose. She stared. We each grabbed an arm and pulled and it took both of us to dislodge her and force a step. Then she began to cry. One big tear –as big as a dinner plate--rolled down her face. Then another.

"Didn't mean to hurt her...." she said and I realized then that it was Tanker who had accidentally broken the running back's leg. My heart splintered like the protruding bone, and I put my arms as far as they would go around her, and held her tight.

The wailing in the background never ceased. Even as they loaded the injured player into the ambulance. It was the eeriest noise I have ever heard before or since.

Laura, one of our rookie linemen, was on the sideline taking off her gear.

"What are you doing?" asked Hayden.

"I'm done. That scared the shit out of me. I'm done." And she was. Laura never played football again.

My family and friends never say much about the horrible injury. Being from Florida and being football fans, the incident didn't spook them one bit. After the game, most of them, including my parents, went home because it was late and they had to drive back to Zephyrhills, about an hour away.

The photo Turpie took is my favorite of all photos ever taken.

CHAPTER 52

THE MEETING EXPLODES

*My hands are shaking as is my voice, but I stand tall and look out
at the people to whom I have tried to be fair, giving and loyal.*

It's a bye week and I'm alone one night in my house singing "I've got the whole house to myself" to the tune of "He's Got the Whole World in His Hands." I am entertaining myself by choosing my own Player of the Week though I have altered the title to Asshole of the Week. But then just as I am enjoying my peaceful moment, the damn little phone tootles that T-Mobile tune that I am so sick of I could just throw this whole instrument right through...

"Hello?" I say calmly.

"Christine?"

"Yes...?"

"It's Erin from your team."

"Hi Erin! How are you?"

Erin is one of our rookies who is the responsible type; always on time or early, dressed and ready to go in advance, and she often volunteers to help which Turpie and I truly need and appreciate. She is a California transplant, a thin but very fit and decent athlete and not only is she coachable, but Erin is dedicated and wants the team to do well.

"Well, I'm good and I hope I am not bothering you." Erin's troubled voice pauses.

"No—not at all."

"I am calling because I just need to tell you something."

Oh, what fresh hell is this?

"I wondered if you will be at the meeting tomorrow night?"

I pause to think. What meeting? I seem to know less and less about more and more. "Nnnnooooo....." I am still trying to think if I called a meeting.

"Well, that's kinda what I thought and I also thought you should know that this meeting is to go over some things that don't sound very positive." She is apologetic.

"Reeeeeeally," I say, still not fully absorbing her words.

"I don't want you to think I'm an upstart or anything, it's just that this team has so much potential and it can all be spoiled with just a few bad apples, as I am sure you know."

Seems we have an orchard.

"True. True." I say. To Erin, it is in the teams' best interest for the owner to know that Kim has puppeteered a meeting through Big Dot. I become more dazed as she gives me the details.

The clandestine meeting has been called at 'Killer Miller's,' our outside linebackers' law office, whose law partners are naive enough to let us take over their conference room on occasions after business hours. This meeting is to be at 8pm. When Turpie and I unexpectedly walk in at 8:30, Kim starts lying. We can tell because her lips are moving.

"I was going to tell you about this, but I thought the team should talk first, then let you know what our feelings were."

"Would you like to know what MY feelings are right now?"

I am staring at her, my body temperature so hot I can solar heat a village. She talks fast, knowing she's been caught, but still trying to stream reasons for, once again, being duplicitous and divisive.

"We just want to discuss the past games and then talk to you about them and the coaches." I am jabbing holes through her with my stare. She sees the calm approach is not working, so she shifts into manic mode. I watch as she works herself into a lather.

"Our practices SUCK! The offense is disorganized, players are in wrong positions....and there's BAD play calling!" she is frothing and rasping with such exuberance, I would laugh if I weren't so devastated by the extreme betrayal. "We were on our own two-yard line in North Carolina and Hayden calls a pitch right!" She leaves the ground a few inches a little on this recollection. "Then Wendy dropped the ball and North Carolina recovered in the end zone." All of this, as if I hadn't been there. "Wendy shouldn't be in the backfield! She sucks back there!"

Several more players arrive, and after seeing me, they skulk down the hall and into the conference room. Wendy is one of them. She has been at the copy machine. She shoves the handouts into Kim's arms as she slithers into her seat without one "heh-heh." I snatch a copy from her pile and scan several paragraphs.

.......want player union........ Christine's taking money......... see actual bank statements......... want more control........ start new team....... want better staff........ want advertising.... want sweat suits........want new coaches ....want...... want...want... want...wantwantwantwantwant......

The pain is overtaking the anger and I want to cry but I keep a stiff upper lip and walk directly into the room and up to the podium as if I had called the meeting. I am happy to see not all the players have shown up. No Sarah, Little Toni, Tanker, Molly and several others.

My hands are shaking as is my voice, but I stand tall and look out at the people to whom I have tried to be fair, giving and loyal.

"I know I am an uninvited guest at this meeting, but as the owner of the Sharks and as a "friend" to many of you before this team began, I need to tell you a few things. First off, my finances. It's none of your business, but I'll tell you since you seem to think I need your money. It takes about fifty thousand dollars a year to run this team. The fees collected from you last year didn't even total thirty. Same this year. So if I kept every cent for myself, it wouldn't even cover expenses. If anyone can do math in here, you will see that I spent a lot of my own money last year to get us on the field and more of it this year to keep us on the field. And since we are still playing and have fields, coaches, buses, refs, and everything that none of you have to even think about, then clearly I am not keeping your money. Your stinkin' 30 grand wouldn't keep my life operating for more than two months." All were dead quiet. Except Jessie, who slid so far down in her chair her ponytail caught on its back. With a cinnamon stick bouncing like a see-saw between her lips, she uttered a dry sentiment. "She had a fuckin Porsche when I met huh."

"I'm not done yet. Please shut up. As for racism...I have an Asian webmaster, a black GM who is also my best friend, and a Jewish PR person. If you feel I've been unfair to you because of your race or religion, take another sniff. It might just be your own shit you smell."

"I've always tried to make this team community property, and let you have a say in things. I bought it as something we could build. It was for us, not me. We all wanted to play and no one else was stepping up, so I did. All I've gotten in return is a kick in the ass and a lot of heartache. From now on, this is MY team. MY rules. You won't be seeing any bank statements, it's none of your FUCK-ing business. If you have complaints, keep them to yourself. I am NOT interested. If you want a better staff, then go to another team. These people, including myself, work hard for this team on a volunteer basis. You should be grateful, not critical. All you have to do is show up and play football. And as far as going to another team, feel free but know this—if you go, don't you ever look back. You will not be welcome here."

The room was pin-dropping silent. Then Kim started.

"Yeah, but..."

"No Kim. Shut the fuck up. You're always playing the angles, aren't you! I have never seen a more divisive, dishonest, manipulating human being than you. All you do is complain, blame and tell everyone they suck. I am sick of it. Stop telling my players that they suck! They don't! You never say one good thing about anyone!" I am now crying in addition to shaking and not sure what else to say. "Don't ruin this!" Cooper is crying, too and Dulce is saying over and over that 'It is in God's hands.' The others have congealed in their seats. The Manhattan skyline is bold and beckoning through the full wall of windows and I am looking at it now as if it holds the answers. "Come through, New York, come through..."

CHAPTER 53

GOING DOWN FAST

'Football does not build character.
It reveals it.'

I live on Prozac and Margaritas. I had lost the love of my life, was hoping to regain the respect of my family and now my football team has turned on me. I never wear a seatbelt anymore, hoping that if I do crash, I will be catapulted into my next incarnation. I am not ashamed of that. It's how I feel. The paleness of surrender has become the color of my days. This women's football has pruned my emotions to the roots. So when the T-Mobile tootle goes off, I don't even flinch.

"If I can't drive to the game this weekend," Big Dot informs me, "I'm thinking of not going." She's smart enough to say it carefully, but ballsy enough to say it all. Her threat is regarding a simple rule I made when I bought the team--that all players ride the bus to games. It builds morale and ensures we all arrive together, hopefully, on time. They can get home any way they like, but I ask that they travel to games as a team. Her call to me is very revealing of her true character. The Coven inspired one of my tee shirt designs that says 'Football does not build character. It reveals it.' I get a good laugh when I see any of them wearing one of those shirts. They are rare characters and she is at the top.

"I'll talk to Turpie and get a feel for how many want to drive, Big Dot. I'll get back to you soon." I should have told her no but, honestly, I don't care any more. They have missed the point of the rule anyway. To deny them means more drama, more angst, more bullshit over nothing more than a bus ride. I tell Turpie about the call and we wonder why they do not like to ride the bus with their teammates? We enjoy the bus rides. We are perplexed.

"There's no team in I, buddy," and this sums up the New York Sharks.

I send an e-mail the next day. I feel defeated and it sounds that way. But I level with them, tell them why I ask them to ride on the bus; the morale building, the fun of unity, the strategizing on how to beat our opponents... I implore them to get on the bus with their teammates and show each other what "team" is all about. Then I push "send."

CHAPTER 54

SHARKS ON A BUS

Even Eve and Wendy,
showing a smidgeon of moral sense, get on the bus.

I am at the bus and ready to go to Syracuse. Players are arriving for the six-hour ride and most seem excited to play in spite of the clandestine meeting and the bus bullshit. I can't stop thinking about either and can't even look at some of the players. Big Dot is top of the "can't look at" list, but even after my e-mail, she, Jessie and a couple of the rookies are driving to the game. The others who might have thought about driving, were swayed by their consciences. Even Eve and Wendy, showing a smidgeon of moral sense, get on the bus.

It is a peaceful and scenic ride along the road to Syracuse. Sunflowers and pumpkin patches quilt both sides of the highway. Not until Wendy loudly calls someone a "cross-eyed turtle fucker," do the Sharks stir. Eve gets up to go to the bathroom in the rear of bus and finds Piper stretched across the one long seat in the back.

"Well, if it isn't Lord Layabout and her concubines!" she chides. Piper shakes her head at Eve—an old friend she sometimes hates and wants to kick. The rookies, expecting a flare-up, stare out of the bus windows pretending that they have often traveled by bus with maniacal female football players and were not nervous or insecure.

Hayden is talking to Turpie and they are laughing about a game when Dulce fumbled right near the goal line.

"I had to go clean out my pants!" says Turpie and Hayden howls. Kim and I intercept glances and she rolls her eyes in disgust towards the back of the bus and the conversations taking place back there. I chuckle to myself. Other than that, the busload of Sharks remains unruffled.

CHAPTER 55

A BONDING MOMENT

I needed to stand up for my players;
forty-five delicate threads that attached forty-five lives to my own.

We arrive in Ithaca, New York where on an autumn like evening we play the Syracuse Bees. The final score is 21-14 with Leah "Tanker" Woods making eleven tackles. The team will stay on the road, playing the Arizona Beasts on September 8th.

After the game, I showered and put on my civilian clothes when Turpie entered the locker room.

"Buddy, we have a little situation."

I say nothing, but look up from my seated position. "That bus driver says we aren't stopping for food."

"That's ridiculous." I say. "Of course we are."

"No buddy. He's serious. He's a nasty piece of work. Says we don't have time."

"Yes we do. Yes he will." I was in no mood to battle this man who had engaged in hating us since we boarded the bus. I tied my shoes and, gear bag in hand, walked with Turpie to the bus. Mr. Personality was hunkered nearby trying to light a cigarette. His mid-eastern air gave off disapproving energy. Most of our previous drivers had fun with the Sharks. It's a novelty—women playing football—and they watched the games with interest, even amusement, but certainly not disdain like this menacing man was showing. He glowered as I approached.

"We're almost ready." I informed him. "We'll make a quick stop at a fast food place close by."

"No time. I'm not stopping."

"We have time and it's paid for. My players have to eat."

"No time. I'm not stopping."

"We will be stopping. They have not eaten since before the game and they have to have food."

He sucked at the cigarette and shook his head reaffirming his decision. I felt my temper rising like an elevator. I wanted to hurt this man and my inner mother bear rose up in his smoke-filled personal space. "You work for us. We have a contract and we are stopping to let my players eat something."

He looked directly into my face and I met him full on. He versus she. Brown eyes versus blue. Black hair versus blonde. Dark skin versus pale. Stubborn versus more stubborn. I was afraid of what I felt. I could have bludgeoned this man with a bat and not felt remorse of any kind. It might have even felt good. I hated him. For his prejudices against my players and me. For the malignity of him not wanting us to eat. For his belief that he was going to win this battle. I felt my mouth fill with saliva and I fought the urge to spit on this man. I was so uncomfortable, one for feeling this dark hatred and another for not acting on it. I turned and walked up the four steps onto the bus and placed my gear on the front seat. I sat down with eyes water-filled and my soul in a panic as though something free in me was trying to be caught and tamed. This was not an unusual feeling at all. Life had made a record of it and played it over and over for me, but this time the volume was disturbingly loud. Maybe because I needed to stand up for my players; forty-five delicate threads that attached forty-five lives to my own.

Turpie boarded and sat across the aisle. "He's crazy buddy. Fucking nuts!"

I was trying to compose myself so I could get on the phone with the bus company though it was late at night and I wasn't sure who would be available. But I needed to be rational when I called, so I was sitting very still and quiet, hoping my own malignity and blind rage would subside so I could speak. As my eyes skimmed the front of the bus I saw the ring of bus keys in the ignition. I slowly got up and tugged lightly at first to see if they would come out. The keys didn't move so I tugged harder. They dropped into my hand and I pocketed them wordlessly. Turpie and I exchanged looks. Hers of delight, mine of satisfaction. He would stop to let the Sharks eat or he would sit in Syracuse until his bus became obsolete.

Slowly the players boarded the bus. Some knew what was going on, and others did not. Either way, Act III of tonight's Shark performance was about to begin.

Finally, all players had showered and boarded. They thought they had been discreet stashing their beer, but Turpie and I both knew we were about to become a rolling brewery. Mr. Personality bounded up the steps, plopped into his swivel chair and aimed it forward, eager to go. He reached to turn the keys and found his bus keyless. He first looked on the floor. Maybe they had fallen out of the ignition. The floor was keyless too, and his dark eyes quickly flashed onto me. I looked at him and shrugged.

"Give me the keys," he demanded.

"Are we stopping?"

"No." So I shrugged again.

He showed his palm and wiggled his fingers, sign language for "give them here."

"We are stopping to eat." I said. He wiggled his fingers again. I turned and looked out the window as the players watched silently. Mr. P. then leaped from his chair and landed in the aisle beside my seat.

"This is illegal!" he declared.

"So is starvation." I didn't look at him and continued to face the window trying to contain my anger.

"I'll call the police!" He shouted and his shouting released my rage and I jumped up from my seat into his face and yelled, "Call them! Please call them! Let them know what a sexist douche nozzle you are! Let them call your company and tell them how you broke this contract, and have been belligerent, rude and hateful to a busload of female athletes. Call them! Go ahead! Call them!" I screamed so loud my voice cracked. People all over New York State woke up and started dialing someone, anyone from fear of disobeying the irate voice they just heard in their sleep.

The story of the "asshole bus driver who is trying to starve us," had trekked to the last player in the back of the bus and they were pushing to get to the front, ready for physical contact should it be necessary. Mr. P. lowered his head a notch, contempt still in his eyes, but he felt my mother bear anger and my cubs' eagerness to take my side.

"We stop. But for one minute. They eat on the bus." His voice was low and rancorous and when I turned the keys over he sat silently for a minute before he cranked the motor and edged out of the parking lot. The Syracuse team, hearing the drama, stood cheering for us as we pulled out. It was a bonding moment that women's football provides so often. We war on the field, we quibble off the field, but somewhere endemic lies a source, an unseen spring that can't be polluted and withstands whatever throws us off balance. It's a solid foundation that sits deep, far below personal and it unites us.

It was a good performance and I felt vindicated. I was settling into the seat when I heard one last remark. It was Wendy, bellowing towards the Syracuse onlookers as we left the field.

"Hey! I thought you said you got better since the last time we played you!"

CHAPTER 56

SHARK CHURCH

The Sharks were truly a different kind of religion, a different kind of faith.
It wasn't sinless, but it healed a lot of hearts.

In my dream, I am peering through the window of the Depot Museum in Zephyrhills. It is housed in the old train depot that sat at the cross of 301 and Fifth Avenue. I cup hands to each side of my eyes and look in. I see a picture of the old church, a Coca Cola sign so prevalent in the south and some trains in a glass case. I read the dedication plaque mounted on the old brick wall beside the door saying it was built in 1927 and served for over 50 years. Ellen is sitting behind a desk and moving WWI helmets around.

Then I wake up.

I can still see the old train depot perfectly and I keep my eyes closed to nurture the memory. Now, as a museum, it sits by the railroad tracks that span the hill where I grew up, which is as familiar to me as the train's whistle. Though bothersome to those who are unaccustomed to it, that whistle is music to my ears. I can hitch a ride back to my childhood every time a train comes rumbling along. Every spring, usually right around Easter, the Ringling Brothers circus train would come through and my mom and I would run out to see the brightly colored cars full of animals.

The last time I was home, the only trains running were freight trains with no passengers—except me, hitching my mind to it and whistling back to the '60s and '70s and memories of the hill as it was long ago. Especially when the scent of orange blossoms is thick, I can close my eyes, dig my barefoot toes into the Florida soil, breathe in that supernal scent and hop the train whistle back to an era gone by.

But it is a Sunday in New York City and I am in my brownstone. It is quiet. My head hurts from last night's wine-filled bus ride home. I get up and walk from room to room. I look at the repairs needed, I feel the memories that have been made. I listen to the floor squeak as I walk to the window, I listen to a horn honk. A bird sing. I watch, I listen. I may not have Ellen, but my life is chock-full of goodness. I will be reverent today. I will send goodness and gratitude into the universe. Thank you, sweet Jesus. Thank you. I go to my computer to check my e-mail.

From: moutzen@earthlink.net

Subject: Re: feeling like shit

I know that you are quite busy and have much on your mind, but I need to get this out to you. I realize that it's important to post when a big newspaper publishes an article and any TV coverage we get goes up on the Sharks website. And yet, when I write an excellent FREE article, nothing happens with it. You said you liked it but didn't ask Lee to put it up. Somehow there is always time for other articles. I'm not sure if you understand how much time and effort goes into getting accolades for everyone and yet, the article that I wrote.....does not get recognized.

Do I feel like shit? What do you think?

Mabel

Instead of anger at Mabel, I feel regret. I didn't mean to make her feel unimportant. I don't mean to discount her efforts and her intentions. And I see that Mabel is possibly more angry at life than I am. Her e-mail is a sinister reflection of myself. I need to find a way to make forgiveness run deeper than anger. My fury has not been extinguished, but I will try to keep it contained to a trail rarely traveled, and I will try not to burn up my world with rage. Conscience has entered the house and I have Mabel to thank.

As I stand there sending more gratitude into the universe, I hear loud footsteps. Conscience must be equipped with feet. I can hear them clattering on the steps. The noise is so great, it appears that conscience must be a centipede.

Then Turpie appears with Erin, Sarah, Dulce and Little Toni. We all hug and I notice Dulce, whose tee shirt says 'It's almost Sunday and we aren't saved yet' is wearing enough perfume to kill small birds. They have bags of breakfast items and want to sit with me on the roof deck to eat and I am happy to accommodate. When we finally sit down, Turpie appears very serious.

"Buddy, we are here to take you to church. After yesterday and that bus episode, we are really worried about you." It takes a minute, but then I begin to chuckle.

"You guys are real knee-slappers. Besides, we were at church yesterday." I say. "Our religion is football."

"Amen sistah!" says Turpie and even Dulce laughs at our sacrilege.

"I don't see any Catholics or Baptists or Jews or Muslims or anyone else with several hundred screaming fans at church!" laughs Erin.

"Amen sistah!" says Turpie again.

"I don't know of any parishioners tailgating in the parish parking lot either!" I add.

"Or buyin' tee shirts and bumper stickers with their favorite temple on it!" Little Toni blurts and we are howling with laughter. Then Sarah gets in on the fun.

"How about someone taping every sermon and breaking it down like game film until they can recite every word!" We are nearly rolling on the roof deck. The Sharks were truly a different kind of religion, a different kind of faith. It wasn't sinless, but it healed a lot of hearts.

CHAPTER 57

SHARKS FLY AGAIN

Sometimes our obsession for the game is like staring directly into the sun.
As long as you kept staring at it, you don't notice the blindness it causes.

It is no less than a Shark miracle that we all get to the airport and board the plane. Kim has talked her way past the rules of "small carry-on" and is trying to stuff a bag the size of a lawn tractor into the overhead compartment. The compartment, however, already contains Dulce's upright church piano so she moves on towards the back of the plane. The doors have not been closed before an argument breaks out. I can't see them from where I sit, but everyone on the plane can hear them.

"You called me an idiot...." says an indignant Shark voice about twelve rows back.

"I'm sorry. Was it a secret? Oh!" says Eve followed by Wendy's 'heh-heh's.' "Cooper, where'd you get that purse?" Eve yells to the front of the plane where Cooper is trying to place the large purse in the overhead compartment. Cooper ignores her. Turpie, shaking her head, says she is going to kill Eve.

"I should have done it long ago, but one keeps putting those things off," I say.

Poor Big Dot is sitting across the aisle from me. She is petrified and clinging to her seat.

"Are you scared of flying?" I ask.

"No! Crashing!" she says and she is not trying to be funny which makes it funny. I smile, trying not to laugh and squeeze her arm.

"You'll be fine," I assure her, but she fingers her large bling Shark on its' thick silver chain like rosary beads and grips the armrest with her spare hand.

Once in flight, the stewardess gives out a box lunch. At the bottom is a small Baby Ruth bar. On the wrapper beneath the name are the words "fun size bars" but they are way too small to be much fun for this gang. Give them one that's two feet long and weighs seventeen pounds. That's a fun size bar!

The Sharks are complaining about not having enough food, and the flight attendants can't irrigate them with cocktails fast enough. On one fin, it's a blessing. On the other, it stimulates poor behavior. Eve carefully removes several cans of beer from her knapsack and fires them with deadly accuracy over the passengers heads to Sarah sitting nine rows behind. Wendy discovers the "fun size" candy bar and tells the entire plane that she will take any "fun-sized poodle turds that nobody wants."

The Coven has started a card game called Screw your Neighbor. How Delphic. With this game comes a little ditty which is sung to the tune of 'Oh My Darling' Clementine.' Each time someone gets 'screwed' which, from the singing in the back of the plane, is often, the catchy ditty is sung.

"You're an asshole,

You're an asshole,

You're an aaaaaaasshole.

You're an asshole,

You're an asshole,

You're an aaaaaasshole."

Tanker and Sarah, two of the more vociferous Sharks, naturally make friends with the attendants who announce us over the intercom. Fortunately, the passengers are amused by our antics instead of repulsed, and high over mid-America is a plane-load of people singing "You're an asshole."

I am amused, but also aware of the lack of regard we display. Sometimes our obsession for the game and all that surrounds it is like staring directly into the sun. As long as you kept staring at it, you don't notice the blindness it causes. Either way, it's damaging. I sit alone in a window seat staring out. The blast of sunlight and the infinitude of clouds is alluring. I picture my body tumbling across them, hurdling towards the unknown with fantastic speed, out towards the end, wherever that is.

CHAPTER 58

STRATEGY AND CORN PLANTS

If we learned to see everyone around us as pieces of a sacred whole,
things would be funny a lot more often.

Lee writes a concise article and, as usual, posts it on the web;

Game Day. Tempe, Arizona, September 8, 2001. New York is playing their last road game of the season while Arizona is playing their first home game ever. The Arizona Beasts (0-1) are a brand new team and play out of Tempe, Arizona.

It was a hot evening in Tempe, with the game time temperature still in the 90's as the two teams took the field. Sharks (5-1) were putting a 3-game winning streak on the line while the expansion Beasts were looking to prove their mettle in front of a noisy home crowd.

Taking advantage of Arizona's inexperience, the Sharks attacked at the line of scrimmage to win the game handily, 20-0. New York kept the ball on the ground and continually ate up yards. Dulce Rodriguez led the attack with 114 yards on 17 carries and scored three touchdowns. The rest of the scoring was done on the foot of Christine Davis who converted 2 out of 3 extra point kicks.

On the defensive side of the ball, there were interceptions by Eve Edwards and Sarah Parham and a blocked punt by Wendy Wayne. Dulce Rodriguez received the Carson Creamery Player of the Week.

The Sharks come home next week to start a 4-game home stand. They will be playing the Syracuse Bees on Sunday, September 16th at 5pm at Kane Stadium in Secaucus, New Jersey. They will then host the Arizona Beasts on Saturday, September 22 at 2pm at Stony Brook University. Tickets are available for these games and the rest of the home stand. To purchase tickets, please contact Turpie Evans, Assistant General Manager. By phone: 616 552-5798 or by email: tickets@nysharksfootball.com.

What Lee didn't write:

It is Wednesday before the Arizona game. Music is blasting from Turpies' Brooklyn brownstone where six Sharks rent rooms. We had planned this night as a film session, additional prep in between our regularly scheduled Tuesday and Thursday night practices. This is what we had planned—to practice—but we are having so much fun!

Sarah who is the best dancer I have ever seen, is trying to teach me to dance to a song where, at some cue that I can't figure out, they shake their hands in front of their faces like palsy victims. The words go something like this:

"Honey came in and she caught me red-handed

Creeping with the girl next door

Picture this we were both butt naked

Banging on the bathroom floor

She saw the marks on my shoulder (It wasn't me)

Heard the words that I told her (It wasn't me)

Heard the scream get louder (It wasn't me)

She stayed until it was over"

My God, I feel old. I used to party in the afternoon at Tea Dances and listen to songs that had words like this:

"Toot toot hey beep beep

Toot toot hey beep beep

Toot toot hey beep beep

Toot toot hey beep beep

Bad girls

talking about the sad girls

sad girls

talking about the bad girls, yeah

Toot toot hey beep beep

Toot toot hey beep beep"

I sit down next to Hayden who is talking strategy with Kim, Wendy and Eve. "We should be fine Saturday but we will miss Jessie at noseguard, since her ankle is sprained. Marilyn may start." The thought of Marilyn starting is not so tragic, except that she is a terrible football player. I am concerned, but Wendy thinks there is no need.

"Their O-line should be called the "O-SHIT" line! They can't keep us out. Whores." she says.

"They're big and dumb," adds Eve. "Like a bunch of throw pillows. Toss them out there for props while their quarterback runs for the light of day!"

"They suck," adds Kim. "A 4-3 defense will kill them." I only hope they are right. I get up and walk to the floor length mirror and try to do the moves Sarah and Big Dot are demonstrating. I accomplish the dance, but catch sight of an unattractive angle of my face in the mirror, which shows crepe on my neck and a round face that is mapped with wrinkles and sags.

God, I look like Yoda's mother.

Mabel arrives, collects numerous hugs until she comes to Cooper. Cooper feels, about touching people, the way natives feel about looking into a camera; that her soul might be sucked in by accident.

"Don't hug me Mabel." She says in her monotone way. Mabel moves quickly onto the next, unfazed, and begins interrogating people for her next article. She starts with me.

"So how do you feel about your teams' execution this season?"

"I think it's a good idea." I say drolly.

"Ha ha! That's a good one. I'm going to use that!" she says "But, really."

"No, really." I say and get up to go to the bathroom. I don't like giving interviews. It's embarrassing and the questions are repetitive. I am standing by myself waiting for the bathroom to become free when suddenly, the corn plant, which had hitherto not spoken, says "'Pssst." I turn towards it and see Kim, who is bent over double behind the large plant.

"What the hell are you doing?" I ask.

"My tooth fell out and rolled behind this bush, and I bent down to find it, and now I can't stand up."

"Your tooth?" I say incredulously and join her search behind the bushy stalks.

"It keeps falling out, and I don't want to go to the dentist," she explains.

Piper walks up and asks, not without reason, why we are crouched behind Turpie's corn plant.

"Kim's tooth fell out," I say, still contorted next to Kim.

"The mother fucking thing just popped out," adds Kim.

"Popped out?" Piper is skeptical.

"Like a champagne cork, and rolled behind this plant," Kim adds convincingly.

"Well come out, the both of you, and we'll pull the plant away from the wall and take a look," says Piper's voice of reason.

"I can't. My mother fucking back went out." Piper and I start laughing. We can't stop.

"Some people ripen…" says Piper "…others rot." We are hysterical.

"It's not funny you fucking fucks!" groans Kim from her bent stature.

But it is. Maybe if we learned to see everyone around us as pieces of a sacred whole with just a role to be played out, things would be funny a lot more often. Kaleidoscopic mixtures of the comically absurd.

Jessie, hearing the conversation, grabs Kim and opens her like a corkscrew. "And here's your tooth." She is laughing as she hands it to Kim, who grabs her jacket from the nearby hook. We see her open the door and the night folds around her and she is gone.

CHAPTER 59

PRACTICE EXPLODES

She seems used to the rejection, which makes me sad for her.

It is Thursday night and we are at the last practice before we leave for Arizona and we have to make sure everyone has a ride to the airport. Marilyn, Gloria and Aniyah, three of our second and third string players are left without rides and my car is already full. No one wants to ride with Gloria because she talks incessantly about nothing. On the opposite end is Aniyah who hasn't emitted twenty words total in two years. They are both like garments drawn from the irregular bin. Their feelings are hurt and I feel sad for them. But Marilyn is not offended. She seems used to the rejection, which makes me sad for her, too. In one form or another, they all just add to my eclipsing sadness.

I asked Big Dot to give them rides, as she slowly strides to the side of the field for a break.

"I'm not sure who I'm riding with," she lies, never even stopping to answer. I am sad for her, too, because she can be such a mean person. I am about to ask Piper who has done more than her share of carting players around, when the fight breaks out. Kim is yelling at Big Dot who is trying to leave practice. I can't imagine why....it's only 11:30 pm and practice is supposed to end at 10 pm.

"Kim, I have to go! I have to work early and I am tired!" says Big Dot. Hayden and the volunteers concur. I have never figured out why they let Kim dictate coaching decisions to them. Especially since she is a player. I guess they give in because, like I am, they're tired of fighting her. Like Chinese water torture, she simply wears people down.

"Nice work ladies. Let's call it a night," mutters Hayden.

"But this is the last chance to go over things before the game! Don't you care?" Kim's raspy voice is getting higher.

"No...no more Kim. I have to go!" Big Dot turns and walks towards the parking lot to her Cadillac Esplanade, which holds the entire Coven and their gear. Her departure means six others are leaving, too. They begin to turn and follow. Kim strokes out.

"You can't leave! You're a CAPTAIN!" Her hair heightens as she says 'CAPTAIN' and her head spins at least once. Then she looks my direction.

"Keep Kim away from me," I tell Turpie "This is a coach's decision and a coach's problem. I don't want to hear how everyone sucks, how the coaches don't know what they are doing and what a thief I am. I can not deal with that lunatic. Just make her stay away from me, please."

"I know buddy, but how do you want me to do that?"

"I dunno....fire a warning shot into her hair. Maybe it will at least slow her down." Kim hovers nowadays, just within earshot, but not too close in case I lose my cool again. She floats in and out of wherever I retreat like an unavoidable patch of bad weather.

"Maybe she wants to kiss and make up buddy," Turpie laughs at her own remark.

"Unless she is served in a wine glass, keep her away from my lips."

CHAPTER 60

IT BEGAN AS A PICTURE PERFECT DAY

A deluge of despair, confusion and shock washes over the City

We fly back to NYC on the eve of September 10th. Early the next morning, I open the kitchen window and look out onto the cobblestones of Bank Street. It is a picture perfect fall day. Cloudless with a slight breeze and the temperature is the perfect comfort zone of low 70's. There is a gathering of people on the corner of Bank and Greenwich Street looking down the road in a curious and concerned manner like one might observe a car accident. I suspect that is what it is. When they are still there 10 minutes later, I decide to go out and see. About twenty people are standing in small clusters and staring south down Greenwich Street. I spot my neighbor, James, and walk up beside him to join the onlookers. We nod acknowledgments and I look downtown to see what the commotion is. I see the usual: the World Trade Center buildings about a mile and a half away. The way they are positioned, they appear to be sitting side by side each in the middle of Greenwich Avenue. The buildings are not an unusual sight except today, it looks like a small plane has run into the side of the South tower. Smoke, black as tar, is pouring from what seems like a medium size hole towards the top third of the building.

"Some idiot ran into the World Trade Center," remarks a stranger to another who has just joined the group.

"It looks like a small plane. A Cessna or something," another remarks. Not much is said. One guy starts his car, rolls down his windows and turns on 1010 WINS.

"Well, good morning and it is not a good morning in New York City. A major disaster, a plane has crashed into the World Trade Center. We are on the line with 1010 WINS account executive Joan Fleischer, a witness to this terrible unfolding scene. Joan could you maybe recap for those just joining us, what happened and what you're seeing."

Clouds of ominous black smoke cascade down the side of the South Tower. The group mumbles a few observations to each other but is fairly silent as we listen to the radio, which has been turned up loud so everyone can hear.

"....passenger airliner ....I'm not that familiar..........no it was over my head I couldn't really tell.......traffic problems resulting from this major disaster.......anything going into the World Trade Center is going to be closing down for the emergency vehicles and of course anything coming into lower Manhattan is also probably going to be off limits...1010 WINS will have more on this horrible....."

"When did this happen?" I ask James.

"I was leaving for work and saw a few people gathering. I've just been here watching for a few minutes."

"The time is 9:02 am and we've been talking with...right now we are going to switch over....saw the whole thing transpire from his vantage point on 14th St. and again we're talking about a plane crashing into the World Trade Center...."

"It looks like a small plane from here," I comment. "How can you hit a building like that? Wonder if he was drunk or something." James shrugs and suddenly, a massive orange cloud explodes in the North Tower.

".....the plane was right overhead. I happened to be looking towards the World Trade Center... NO!! another explosion coming right at this moment in the other building which means..."

We all turn towards the car radio and then back at the towers. The Twin Towers have twin holes, the North Towers' being in almost the same place as the South's. More black smoke billows out and wafts slowly towards Brooklyn. Debris is visible and the light breeze carries innumerable tons of paper spiraling to the ground far beneath.

".....it looked like the pilot was trimming the rudder in order to hit the building.........a second plane has hit......something that looks more like an explosion immediately at the corner of the building, it looks like it would be the North East Tower of the World Trade Center. I'm going to switch over...I have a clear view of the World Trade Center from Brooklyn and I am looking out of the house. The World Trade Center is definitely on fire, there is black smoke coming from both of the towers..."

"There are things falling from the top. Look." I say to James. "What is that?"

"....not sure....." he asks to borrow a pair of binoculars from a man standing a few feet away. He turns pale as he focuses on the towers and then his arms fall limp to his sides, binoculars in hand. I take them and look. Bodies. Live humans are falling from the towers. Arms out, spinning and cart-wheeling and I am breathless as I try to assimilate what my eyes are seeing. As we realize the tragedy we are witnessing, the clusters of people become tighter and murmurs can be heard. I stand and watch in terror. My heart is pounding, my eyes are tearing and I can't accept the pain and terror the people are experiencing. This is a horror flick out of Hollywood. This can not be real. My emotions are frozen and I turn away hoping that if I look in another direction, the south end of Manhattan will be perfectly fine. And I do look away, but the deluge of despair, confusion, and shock has washed across New York City leaving tokens of our past embedded in a disparate world.

Then, as if to punctuate these indelible changes, the South Tower, in a slow, spectacular implosion, folds in on itself and disappears from the New York City skyline. My neighbor and I grasp each other's arms. We do not believe what we have just witnessed and a silent chill overtakes our small group.

Then the radio announcer's voice becomes frantic. "Oh my God! Oh my GOD!......I want to....the South Tower of the World Trade Center has just collapsed in a pile of dust!! The South Tower has collapsed! The situation that started bad just gets worse and worse and worse. World Trade Center South Tower which was hit by a plane approximately an hour ago, has totally collapsed. The North Tower is still standing at the World Trade Center. The South Tower has collapsed."

Although we are shocked, no one yet understands the significance of what we've seen. No one even knows exactly what has happened, or what to do. The news reporters are also panicky and confused at the scene unfolding.

"....the Capitol building has been evacuated and the Treasury department..... clearly thinking that we are virtually under siege here. We don't know... ......striking at the heart of the national government and......we are getting reports that part of the second tower has collapsed...we are checking on that again....the south building is completely gone......"

Ellen... my heart stops. Where is my Ellen? What if she has gone down to get "two-for" tickets to a play this morning? She does that a lot. I run towards the house for my phone. For the moment, I forget that I hate her and dial her number. She doesn't pick up. I want to, but don't leave a message. I don't hear from her that day or for months after.

My mom and dad. I have to let them know I am ok. Then I see the answering machine is blinking and push the button.

"Christine!" my mom's voice calls to me from the machine. "Christine!" the second time is more frantic as though she has entered the room and still can't find me. "The city is under attack! Where are you? Where are you?" I hear the panic in her voice and immediately call her back. I can hear relief in my parents' voices as they listen to the recounting of what I have just seen. My voice cracks and I begin to cry. "Those poor people! They must have been so scared...so scared..." and I weep into the handset. Dad is quiet, but I know he is there and I feel his familiar warmth. Mom tries to make sense of things with her words, attempting to patch where my hearts' frail seams have ripped.

"I have to go." I say. "Maybe I can help somehow." I know they don't want to hang up for fear of never hearing me again, but we do and I stand in the middle of the room, still not knowing the impact of what has happened or what to do about it. I literally ache for the people who jumped and I know I will never get those images out of my mind.

Oh my God! Turpie works down there! In the Century 21 Building right across the street from the towers.

I dial her number frantically from the landline but do not get through. All cell phones have lost connection.

Where is she? Where are all of my Sharks? How can I find them? What can I do to help people? Anyone. Everyone.

I run down the stairs several at a time, back outside where so many people are milling around in a daze. Some have walked up from the Trade Center and are covered in white ash. They sit down on curbs, feeling a safe distance from the horror of what has happened. Radios are still blaring and many stations have been tuned in and are giving recounts.

"Obviously, there are going to be more than a few casualties in the wake of this. If you're just joining us this morning you're in for a horrific surprise, both buildings of the World Trade Center have been hit by aircraft and the South Tower of the World Trade Center has apparently collapsed in a pile of dust...top witnesses reported hearing a huge explosion, heavy black smoke pouring out of the building and wreckage was also seen embedded in the top floors of the skyscraper ...."

I see a lady wearing only one high heel and covered with white ash. She is sitting down on the curb of Greenwich Avenue, crying and trying to reach a loved one on her cell phone. She tries over and over, but cell phone calls will not go through. I run inside and bring the cordless handset to her. By an act of God, it works from this distance and, after a few tries, she connects. She explodes with tears and, relieved, crumbles onto the cobblestones. I begin passing the handset around to people who are trying to make connections. There is sobbing, there are vacant stares, many in a hurry to reach home which could be as far as Connecticut and they have no way to get there but to walk.

"....air travel in the United States has been suspended until at least 5 o'clock in the wake of this....you know these are enormous buildings....no reports of the casualties....

people walking around with the cell phones in tears....people milling around not knowing what to do, not knowing where to go with the dangers of utter chaos....."

When I go inside much later, I am finally calm enough to sit down and check my computer thinking our loved ones might have tried communicating through e-mail. Hayden has started a trail of correspondence and I expel breaths of gratitude as I read each Shark response.

"*I'm here,*" is the numb response from most.

Tanker added a few more words. "*I love my Shark family. Be safe!*"

"*I was right there and had to run from falling body parts,*" came another.

"*Thanks for emailing. I am fine but we can't find my brother. A picture is attached.*"

"*There is a vigil at Union Square tonight if anyone can come.*"

"*PLEASE!! If anyone sees my aunt, call me,*" another picture to accompany the panicked plea.

"*My brother was supposed to be there, but had to take my niece to the doctor. We are so blessed.*"

Though many of us lost people we know, our team is still whole. Physically. The mental toll, however, is just being tallied.

CHAPTER 61

SPORTS AND SORROW

It isn't the smell that is so wrenching as what untenable loss it represents.

All sports in NYC are postponed for the next three weeks, as it is difficult for teams to get flights or even drive into New York City. Playing football doesn't seem right with Ground Zero, as it is now known, being only miles away.

Somber is a well-employed word to describe the mood of the entire city and its dwellers. The Sharks are no exception. The smoke swelling from lower Manhattan blows towards Brooklyn as it had just days ago after the attack. It is an odd sight. An odd feeling. And it smells. It smells awful—acrid and burnt. But it isn't the smell that is so wrenching, as what untenable loss it represents.

One morning the Sharks are to appear on the local Channel 7 News. They are desperate for non 9-11 content. It's great to get coverage even though we already know the drill: "How did you get into this, is it full-tackle, how do you protect your breasts?" and then the newscaster, male or female, suits up while the Sharks chase them around and 'lightly' tackle them. Make sure we mention our website during wrap-up: **www.nysharksfootball.com**. Segment over.

This morning, we have to be at the station in Manhattan at 4 a.m. to prepare for a 5 a.m. appearance. I arrive and am sitting in the green room when Sarah walks in. She is holding her jersey and tells me she had to remove it from a frame where she keeps it when not in use. I look at her in disbelief. In a frame? She grins and shrugs her shoulders. Then she tells me that she wants to volunteer to feed the cops and firemen who are working at Ground Zero.

"It's this place called Zeno's and the guy who owns it is giving meals for free to the firemen and cops who are working down there," she tells me. "So I thought the Sharks could volunteer to cook and serve. We'd get great exposure and....." her grin gets bigger if that were possible, "we would be helping the cops and firemen. God, they are cute!" I laugh. How could I say no?

"Ok. So now let me pass this by you," I say. "There is a new league starting. It's based in Dallas, Texas and Judy Van Brenson, the East Coast Director called me and really thinks we should join. I think a new team is in New Hampshire, there's a team in Texas and a few out west."

"Are they good people?"

"They seem to be in it for the right reasons and the two that will be running it appear to be legit. Not crooks or idiots."

Sarah becomes serious and looks at me. "You've given all of us a dream come true, Christine. This is the best thing I've ever done in my whole life. Whatever decision you make, I will be there, every step." She brings her jersey up to her face and hugs it, then reaches out to me and we embrace. The feeling of love-- and her approval-- is so overwhelming, I am going to cry. We both tear up, smile, wipe tears, then don pads and helmets to go kick some ass on camera.

Zeno's, though somber in mood, was full of firemen and cops. Sarah and Dulce worked the place while Erin, Turpie, Tanker, myself and several others crowded into the kitchen to crack hundreds of eggs into extraordinarily large bowls and whip them for scrambled eggs.

"Ya'll sure do look funny in those hairnets!" Tanker rolled her eyes over the nets we were asked to wear. "Ya'll look like real kitchen help!"

"You look like you ate the kitchen help," muttered Turpie and we all chuckled.

"Now, now! Don't be hatin.' I ain't mad at 'chall. We doin' a good thing in here helpin' these guys. And helpin' women, too!" She added loudly and laughed. "Ol Piper down there in the rubble jus' trying to find someone…God bless us all." And the somberness returned.

My sister Annie started dating Greg when she was in seventh grade. Like us, he and his family—his dad and seven brothers and sisters, had been in our town all of his life and he was almost like one of the family. He was a basketball star and we would all go to his games on Friday nights and he swam in our pool a lot and was always there for meals probably because his mom had died when he was very young (he was the baby) and he didn't like what his sisters fixed for him. When he turned eighteen, he got a notice that he had been drafted and was going to Vietnam. After hearing the news, Annie threw herself onto her blue bedspreaded bed in her blue-walled, blue-carpeted room shrieking and blubbering and refused food or consolation from anyone, even my grandmother, for several days. Except from Greg of course, who had to come over and coax her out of the bedroom and back into daily living. Although the rest of the family did not have the same reaction, it was a somberness that felt similar to today. We were stiff, like over-starched shirts and fretful, reluctant to comment about the possibilities of Greg not coming home. It was hard to be normal because nothing was and nothing would be again until the day he finally came home safely.

This was different. This time, there was no 'home.'

CHAPTER 62

HOLES IN THE SKY

There was the fear that the New York Sharks
could not guarantee the safety of visiting teams.

Lee puts up a post.

The Sharks re-started the season on October 7th. Game Day. Secaucus, New Jersey, October 7, 2001. Playing for the first time in a month, the New York Sharks (6-1) hosted the New Hampshire Cobras (2-5) at Kane Stadium in New Jersey.

Before the singing of the national anthem, the Sharks honored seven of their players who have participated in the rescue effort at the World Trade Center. There was also a moment of silence to honor those who perished in the national tragedy on September 11th. It was a very poignant moment with the New York City skyline in the background.

It was a nice autumn day at kickoff time. It was blustery but the skies were clear and blue. The temperature was in the low 60's.

The Sharks got on the board first with a touchdown in the first quarter. New York quarterback Eve Edwards handed the ball off to Dulce Rodriguez who ran off-tackle and bulldozed her way to a 6-yard touchdown run. Christine Davis kicked the extra point to give New York a 7-0 lead. The momentum continued with the final score 19-0.

Overall a good day for New York City football, the Giants, Jets, and the Sharks - all winners on Sunday. But on this day, the United States started bombing Afghanistan in retaliation for the World Trade Center attack. After the game, the decision to cancel the rest of the season was made. It was not known at the time how difficult it might be for teams to travel to New York. It was said on the radio that the New York City mayor, Rudy Guilliani might seal the city off as was done on September 11th and there was the fear that the New York Sharks could not guarantee the safety of visiting teams. I have arrived at the stadium in Secaucus and am sitting in a rickety chair in the press box. When Turpie walks in, I am staring at the smoke and smolder of lower Manhattan and the obvious holes in the sky where the towers once stood. She says nothing but opens another rickety chair and sets it next to mine. We both sit and stare in silence.

204

"When I was little," I begin "Maybe 7...8 years old, I noticed a sadness in my mother. So at an early age, I made it my mission to make her happy. I was very shy, but I found ways to combat the sadness that didn't require extreme outgoingness." I pause to watch a jet pass over the city. Turpie, my rock, is still and listening. "So I would tell her jokes. I didn't know many, so I made them up. When I went to school, I'd try to remember any funny events or things people said, so I could tell her about them when I got home, make her happy. Sometimes at night before bed, I'd go into my parents' room where she was always reading a book or magazine. I would do this crab imitation, something silly I made up in the way I held my arms and lurched around the surface of the big king size bed. It always made her laugh. But that didn't seem to last long. I became very protective of her. Protective of her even from my sisters, when they were being typical teenagers and saying ugly things or treating her with indifference. It was excruciating for me to watch. I never went through that stage. I was never embarrassed to be seen with her and always wanted to show off my pretty and brilliant mom.

In school, the sad people, mostly girls, were the ones I paid attention to. I was one of the popular ones, but kept myself on the periphery. It was more comfortable there for some reason. I became the Jester....I even played one in the school play...I wore those curly pointed shoes. And the audience laughed. Not just at the play, but whenever I was around. I had become fearless in my quest to bestow laughter to the sad. I was blessed with the ability to be good at most anything I tried, and I always wanted to bring people along with me, make them feel that success and be happy. Sometimes it even worked. It made a difference in their lives when all I was trying to do was get them to laugh. Or just not be sad. But for my mom, at the end of my efforts, the sadness remained." Turpie turned and looked at me, and I slowly turned to her. "Look at our city," I say. "That smoke has human flesh in it. And those people I saw jumping..." I begin to lose it. "Daisies and jesters will never bring the smile back. There is nothing anyone can do to make New York City happy again."

CHAPTER 63

THE
NEW LEAGUE

And the dirty job is done.

On October 19th, it is announced via Lee's rockin' website that the New York Sharks will be joining the International Women's Football League for the 2002 season. This 12-team league will start playing in the Spring of 2002 and gives the Sharks a chance to play a season which includes playoffs and, hopefully a Championship. Because it's a spring league, we will have no 'off season' and will begin mini-camp and practices immediately. But before this happens, I have to fire Hayden. For several reasons. After the season was cancelled, at least 3/4 of the team, including those I trust, reported that the team had become Hayden's dating ground and if he returned as a coach, they would not. I sympathize, agree and with a heavy heart, I set out to do the task. Turpie comes with me to help.

We are very nice to him. We love Hayden and are tactful. I talk unperturbed about his attraction to the players. I say, and Turpie agrees with me, that it must be hard for a single guy to not look around and anyone would have trouble doing that. It is probably, I say, and Turpie thinks so, too, harder than he realized it would be. I conclude by advising Hayden, and Turpie says the suggestion is good, to take a year off while some of the players became less irate at his sexual advances. He translates this as being fired and I, along with Turpie, concur. This is one of the most awkward and excruciating things I have ever done and Turpie, too. He is my personal friend, and Turpie's too. But we know it is the best thing for the team. He says he will not speak to either of us anymore. I believe him, and Turpie does, too. But the dirty job is done.

CHAPTER 64

THE CHRISTMAS MORNING PHONE CALL

"It can't be... please check again and call me back"

It is Christmas morning and my dad has squeezed fresh orange juice and is cooking his traditional pancakes and bacon. My nephews are gift-poking and my mom, grandmother and two sisters are sitting with my brother-in-law William by the tree in their pajamas. My phone rings. Not unusual. Nor is Turpie's voice on the other end. I greet her with holiday enthusiasm.

"Hey Buddy! Merry Christmas!" and I take the phone out into the yard so I can hear better over the Christmas morning festivities. I figure she wants to say the same, but she is mumbling, something she does when things are not as they should be. Piper, who is on duty this morning, called and said there was a car accident. That it was a Shark. That the boy driving is ok. That Sarah is dead. Our Sarah. My heart rushes and my arms feel a strange heat move down to my fingertips until the phone itself feels on fire and I want to throw it. Not let it burn me. I tell her it has to be wrong. They got it wrong. She is crying and says no one is for positive sure, but Piper says that is what the report says. That Sarah Parham was killed instantly in a car crash on her way home from a family Christmas party. It happened at approximately 3 a.m. this morning.

I cannot find words even to hang up and how can that be, that our pink-loving, life-hugging, Sarah has left us? So much is in my head that I can barely form words and I cannot...I do not....

"I have to go...please let me know. It has to be a different Sarah." I hang up and my arms fall to my sides and though I am silent, tears are beginning to spill down my face. Kim calls and when I answer, my weak voice utters the plea.

"Kim, tell me it's not true. Please tell me it's not her. Please..." Kim can hardly answer me and says Piper is sure. Even though she is not supposed to release info like that, in this situation, friendships are king. Kim was gathering the Sharks who lived in the neighborhood and going to Sarah's parents' house. She doesn't think they have been contacted yet. She says she will call me later, but she doesn't. What could she say to prepare for yet another change our lives were going to go through? I walk towards the house and into the room where my family waits, and I stare through the blurry pane of tears, but can say nothing.

"...Christine...what's wrong..." asks my mother whose pain for me is already surfacing. I am silent. I can't utter a sound, until she touches my arm and then in a torrent of emotion, I tell them.

"One of my Sharks is dead! Killed in a car wreck late last night...our Sarah..." Christmas is, as of that moment, no longer a celebration for us. I feel guilt on top of sorrow, for Christmas is a joyous holiday, but my family, knowing of this sadness, shares my grief. They attempt to get to know Sarah right then, attempt to bring her back to me through the many memories she created. My two nephews and my niece, Julia sit on one couch with Dad and William and try to be upbeat.

"Toady, she was your linebacker, right?" my dad asks and I am touched that he knows her position so I cry harder.

"Yes, Dad. She was a really good linebacker." And I blubber louder while Chris, my oldest nephew, gets up to bring me a tissue.

"I think I met her when I came to visit one time." Julia says softly. "She was so pretty."

"I remember her, too, Toad. It was when you were playing flag. She was dancing after a touchdown and everyone stopped to watch her dance!" says Andy, my youngest nephew. I smile, remembering the exact moment and shake my head to confirm. Yes, that was her.

"Did she have brothers or sisters, Toad?" asks Jan.

"Two sisters. And she was very close to her parents, Sylvia and Thomas. Thomas was her best friend." I answer solemnly and look at my dad and begin to sob again.

"Oh dear child…" Grandma says and her voice trails off.

My mother is sitting close to me on the other couch and my two sisters sit on the floor in front of me. My grandmother is leaning in from her position in a comfortable chair she settled into early this morning. They want to know all about her job, her family, her position on the Sharks, the things she liked best in her life. "She was special. Tell us about her," Annie says and pats my knee. I tell them how she loved the color pink, how her energy was limitless and she never sat still, how when she danced, everyone would stop to watch her, how her Brooklyn accent and non-stop chatter was so funny and how people always complained about others, but no one ever had a complaint about Sarah Parham. I tell them how Sarah was the only player to ever stick up for me when it came to my position as owner of the Sharks and the decisions, both good and bad, that I had to make for the team. I tell them that it was

Sarah and only Sarah who would tell people to shut up when they interrupted me, when I was addressing the team. It was Sarah who never missed a practice, an event to help raise funds, a shot at publicity for the team, a chance to further the game of football...the chance to dance. Sarah always showed up for life.

It was Sarah, the one who didn't drink, smoke or have any vices of the sort who gave any party its life. I tell them these things, and my sisters and mother are crying with me and then we all laugh because we are all crying. Jan moves to sit on the other side of me and holds my hand. "I feel so bad for her parents!" she wails and my dad gets choked up and gets up to tightly embrace each of his three daughters and three grandchildren as if to reassure himself that it wasn't us in the accident. The seven of us are bunched near the Christmas tree. When he holds a hand out to my mom to join, she does and William gets up to help my grandmother out of the chair and they lumber to the clutch.

We are in a football huddle, my dear family, when William says he'd like to say a prayer, so we grasp hands and he begins to thank God for the family we are and asks blessings for Sarah and her family and friends. "And please look after the Shark family and be with them during this loss of Sarah, their special teammate. Amen." We are silent for a few moments knowing that Sarah's sisters and parents will forever wake up on Christmas morning and re-live the loss of their youngest and magical daughter, Sarah.

My family is sensitive and kind and I will always try to remember that Christmas for the gift of gentle concern they gave to me, instead of the tragedy of losing a loved one. My dad opens more champagne and makes Mimosas with his fresh orange juice, and we cry and we toast to the White Light named Sarah.

CHAPTER 65

THE SHATTERED SHARKS

"We will never let you down," Tanker whispers softly to Sarah.

When Sarah left, it carved out the team's center and we became hollow. We stood staring from our straw houses of disbelief, a group who once could fill an entire field with just our presence, was now drowning from the open floodgates of grief. 9-11 was still fresh in our blood, as were the months afterwards spent at wakes and funerals mourning or supporting those we loved. Like the Twin Towers, our spirits had been crushed in the devastation. Now our Sarah was gone and with her, went the well-known Shark swagger. On this cold Friday in December, just days after her 28th birthday, we are attending her wake.

The team meets in the foyer of the funeral home. Tanker has brought Sarah's jersey and we all want to sign it before she places it in the casket with Sarah.

It is clear to see, looking around the room, that our formidable ways and the fear we unconsciously instill in our opponents consists of pure heart.

The boy driving the car the night of the accident stands in the road outside the funeral home, his broken arm in a sling. He is unable to pass through Sarah's teammates who stand like faithful sentinels at the door. The Sharks place blame on the poor soul who is only playing his scripted role in her exit from this planet.

Little Toni is in her three-piece unfashionable suit. We tease her, even then, but with deepest affection. She is accepted, as each of us, in any form she chose to be on this team.

Eve is inconsolable and weeps unabashedly in front of the coffin or in one of her teammates arms. At one point, she stands near the coffin, alone in her own space, head hanging, tears streaming and eyes stealing sideways glances at the shell which is no longer our Sarah at all, and whose body no longer holds any of her singular essence.

Tanker lays her number 77 jersey at Sarah's feet and bends down to kiss her forehead.

"We will never let you down," she whispers softly to Sarah. Tanker's eyes, which already bug slightly, pop a little more as she attempts to hold in her tears. After that, her massive frame slumps in a chair towards the back of the room. She never hangs her head, but instead, stares out at something only she can see and for months afterward all she can do is stare and shake her head. Few words ever emerge.

The Sharks carry Sarah's casket to the waiting hearse. Tanker, Dulce, Kim, Big Dot, Jessie, Wendy and, through a veil of non-stop tears, Eve.

The procession to the cemetery is slow and the winter wind rocks us with stone arms. The deep pocket in the ground where Sarah is to be laid, is gray and heartless. Clusters of tearful teammates cling to each other for warmth and support. Jade Max and I hold each other through shivers and tears as the coffin is lowered into the ground. The Sharks are the last to approach. Piper huddles us up next to the dark hole where our friend lies, to shout our Shark cheer, one last time with Sarah. We have added a line in her honor; Sharks Hoo-Rah, Five-One, Forever.

Then we file by, each player dropping a white rose into the chasm amidst the letters, trinkets and photos added by the many people who love her. Friends, family and teammates who shared this time on earth with her now watch until the last shovel is emptied over her casket. It is so cold down there. How can we walk away and leave our Sarah in this raw, ashen earth? More pain, numbness. I can't imagine the anguish of her family. None of us could bear anything more. Our Sarah was gone, and when she left, she took her light. It was as if she reached up and turned off life for us all.

CHAPTER 66

THE COMFORT OF HOME

My father shows his age the most. I react as though it irritates me,
but really, I am scared to lose him.

I am at home with my parents. I had left home to set the world on fire, as so many do, but now in my forties, I am back for more matches. I have resigned from my coveted, well-paying job due to my lack of interest and focus. I can't concentrate on anything without suddenly crying. I feel nothing but extreme love or extreme hate and sometimes both. As if I want to serve Ellen love letters on the pointy end of a steak knife. This Shark shit is making me feel, "Get off my property!" old and I try my best to keep the recent sadness at bay and ignore the negative energy surrounding women's football.

The losses have been too much for me. I need to sort out the tug of the past and the pull of the future. Here, I can safely note the autumn that floated me down to reality and the white winter snow that couldn't cover the imperfections. I needed home's solitude to form a spring season of budding freshness, a flourishing newness. Happiness. Here, I would wrap myself in warmer seasons and await the sails of summer.

My father is leaning over the sink, cutting oranges. He is wearing bathing trunks I bought him back in high school. I remember it distinctly because I purchased them with the first paycheck I had ever earned. Raybelle got me a job at Godfreys Hardware Store in the bait and tackle department. I hated it. But it was a summer job, and I suffered through it even though I had to work with Bubby Johnson, a boy in my class who had a crush on me although I did not have one on him. I liked the fact that he was on the football team, but I sure didn't want to kiss him. So when I got my first paycheck I was especially proud of it, as I had endured two weeks at Godfreys Hardware Store with Bubby.

Dade City is a small town, much like Zephyrhills. All the stores are owned by people who live there. No chains except for the Royal Castle hamburger joint where my two sisters spent much of their time when they were in high school, circling to see who was there. Sandler's drugstore has been a part of Dade city for decades, passed down for generations. Today I go in because I see in the window, a pair of blue bathing trunks with fish on it that look like largemouth bass—the kind my dad and I fish for. I go to the part of the drugstore where there is clothing and other articles not typically found in a drugstore. I am pleased to find the trunks in a size that looks like they will fit my dad so I buy them. For my grandmother, I purchase an eight-track tape of Clarence Welk. I know his name is Lawrence but for some reason my grand-mother always confuses his name and calls him Clarence. She sits in her cypress-clad den and watches Clarence every afternoon. She loves 'the beautiful costumes' and tells me the music is "the best you'll ever hear." For my mother, I buy a filigreed pill-box. Sterling and small. Strong yet delicate. My sisters each get an extra large bottle of suntan lotion. Annie is in school in Tallahassee and Jan is in Gainesville. I think it is the perfect gift since they spend most of their time bronzing their skin in the Florida sun. And for Raybelle, because she got me the job, plus, she's like my second mom, I buy a citrus scented candle. I feel bad that everyone is getting something except Sam, Raybelle's husband, so I buy him a fishing lure. He often goes with Dad and me to the Withlacoochee River to fish for brim and largemouth bass.

It uses up all of my paycheck, but I am excited to put the items in the car and motor back over the ribbon of hills to Zephyrhills to declare my treasures. I remem-ber each recipient was pleased and now, many years later, I am happy to see that dad is still wearing his swim trunks and I say so.

"Hmmmph." he says and smiles at me. Then he gives me a big hug. "You know Toady, when we were young, my brothers and I used to skinny dip in the lakes around Land O'Lakes. We'd play baseball with a stick and a rock and when we got too hot, we'd run down to a lake and jump in. Course, there were no fences back then so you could go anywhere and swim or hunt. But I was always watching for water moccasins. They're mean you know. I've had them come right at me. They aren't afraid of you."

The image of a water moccasin takes over the image of my skinny dad and his skinny brothers horsing around in a lake. Makes the back of my neck wiggle with horror, so I return to the topic of skinny dipping.

"That must have been a good life dad."

"We didn't have any money, but we had all we needed. Didn't need a bathing suit at all. But if you have to wear one, this is a fine one." I hug him back while he pierces a fresh and juicy chunk of orange and holds it in front of my mouth until I eat it whether I want it or not. It's a pastime he enjoys, both slicing and vending. I noticed his ears are hanging lower than they did ten years ago. I speak in what I think is a clear and audible voice, but the sagging auricles do not perk at all. I frown and repeat myself many decibels louder. He is aware of a noise in the room, but can't pinpoint its' source. I wave my hand. A non-audible clue. It works.

"Did you say something?" The ears are twice as big, yet do not function half as well. "Why?", I wonder?

"I said they are delicious, these oranges." He grins, but says nothing, then appears with a bowl of the beautifully cut fruit. "Take this to Mama," he shoves it under my nose and I take the bowl in self-defense.

"Ok. She'll like this!" and she does.

My mother and father have been married for 43 years. Over-all, I'd say they still like each other regardless of life from then until now. My father shows aging the most. I react as though it irritates me, but really, I am scared to lose him. How dare he get old? He could die if he continues this shit! Stop it, Dad, you're making me mad. And fix your hearing, for God's sake! You have good, big ears. Use them! Stop making us repeat ourselves in loud voices! Stand up straight while you're at it. You're taller than that! And quit pulling out in front of cars and telling us you had plenty of time!

That evening, I listen to Mom and William speak opinions about the Civil War. General Lee, Ulysses Grant, battles and ancestry. My mom's side of the family is from New York State. My dads is from Alabama. William's family comes from Georgia. The Confederates attacked Fort Sumter back in 1861, but they refer to the great unpleasantness like it happened last week. After that comes past presidents. How Kennedy money came from importing Scotch whiskey. Had JFK's father supported the Nazis? Could it have been the CIA who assassinated him due to his ever-increasing anti-Americanism? Was Hoover knowledgeable of this assassination? Teddy Roosevelt was the good guy, not FDR, who married Eleanor, his first cousin...for her money. LBJ was a crook. Stole all of his elections.

My father, nose buried in a University of Florida Alumni magazine, never lifts his head but imparts news he learned from his Texan friends who knew Lyndon personally.

"He was a son of a bitch."

I listen, knowing that at some future point I will probably, like a parrot, squawk this information out to others as though I am knowledgeable on these subjects and have formed my own opinions. Everyone does it. Everyone is so full of shit.

My mind drifts off as it so often does. Unfortunately, it beelines to Ellen. It has been many months since she left, and my self-esteem still hasn't crawled out of the toilet and toweled off. I hate her—love her—hate her and not because we aren't together, but because she never offered closure. She had, without a thorough examination, pronounced our relationship dead, but didn't bother to tell me I was the corpse at the funeral. I guess to offer closure; one has to accept responsibility.

Even if she returned, I wouldn't know how to love her without the paralyzing fear of losing her again. I am angry that I still love her, but I don't think I could take her back. Something frightens me about her theatrics. True hell is the life we love that cannot exist. I feel I should spill these thoughts onto paper, so I say goodnight to my parents and fade into my room.

CHAPTER 67

SINKING LOWER

We have no money, no field, no coaches.

I am scared to write for fear the flow of words will carry me too far from shore. I need stable ground having been afloat in cold waters since February, when it became evident that our relationship was in turbulence. When I tell you these waters are shark infested, I mean it in a good way. It was the loss of Ellen that drew me from my safe shore. 9-11 capsized me. It was the loss of Sarah that finally sunk me. Where can this story take you but into the dark waters with me? I am cold and afraid, but not of Sharks. The Sharks saved me.

I bought the team, but the real reasons are more intricate than I realized and scratching them into existence through the tip of this pen is painful. I know that sometimes we hold on too long to things and our knuckles turn white and our fist hurts from squeezing so tightly. When we are finally able to let go, it feels much better, but our hand is empty. Buying this team was both holding on and letting go, an odd immersion and acquittal of myself. Comfort out of my comfort zone. One hand is hurting and the other feels empty.

Many times since that purchase I have wanted to sell the team. Disband. End the negativity. Women's football has been toxic. Jealousy, accusations, deceit, and cruelty exist in solids and shadows and it has been too much for me. I need to sell the team. Maybe it's better for them as well. I am not my blue-ribbon self. I live on a frayed string, continually losing balance. On good days, when the line is taut, I slide the soles of my feet towards new worlds that aren't riddled with judgment and inequity. I saw possibilities when I bought the team and that is what kept me tough even when it got scary.

Fear, when it reaches a certain level becomes tangible. At the ranch my father shows me tracks in the sand. Of animals running. The scent of fear is still fresh on the ground and their toes are splayed and the dirt is pushed out behind like a spray of steel pellets from a shot gun. My passion is and has always been to play this game I love, but so many years have passed and now, I juggle urges to either run joyously towards the opportunity or flee from the burden. My team was my child. I love its lightness and its significance but, like everything you birth, it eventually becomes too heavy to carry.

So I retreat to the dark safety of my interior self, where I grapple to believe that this football team can come together in the way I envision it; that it can really happen. I, like the other women who share a passion for the game, understand how it feels to be a part of it and to want so badly to believe in its possibilities. Admittedly, it's an unusual love story, but a love story all the same.

I come to believe I am 'stuck' with the Sharks, but it's they who return light to my world. It's those 'Goddam Sharks.'

I am flailing in my own abyss when Turpie calls.

"How you doing there buddy?"

"I'm alright. Thanks buddy."

"You know I'm worried about you," she says.

"Naw, I'm alright."

"Well I'm worried about the team. You know this team don't exist without you."

"I'm sure the team would exist just fine. I can't do it anymore, Turpie. It's just too much and I'm not in a good space...it's done for me."

"You can't say that buddy. This team wouldn't be playing without you. It needs you. I need you. I'm gonna come down there and get you if you don't come back soon. It's time to get started again."

I am silent, but I'm shaking my head. I don't want this team. I don't want anything to do with it anymore.

"Buddy, we have no money, no field, no coaches. Even the players are talking about going elsewhere. I don't have it in me any more. They don't appreciate what we have done. Hell, they don't even like me!"

"They do like you, but you spoiled them."

"Spoiled them? I 'spoiled' them so bad they think everything I have done is wrong and I stole from them! I'm not overly sensitive Turpie, but I've done right by this team and all I get is accusations and criticism. No more." I say emphatically. "Besides, they are gone, Turpie. Between 9-11 and losing Sarah, we all scattered and no one even cares about football anymore."

"That's not true. They're still there and they waiting for you to come back and get the team started again. We're waiting for you buddy. You are our leader. You gotta come home and get the team back together."

"With what? I don't have the stamina or the money. Oh, except the money I stole from them," I add sarcastically.

"We'll find money. We'll get sponsors. You just gotta come back."

I continue to shake my head. I do have to go back, but I do not want to keep the team. I am in no physical, mental, or financial state to focus on the New York Sharks.

We sit at breakfast, my mom and dad and me. My mom is concerned with Gorbachev's inner thoughts and is talking to us about this. My dad is concerned with the college football polls, Steve Spurrier and the Florida Gators. He has always been passionate about these things. I know this and wish I could have been a great football star for him. Some say it is my dad's fault, that I am strange and gay. And I wonder why it is expressed as a "fault," as though everything I am is bad and someone needs to shoulder the blame? I have a pretty respectable list of accomplishments, but that's not enough for me. And, maybe not for my dad. He is proud of me in many respects but is still overly concerned with Steve Spurrier and the Gators. It is they who are his passion. I would have done that, Dad. I would've been that for you.

He finally puts the paper down. "Toady, I thawed out some of that good salmon like the ones we caught in Washington. Let's go check on them." We do.

A long time ago, we went salmon fishing off the coast of Vancouver, BC. He, my mom, me, and the two dogs decided to go there to look around. They both had fond memories of Lake Louise and wanted to see it again, and I had never seen that part of the country.

So we flew to Portland and rented a car—Mom and Dad and Mocha the poodle in the front and me and Tigger, the Scotty, in the back. I hate riding with those dogs; the stench of poodle breath from the front and the pong of Scotty farts in the back. The windows, all but mine because I won't let them near me, are fogged and snotted from their constant compulsion to look out. I can't blame them. The Cascade mountains are magnificent; evergreens coating entire sides of steep mountains, javelins of pikes and peaks storming from their tops towards infinite blue. We are close to the border when my dad spots a short runway and several small planes parked next to it. There is a handmade sign next to one of the single-engine Cessna's that says 'Flying Lessons.'

"Lookee there Mimi," he says to my mom. "You wanna fly?" she says "No," but he pulls over onto the side of the winding road anyway. For a minute, no one says anything, but I know what they are thinking. My mom met my dad when my grandfather gave her flying lessons for her 21st birthday. There was a small airport across the field from where they lived—the same one I grew up next to—and my father, having recently returned from England as a B-17 pilot in WWII, was employed as a flight instructor.

"Were you scared to take lessons, Mom?" I ask her.

"No. Not really. Not until the day he got out of the plane and told me to fly solo." I laugh and shove encroaching Tigger to an arm's length away. She farts twice and crawls onto the floor.

"What did you do?"

"I said 'No, no, no! You can't leave me! Don't you get out of this plane! I'll come back tomorrow and do a solo flight but not now!" she is laughing and my dad has turned part way around in the driver's seat, so he can see us both better. He is beaming and I can picture the two of them, youthful, daring, love-struck.

"What did you do, Dad?"

"I agreed to the next morning and we taxied back to the hanger."

"I was there bright and early and I did it," says Mom.

"That's right. I told her she would be fine, and that I would be right there waiting when she landed."

"I sat there for a minute, then taxied on down the runway and took off, I had to go to a certain altitude and fly around and land."

"She did everything right. I had to watch her from the ground and grade her. I gave her an A," he squirms a little and reaches over to pat her leg.

"But I was mad at him!" says Mom. "I picked him up and we took off again and I had to do some maneuvers to complete the test. I spotted two pine trees just wide enough to fit through and I dove down and put that little plane right in between those two pines…"

"It like-ta scared me to death!" he hoots. We are all laughing even though the story has been told and heard a hundred times. "Worse than the damn Krauts, she scared me!"

"I knew we would fit." She says, referring to the plane between the pines. Her smugness is appealing. It is a confidence I admire in my mother, one of so, so many things. We sit a minute more looking at the small crafts and the 'flight lessons' sign until my father wordlessly cranks the car and we resume our drive.

When we get to Vancouver, it is natural for Dad and me to want to go salmon fishing, but it is cold and rainy and the waters are deep and black. I didn't want to go but hated to let him down. I was in my teens and feeling rebellious so I went, but I was a pill. I sulked and whined, and was unappreciative of the time I was given with him.

I will never forgive myself for that and am beating myself up badly, as I stare at two salmon in a large plastic bucket by our back door. The one on top has its mouth open like it had something important to say but ran out of time. I look at the poor bastard, its eyes open and mouth relaxed. As if it decided that what it had to say wasn't that important after all. Or perhaps it, too, has realized that nobody listens.

I'm thinking way too much about these fish. I guess I do need to go back to New York City.

CHAPTER 68

BACK TO THE LAND OF YES

By purchasing this team, I had dared to create my own picture.
A self-portrait running directly counter to others.

My flight is landing at JFK and I am looking down at the many lights stitching the blackness together. I am back to a life that I worked so hard to create for over fifteen years. New York, New York.

I want to wake up in the city that never sleeps...

The plane banks left and I look for the off chance of spotting our field.

'Come through New York, come through!'

The city's lights section off areas like electric fences with cars wiring the way. I wonder if my New York chapter is closing. Maybe there's not enough here to hold me much longer. The tiny lights below illuminate dim paths. Where will they lead?

Back home, I put the key in the door, but so much mail has been shoved through the mail slot, I can hardly push it open. I tug my suitcase up the flight of stairs onto the main floor and set it down. Then I go back downstairs and fill a garbage bag with the accumulated mail and lug it up the stairs. I will go through it some other time. I see my Sharks jersey reclining on the rocking chair, which moves my thoughts towards Sharks instead of Ellen. It has been close to a year since we split, but I still seldom think of anything but her.

And now, though every arrow points to getting out of women's football, my soul speaks differently. I have tried to paint the portrait of who I really am, but I have, as most young people do, composed my portrait using someone else's sketches: religions, governments, media, all part of society's woven mural of half-truths and inconsistencies. I have not been happy living in these confinements.

By purchasing this team, I dared to create my own picture. A self-portrait, which runs directly counter to others' view of me. My hope was it that it would lance the boil of inner conflict, create a self-portrait painted from a different palette than that of my family's: my mother, who denied her own abundant talents and gave her power to my dad; my sisters, who married dependence and sought no self of their own making. They relinquished their last name for another's—a name foreign to who they are. They live for the shiny nuggets their husbands' successes provide, basking in the reflection of those accomplishments, instead of looking to their own.

I don't want that for myself. I want to be my own person with my own name, my own accomplishment or failings. I want the responsibility and the challenge.

I go back to Florida now, aware that I am a New York transplant. I drive down a canopied road. I look across the fall-hued scene of a black-watered pond filled with lily pads fingering into the deep stillness. My nephews, sunken into waders, duck hunt these ponds. They leave the house at 3 a.m. and walk out into the grassy waters before sun up. They stand in the coldness and float decoys around them. They come home frigid, and often duckless, but it is who they are. When they were small, no one questioned their love of this seemingly absurd ritual. The encouragement they received nurtured them as they grew taller. The south is their constitution and it gives them a strong sense of self.

Florida is still home in my head...but my heart aches. I love New York City, yet I love this canopied road. I love the way a southern winter speaks to me with the flicker of russet leaves reflecting off coffee brown creek beds. It is everything I am made of, but nothing of who I am. I was denied the ease with which my nephews navigated through their boyhood. Southern rituals were a birthright for them as boys. To participate was a privilege for me, a young girl.

There seems nowhere to go, but inward. It has been that way since I was a child. I am easily outraged at unfairness. The pettiness people display is just an x-ray of the glow of anger that resides in each of us. What is the cure?

I light a fire, pour a glass of wine into a beautiful goblet my mother gave to Ellen, and stake out a post in front of the fire to reflect. One time after we had had a big argument, she left the house for a few days. On the third day, she had slid a message under our front door. It was a collage of cut-out words and images from magazines that she had clearly taken some time to create. It was an apology in ransom note style and I called her when I got it and she came home. So much time has passed and I have received nothing. I fill the glass to the top.

My trust has become jagged and the loneliness is piercing. I used to run to my partner's arms, but walls grew tall through the years. I couldn't talk to her without criticism or indifference. I was "remiss" or I "should have" or she had "no investment in this conversation." All I wanted then and now was for her to listen and not interrupt with opinion or advice. Just listen. Hear me. See me. But neither interest nor empathy was given, and those formidable walls of self-protection are now holding me prisoner within. I don't want to be here anymore. If we are what we believe, I will unbelieve myself.

CHAPTER 69

DEEP GRIEF

The grief of all who loved Sarah is as sharp as our first day without her.

I have become so listless that I seek the easiest way to accomplish whatever is in front of me. Sleep is hard to come by, so I take a pill. No meditative music, no whale noises for me. Just eat the pill and become unconscious. Days go by without human contact, until I finally write a message for the Sharks website, a thank you to all the wonderful people who have been so supportive in our loss of Sarah. Lee posts it.

It has been many weeks and the grief of all who loved Sarah is as sharp as our first day without her. We love our friend. She was white light, spilling over with goodness. Her constant chatter, making us laugh. Her many talents, pushing each of us to be better. Her collection of zany, pink clothes, making us shake our heads and smile. Her energy, making us marvel just to watch her! Her love of humanity, making us rethink our often petty views. Her leadership, helping us believe in each other and ourselves. Stepping onto the field this season will be hollow and fragile without Sarah. But the messages, flowers, phone calls and letters from all of you who share our sadness, reflect Sarah's own essence of true kindness. There is much good in our community of women's football and on behalf of the players and staff of the New York Sharks, we thank you for helping us and Sarah's family through our tragic loss.

Then, I retreat again. The team tries to remain tethered, but falters and I am no help. Several times a group makes plans to get together via e-mail, but it is hard to make this happen. Turpie participates and she tells me that Tanker has ceased to show up at Shark events, that her communications have halted. Even Turpie cannot reach the giant's soul. Tanker's heart is unmended.

Slowly, the goodness of the team reaches me. It arrives in the form of an e-mail from Janet.

> *hey Gramma A,*
>
> *hope you're not too down today. guess i may just have to stay ONE MORE YEAR!! i wanted to let you know how much it meant to me when you told me that you were proud of me. i had a tough year as you know and finally got a chance to prove that i deserve to be out there. i think i did a good job of it, but*

to hear it from somebody else, especially you, not only confirmed it, but again, really meant something to me. thought i'd let you know that. i'd also like to tell you that you believing in me and going to bat for me was the sole reason why i just didn't completely take myself away from the sharks this year. i was sooo close. thank you for that as well. everything happens for a reason and SOMETHING is forcing us to come back next year. again, 2001 just wasn't it for us but 2002... how does the 2002 IWFL National Champs sound to you?? ok, talk to you soon and again...thanx again from the bottom of my heart.

love ya...Gramma J

I feel a flicker of response to this email. I stare across the room and fixate on an ornately wrapped little box Ellen gave me last Christmas that still holds the Skeezix marble I had hoped for. I take it out and roll it around in my cupped hand to examine it closely. I close my eyes, feeling the marble with my fingers and I hold it to my heart knowing it is the closest I can get to her. I had wanted to spend my life with her, yet we are not together. Except, it seems, through this tiny marble.

I look over at my collection of antique marbles. Hundreds of miniature worlds, with miniature gravitational pulls. I am still feeling that tug of the past, that force of the future. Or is it the other way around? Either way, to stay in the present is to be split wide open, bearing the pain of vulnerability. It feels so much safer to stay deep within. On my globe, I search for a land of "yes," not "no." Janet's words are a bright fork of lightning piercing my darkness and telling me that someone is there. Someone has acknowledged my efforts. In that moment, I see the land of "Yes."

CHAPTER 70

A HEAVENLY CHECK

"Buddy, you gotta understand...this team needs you. And we need them."

I am going through the trash bag of mail, when Turpie calls and she is mumbling. I know she is excited or guilty if she's mumbling. I am hoping it is the former. "What's up buddy?" I ask.

"Monster is coming back. I just got off the phone with her!" Monster is a pro boxer who played defensive end and instilled unequaled fear into QB's league-wide. "She took a year off for bad relationship reasons, but is coming back."

"Coming back to what?" I say stubbornly. "I'm done. I mean it." I have the phone cradled between my head and shoulder, pitching most of the mail into the garbage bag, when I spot a letter that doesn't look like junk.

"Buddy, you gotta understand...this team needs you. And we need them. We're all we got right now. We have to do this for Sarah. All of us."

"Turpie, I am barely alive here at Bank Street, since Ellen left. I don't have a job and my family has never fully supported this football deal. I can't spend any more money to pay coaches and fields and buses and refs and any of the million things that need paying for when you own a sports team. The fees we charge don't cover half of it! There are things we don't even know we have to pay for yet, I'm sure!"

I rip an envelope open with a bit of aggression and see what looks like a check. I see it is made out to the New York Sharks and the amount is for $25,000 dollars. I am silent as I look for a name and address at the top of the check but it is blank, like a starter check from a new account. In the lower left corner a note is scratched in handwriting that I don't recognize. It says: "From Sarah Parham for 2002 season."

I drop the phone, which clatters to the wooden floor and I jump up as though I've seen a ghost. And maybe I have. I hear Turpie's voice. "Buddy, you there? You there?"

I pick up the phone still staring wide-eyed at the check, which has floated with angel wings to the floor. Who would do this? It must be Sarah's parents or someone close to her family.

"Turpie..."

"I'm here. What was that noise? You ok?"

"Yes." I pause, still staring at the check. "Sarah mailed us a check..."

Sarah's life had been so full, yet the Sharks football team was her focus. It had given her an odd kind of physical freedom, a sense of endless durability and death-lessness that only the women who play can imagine. I think about how she always defended me, never once showed signs of mistrust, and constantly found ways to demonstrate her gratitude. She always told me that I'd made her dream of playing tackle football come true when I purchased the team. She had a pure passion for the game and filled anyone lacking it to the brim. What we lacked now was our friend, whose inspirational effect was never more clear until her death. We had not been shatterproof. Our pads and helmets did not spare us from an imperishable existence, but perhaps we could channel our passions into a common goal. We could unite our energies for her.

With this surprise check, Sarah walks us off the ledge of impending disaster. She had been our jester, our inner child, our friend, our conscience, our bright light in the darkest moments, and now, a financial angel and benefactor we could never have expected. She is still with us. The Sharks have a job to do and it isn't just for her. It is for us.

CHAPTER 71

WINGS

The Sharks begin to rebound and re-bond

It is late one evening when Sarah's mom, Sylvia, calls to ask who on the team wears number 77.

"I'm there at the gravesite every day and find so many things left for Sarah and most of them are from the Sharks. Usually they sign their names," Sylvia tells me "but this one just had number 77 on it."

"That's Tanker, Sylvia."

"Oh Tanker!" she says with wistful fondness. "You know, I know them all, but not by their numbers," she explains unnecessarily. "This card was so sweet and it had a little gold 51 charm inside. I just wanted to know which one it was..." her voice trails off. I have not been to the gravesite since the funeral, but Sylvia tells me about things she and Thomas find on their daily visits. Handmade cards, bundles of flowers, notes, a T-shirt with number 51 on it, wooden plaques of gratitude, all tokens of love for number 51, Sarah Parham.

Tanker had worn the '51' charm around her neck since Sarah's death. When I tell Turpie the story, she believes that putting the charm inside the card signified the conclusion of the deep mourning Tanker had slipped into. Perhaps, like me, she was ready to emerge.

With a plentiful personality, Tanker begins to unfold herself back into our lives. She infuses others on the team with newfound aggression and a fully restored wit. She is the Pied Piper, and the Sharks begin to rebound and re-bond.

"We gonna do this season right, I tell ya! We gonna do the whole thing!" she says. "S'like I always tell my kids when we have pizza, and they just wanna eat the cheese off the top. I tell 'em that that slice of pizza is like life. Why anyone wanna skin the topping off of life and not enjoy the whole thing? Just eatin' the cheese off the pizza gets boring at some point and eventually, it'll stop you up!"

The phone is ringing. I know I shouldn't pick up. I still have little to say to anyone. But I do.

"How's it going buddy?"

"Merrily, merrily," I answer.

"He's openly Latino."

"Who is?" I ask. Turpie has a habit of going places and not telling you you're going with her.

"That guy Dulce said she knew, who was a really good coach. I called him and he's going to call you, and I'm gonna call the NFL for anyone retired who might want to coach us."

"Please ask for someone who can control themselves in behavior that dates later than the Cro-Magnon period," I add, just in case we get a choice.

Turpie calls the NFL while I search the local high schools hoping to find a good head coach. I also call the IWFL. They have no clue either, but will place some ads for us. No one replies. I am not surprised. Women's football was routinely derided and pilloried just a short time ago. After two years, we have moved on to merely being caricatured and lampooned.

Finally, we get a break. Dulce's friend calls back, and sounds so respectful and knowledgeable that I ask him if he will take the coaching job. He says he can't, but he knows someone who might. Enter Coach Rex. Young and spirited, khaki-clad and polo-shirted, Rex fits the bill. The Sharks will be very happy with a coach who emphasizes regimen, structure and knows the game far better than any of us. We are all comfortable knowing Dulce's friend thinks Rex will be the perfect fit and when he agrees to sign on, I feel a huge relief.

Turpie and I also want to ask Erin to join the staff. She is eager to help and we need her. She is organized and thorough. Anal, in fact. She tackles tasks and problems with zeal and determination. Instead of hot chocolate in her thermos after practices, a pair of warm socks, still warm from the dryer, are pulled out and slipped over her hands.

"Let me ax her ok buddy?"

"Sure," I say and one day after all Sharks have disappeared and Erin has lagged behind to help clean up, Turpie approaches her. She looks around as if unwilling to let this priceless shard of information fall into the wrong hands. "So Erin...how would you feel about being a volunteer on the staff with Christine and me?"

Across her sharp features blooms a smile she must have had as a baby. There was a softness in Erin; a yearning for place and purpose. Still, she is wary.

"Well...what does it entail? I'd like to be involved, but I don't have a lot of time," which seems like an incongruous statement since she already spent most of her days either attending practice or hanging around asking to be of help.

"Why don't you just give it a try and see how it works. There's so much to do—you can just take your pick," Turpie advises her.

"Ok. I'll do that." She seems the perfect complement, and I envision the three of us, popping in and out of each other's days trying to master the art of running a group of highly dysfunctional, athletic women and a few maladjusted men.

CHAPTER 72

EMBRACING PAPA SHARK

We need him. He needs us even more.

Mini-camp arrives and so does Big Dot. She clamors out of her car, scowl intact and lumbers to the edge of the field.

"How ya doin' Big Dot?" I say cheerfully.

"I'm here," is her sunny reply.

"So much sunshine to the square inch," I answer, enjoying the opportunity to poke at her. She looks at me with an increased scowl.

"Walt Whitman said that. You don't recognize it?" I chide while moving on. We have quite a crowd and Erin is collecting vet fees, while Piper is fitting the rookies with their new equipment. You can tell they are excited. The helmets, gleaming silver, are their favorite new toys and they walk with joy beaming beacon-like from behind each facemask. Eve and Wendy pull up in a Mini Cooper, which makes me laugh. Two clowns. I give them each a big hug, my heart truly glad to see them. Then Thomas, Sarah's dad arrives with Tanker.

"We got us a Papa Shark this year, Mama Shark!" Tanker says to me while pointing at Thomas. A smile flares and he shrugs, gray hair eclipsing his state of melancholy. The Sharks are his refuge from the grief that comes in large parcels of unmarked time. He is searching for his Sarah and anything that might dissolve his loneliness. I hug him, and Sharks gather around taking turns at squeezing him tight. He has sat in the stands at every game since we started, a loyal dad who thinks nothing of safely harboring the players' necklaces around his neck and forearms and filling his pockets with earrings while they play. Thomas knows Sarah's closest bonds were with Sharks and his need to be around the team is apparent. We understand and immediately adopt Papa Shark for practices, games, events, fundraisers, and dinners. This season, he will be on the sideline with us.

Thomas, a retired Brooklyn cop, isn't shy and takes any opportunity to talk about Sarah, which we all enjoy. She was his pride and joy, the baby of four girls. Thomas had been something of a chauffeur to Sarah, taking an interest in her many activities. The two of them had been inseparable even though Sarah's antics, he admitted, wore him out. She had that effect on all of us. Her high energy level was wonderfully inexhaustible.

"My other daughters are just as wonderful, but no one kept me on my toes like Sarah did," Thomas tells us. "Must have come from Sylvia's side of the family, because I never saw anything like it before. I remember one time when she was about nine years old, and we were traveling and our plane got delayed. We sat in the airport for about 15 hours and Sarah didn't sleep a minute. She started dancing to the music coming out of the bar. No one ever taught her how to dance! And she was entertaining everyone at the airport by dancing and asking people questions... amazing questions about people's children and where they were going...even then she had a way with people."

I relate to their bond. My father, though he loves not one of his three daughters more than the others, identifies with me the most. The years have robbed him of his vitality, but I am sure he can see himself in the way I walk, the way I set my jaw and the way we both love in ways indistinguishable from passion and obsession. I wonder if he truly saw himself before his mirror of me arrived.

"He "made out" at me!" I hear this remark as Sharks begin to arrive. I hope that this expression does not mean that Rex has already put a move on a player.

Erin handily carries a twenty-pound briefcase full of paperwork to be dispensed. She is chipper as always, humming a tune as she unlocks and proudly exposes the handout sheets in her case. She then hides the key in a small leather pouch and tucks it into her jeans pocket. Seeing Mabel arrive, a scowl takes over and she crosses the room, refusing to dole out Mabel's requested embrace. Mabel is affection-challenged and continually seeks hugs and begins conversations that occupy personal space. "I'm not hugging her. She holds on too long and it's gross," says Erin matter-of-factly.

Mabel greets me with her customary hug, that is, she almost suffocates me and while doing so, she unloads inane information into my ear. "Just found out that there is a Jewish Sports Hall of Fame and Museum, so first I'm setting it up for Jade Max to have her own display and then I have to wait until next year to nominate her and get her inducted."

Stand back, while I leap around and bang the cymbals.

"Really?" I respond, trying to sound enthused and free myself at the same time. When we become separate entities once again, she grins and shakes her head letting me know that yes, it is really true.

"What I always say..." she begins and whatever it is that Mabel always says remains unrevealed, because two Sharks begin a distracting conversation.

"Weight's up, Pussycat!" yells Eve to Cooper as she approaches the field.

"Fuck you Eve. I've been dieting and my weight is good."

"What kinda diet makes you gain weight?"

"I didn't gain weight, you jerk. It's a healthy diet that consists of the seven food groups."

"Yeah. And there's only three left. OH!" We all laugh including Cooper.

"You know, I'm not faaaat," whines Cooper. "My mom says I'm just big-boned."

"Yeah. You're stomach bone is immense!"

"Eeeeeeeve!" Cooper moans and gives a hurt face.

"Come on Prada," teases Eve. "You got work to do on that 'O' line."

Further distractions arise as we watch the Coven close in. "Well, look who has seen the light!" says Erin.

"Yeah. Must be the light on the inside of the refrigerator because they got fat, too!" Eve again.

"I told you they eat everything buddy. I told you!" Turpie is aware of this because her brownstone in Brooklyn is still jammed full of renting Sharks—namely "the Coven." It remains a team dorm of sorts.

"We better start before something awful breaks out." I climb the stairs to the small room above the concession stand. Fortunately, the windows open and Little Toni swings them wide. Turpie brings in an armful of edible morning goodies.

"Christine, want a donut or coffee?"

"No thanks buddy. Actually, coffee sounds good." Turpie pours a cup from the Dunkin Donuts cardboard carafe, adds a little half-and-half and hands it to me. I find it sweet that she knows how I like my coffee.

"Thanks. Guess we should start..."

"Did you make any changes in your speech since last night?"

"Yes—in the paragraph about Wendy, I moved the apostrophe in Horse's ass," I say and smirk at her.

She is flashing that grin. "It's time buddy." And I know she's right. It is time to lay down Shark law. There have been too many players acting like they are in charge. There have been coaches more concerned with their popularity than winning. Opinions are hard and emotions are high. The line between folding the team and continuing is taut and brittle, and if I don't present the right tone, it will snap.

"SHARKS!!!" I bellow across the small room. It takes a minute, but the twittering stops and they fall silent.

It is the sort of short silence, however, which precedes a tornado for a few seconds before it touches down and really gives a town the works. I brace myself.

"Welcome to the 2002 New York Sharks!" They applaud and whoop, then settle back in. Except Jessie who slumps in her chair, arms folded, bottom lip hanging down to her boobs and occasionally chewing the end of a cinnamon stick.

I take a deep breath and begin. "On December 25th, 2001, we lost Sarah and the New York Sharks changed forever. So did I. One of my favorite sayings is 'To thine own self be true.' For several reasons--many really--I was not true to myself last year. I was in a position where any choice I made was a losing one. I ended up feeling isolated and trapped. Decisions were made that were not in keeping with my true beliefs. I let some of you run roughshod over me, fearing we would not have a team if I didn't give in to certain things—like not riding the bus with the team or accepting stupid excuses for missing practice and events. Some of you blatantly flirted with the coaches, yet you refused to play if I did not fire the coaches who flirted back. These are just a few things. In short, this year will be very different. The rules set forth today will be adhered to by you and the coaches or you and the coaches will not play or coach for the New York Sharks."

To my surprise, they are quiet and even appear to be listening. This is very un-Sharklike. I begin listing what I expect.

"One: You will be committed to the team on all levels including practices, public appearances and sportsmanship to each other.

Two: When we travel by bus, you will get on the bus to the game or you will not play.

Three: Any flirting, dating, surreptitious meetings, etc., with the coaching staff will cost you your position on this team. Same for the coaches. Treat each other with respect and professionalism.

Four: Your sponsorship commitments must be adhered to on the dates set. No exceptions.

Five: If you tell me you will be at a function and you don't show up, look for yourself on the bench come game time. Make an effort to be a part of these things. It makes a difference."

I continue to explain some things about the field, or lack thereof, and I talk about the fees and where they are applied.

"The coaches alone run at least 10k. Fields...another 10-12, buses, planes and hotels, add another 25 then you have the miscellaneous things that add up quickly, all told around 50k minimum. And that does not include playoffs. If—no WHEN—we get to playoffs, we will have to fundraise in order to travel there. Meaning, you Sharks will be pimping yourselves out in the meat packing district," I tease them.

"Eh, gonna be giving back a lot of change," chirps Eve which brings a good laugh from the group.

My speech continues. "This team exists on passion which is part of its magic. It was founded on love of the game and, despite our setbacks, we move forward. It's one big relationship. Sometimes bad, sometimes good. Players leave, coaches go away. Some take a year off for personal reasons, some retire, but most of us are still here. I will be here as long as people are loyal. The New York Sharks are a storybook team from a storybook city and I don't want to see it end. But it will take a lot of hard work from a united group."

I scan the room now and ask, "Are you in?"

There is a pause. I know they are not used to me talking uncompromisingly. I am struck—not for the first time—about the mix of people staring back at me.

Blue hair is coming from under the back of Debbie's helmet. Red glasses are strapped tightly to Joy's green-eyed face. Various hues of skin on various sized frames have filled the small room. We are a collection of vivid egos and personalities. Most of these women are rugged individuals chasing a type of personal freedom and self-expression. But the paradox is, to get it will require compromise, selflessness, bonding, and a commitment to properly channel our aggression towards our opponents -- not each other. Loving to play won't be enough to win; we're going to need to find a way to love each other enough to stick together through thick and thin.

"Are you in?" I ask again, only louder.

"YES!" the group yells back, including Thomas, his voice containing the sounds of hovering grief, a quiet despondency.

I am shocked at the apparent acceptance of my new laws and attitude. I expected moaning and gum-snapping, and the rolling of beady Shark eyes. Instead, I feel a weird relief from them, like kids who feign anger at discipline, but are happy because it spells caring. We are odd "goddam" Sharks.

"Who-the-hell knew?" I softly say to Turpie and we shrug at each other and the team breaks to begin our first practice of the new season.

CHAPTER 73

SEARCHING FURTHER FOR FUNDS

Obtaining coaches, practice and game fields is repetitive,
daunting and tiresome. Funding is impossible. Advertising is nil.

If the kick-off party is an indication of the season, we will win, but with great drama. It starts off quietly, as always and the usual stuff crosses my mind: What if only a few people show up? What if they don't have fun? I feel responsible. But they do show up and we do have fun. The rookies bond over the drinking game of "flip cup," during which some extraordinarily personal questions are asked and private admissions are squeaked out and chased back in with beer.

Mabel arrives and approaches me and somehow I escape the hug. She does manage, once again, to invade my 'Soviet airspace' and I want to shoot her down, but I don't. She works hard to get us exposure. She has gotten lots of press for us albeit small newspapers around the five boroughs. We have been acknowledged by the Mayor of NYC, the borough presidents of three boroughs, Carl Prescott, New York City's Sports Commissioner, and several restaurants have allowed us in to pay less than the posted prices for an evening of beer and food. Mabel has attempted local and national television and magazine coverage and even sponsorship of the team. She says she does it from her heart, though the topography of her heart is mysterious, given its' curious and antagonizing tributaries.

"I googled New York Sharks and a track team came up! I wonder if they had that name before you? Is it allowed? The website is w...w...w...nys...runners.com."

"I don't own the word Sharks, Mabel, only the logo. I'm sure a track team wouldn't be confused with us."

"Uhhhhhh....yeahhh....." is her skeptical reply. Her travel website is constantly dishing up strange adventures such as underwater diving without getting wet. She tells me about the odd escapades and invariably, there is an incident in which Mabel argues with someone. She is now intent on sabotaging the track team. "If I wrote a letter threatening them, we could get some money out of it for the Sharks. Their logo may be too much like the Sharks."

"Please do no such thing Mabel." I look her straight in the eyes, but it's hard because they are shooting around the room like a laser show. "Leave the track team alone."

The next day, at Mabel's behest, I am faxing council-people in Brooklyn and Manhattan, requesting funds. I dial. I push start. The letters are clicking through and, waiting for them to finish, I stare out the window at the pageantry of people. Sunlight falls off the bricks of the old brownstone across the street. There is something sultry about a cityscape and I lean into distant thoughts as I fax.

My mom and I are standing in a gallery in San Francisco. It is full of photographs of the city; the Golden Gate Bridge, Alcatraz, Lombard Street. I am in 9th grade, but my mom has let me miss a week of school because she says travel makes you smarter than any classroom. I am into photography and am staring at a night photo of the bridge and its reflection in the waters of the bay. You can see a faint outline of Sausalito in the background. It is clear, sharp and so colorful.

"That's a nice shot, isn't it?" She says standing next to me.

"Yes. I love it."

"Yours are that nice."

"Hmmmph," I say, sounding like my dad.

"You could be a famous photographer and artist one day. You might even live here or in New York City."

"Hmmph." I repeat, but my mom always knows.

The ringing of the phone returns me to present day. I answer it and Kim says, "I watched D.C. again."

"AGAIN?" I am amazed. "Why? We don't even play them until mid-season!"

"I know. What happened to that number 99 that used to play flag?"

"That HUGE one?" I ask. I have not seen a human that large. Ever.

"Yes. Where did she go?"

"A crane came and got her," I say dryly, and then feel guilty for saying such a mean thing.

"Well, I'm glad because I think she's the one that sat on Barb last year and blew her knee out!"

"I know. And Wimples' leg, too. She was yelling 'My leg! My leg! and you could see Wimples' stick of a leg poking out from under number 99 like she was hatching something." Kim laughs. "I'm supposed to go to practice tonight, but I can't go until Thursday."

"Why?"

"Because we have other issues like fields. Donny, at the Staten Island field got pissed at us, because we tried to use the indoor bathrooms instead of the provided port-a-johns." This in addition to Erin putting a stop on a check for seventy-five dollars for a practice field, instead of being patient and letting it arrive. It cost more to stop it than it's worth. But that's Erin. She means well. So I get out the bucket and mop again and clean it up via phone, but now I need to make a physical appearance to smooth the last feather. If we lose this field, which is no more than a bulb hanging over a mosquito breeding pasture, we have nothing.

In all of NYC, we, the women's pro football team, have no field. After two years, nothing seems to be easier for us. Obtaining coaches, practice and game fields is repetitive, daunting and tiresome. Funding is impossible. Advertising is nil. But, somehow, Turpie gets us a meeting with the NFL about partnering with the Giants at a few of their functions to get some publicity. It seems positive. We sit in the car outside of Giants Stadium waiting to go into our meeting. As we sit and wait, we watch a Giants player come out and get into his Hummer.

"That's that asshole that was at Kim's banquet that night. A few Sharks were talking to him about being a Shark and how cool it must feel to play in the NFL. He was so surly! He said he only did it for a paycheck and then refused to sign his autograph. He was an arrogant jerk," she says.

We are here to beg to work at any Giants function just to get the word out that the New York Sharks exist and all I can think of as he loads his NFL bag into the passenger seat of his expensive sports car is how much that asshole makes doing something he loves to do. My players are sending sponsor request letters and having fundraisers to pay the $750 bucks each to play.

"He's been working out," I say. "I bet that is one beautiful workout room in there."

"Yeah, buddy. Your Sharks need to be working out. Diamond, Laci, Big Dot, Wimples, they all gained 30 pounds in the off-season. You saw them! They have over 45% body fat and are all over 200 pounds. We were sittin' there the other night—eatin' more shit—and Diamond looked 'body fat' up on the computer and by that standard, they are all obese!" Turpie is laughing.

"What did you say to them?" I ask.

"I said 'You fat motherfuckers need to lose weight! They can't. Laci hung her head. Big Dot said she was going to zip her lips. No more food. Then she drank 10 glasses of water. Just kept drinking water. Diamond didn't say much. Next day, she went and bought a Tai Bo tape and moved the furniture around and called them down to work out but they never showed up. Went to Ruthie's to get soul food instead."

I am laughing out loud. "They eat everything buddy!" Turpie continues. "They came in the other night about 4:30, woke me up. They were drunk, jumped in my bed. Wimples said she couldn't go upstairs to her room 'cause she was drunk and would get in trouble. I said "Go home and lay down. Get out of my room!" She says, "You got anything to EAT? They ate everything I had! I had a leftover bag of fish and shrimp and they ate it all. I looked in the bag and there were two shrimp tails." I am cracking up. "But they didn't touch the salad!"

"Everyone is getting bigger," I say. "Even Little Toni. Did you notice that at the last meeting?"

"Yeah, she needs to work out a minute, too. Same with your fullback! Her ass blew up like she got a shot and it swelled up. Or like she sprained a muscle in it."

I belly-laugh again. "Should we go in?" I ask, as I grab a sweatshirt out of the bag in the back seat. "I'll bring the lady this Shark sweatshirt. A large should do, right? I only have a large and a double X."

"You better take both buddy. She may be blown up like everyone else."

We are introduced to a nice woman named Melinda who, we both notice, has not blown up. I give her the large tee shirt and apologize that it might be "a tad too big."

"That's fine! I'll sleep in it!" she says and begins talking about how the Sharks can help at games.

"I had never heard of the Sharks before you called," she says.

You and 8 million other New Yorkers.

"I am so happy to hear about you! I already had some thoughts and wondered how you guys would feel about working the bubble for pre-game activities?" The bubble is the Giants practice field, which is encased in a white, plastic, blow-up dome. We learn that before each of the Giants home games, VIP ticket holders bring themselves and their kids to the bubble to participate in a carnival of sorts: booths to throw footballs or try out a tackling dummy. Food and beverages are served and there are lots of giveaways for the kids. Melinda thinks we would be perfect to run the booths and demonstrate the football-related activities. "You can wear your jerseys and tell people all about the Sharks and everyone that helps will get a free ticket to the game."

The thought appeals to Turpie and me and we know the Sharks will like the opportunity, too. The three of us talk further, but I don't hear much. So many odd thoughts are bouncing dreamlike through the outer space of my mind, and like all dreams, the details are strange. Is it really possible that the Sharks will be working with the Giants?

Outside, Turpie and I high-five each other for our small accomplishment while another Giants player nonchalantly drives away in a truck large enough to consume the annual energy output of Texas.

CHAPTER 74

DULCE AND LITTLE DULCE

"Tomorrow, I am taking my mom to school for Show and Tell."

It is a Thursday night practice. Erin jolts her car to a stop grinding the brakes. I have learned from experience, that sharing passage with this road beast behind the wheel is not advisable. I am sure she hit such speed from the time she left the peaceful backside of Hunterdon County until she arrived here at practice, that her Honda only touched New Jersey and Brooklyn in odd spots.

Erin found the Sharks shortly after her mother died of cancer. A controlling woman, her mother had been very adventurous, something Erin was not. Perhaps out of rebellion. In any case, Erin spotted the Sharks while trolling the web and thought it might be a place to honor her mother's adventurous side, as well as Erin's athletic side. Confronting day-to-day life with the greatest, white-toothed smile in the world, there appears to be a smidgeon of anger and resentment in Erin's demeanor. Was it from her mother's choices while raising Erin, or the fact that she had left her to fend for herself on this planet—we were never sure, but as my grandma always says; "You never know what shoot she's gonna come out of."

Today is no different as she walks over with clear purpose, and that purpose is to inform me that a lot of the players have "Skipped out on paying for these jerseys." In one hand, she has gripped a half dozen of said jerseys around their mid-sections and is carrying them like a flower bouquet. In the other, the familiar clipboard. She points emphatically at the names on the board.

"They aren't getting the jerseys until P. I. F!"

Paid in full.

She shakes them at me. I nod in agreement, while several players, eager to get their jerseys, begin lining up. Tanker stands in mid-line appearing as circular as possible without bursting. Her turn comes to face Erin and the event turns sour when Erin folds Tanker's tent size jersey and places it back in the box. "You owe $9.75 additional since it's a 4X."

"You didn't tell me that when I ordered it!"

"Erin didn't know she'd have to convert a Buick cover into a football jersey either!" comes the familiar voice of Wendy. Snickers are heard down the line.

"That ain't fair that I gotta pay more because I'm bigger! You need yo big girls ya know!"

"Nothing personal Tanker," says Erin. "We are only charging you our cost."

"Well that's discrimination against big girls!"

Oh dear. Here we go.

I turn my head, and for a good 30 seconds I look off and daydream of having more agreeable people on my team. When I turn back around, Tanker is in front of me with an expectation of getting the $9.75 waived. She looks at me and waits.

"Tanker, we can't absorb the cost for everyone, or we'll go broke," I say. "Please pay Erin the $9.75." This is hard for me. I want to say, "Oh forget the damn $9.75," but what about the other large players who will owe it? If I do it for one, I have to do it for all. I remain firm out of loyalty to Erin and her efforts to enforce policy, and shake my head. Tanker stomps her foot which, though intimidating, is so much better than kicking an owner with it, an action she clearly wants to perform. I sigh and she lumbers away.

Practice begins and I'm on the sideline babysitting Charlotte, Dulce's precocious eight-year-old daughter. Charlotte has been to several practices and Shark events, so it is not unusual to see her.

"She actually wanted to come this time and I was having trouble finding a babysitter so here she is. I'm sorry, Christine. I know we aren't supposed to bring kids to practice, but I didn't want to miss it," says Dulce as she buckles the straps on her shoulder pads.

"I'm glad you are here, Dulce, because it's a big game coming up and you need to be here." I tell Dulce that I'll watch Charlotte since it is more important for Dulce to be on the field in Saturday's game than me. It's just me and the eight-year-old, so I take her across the street to get a slice of pizza and some ice cream.

"Tomorrow, I am taking my mom to school for Show and Tell," she says.

"Really!" I say. "What are you going to show and tell about her?"

"She's gonna suit up in her football uniform and talk about the Sharks." She has a slight New York accent and pronounces it "unifwom" and "Shawks."

"Yeah," she answers nonchalantly. "At first I thought they'd laugh at her, but everyone thinks it's kinda cool that she plays tackle football."

"Do you think it's cool?"

"Yeah...but..." she contemplates her next utterance. "We've both sacrificed a lot for her to play. I don't see her as much as I'd like, and I'm certain her job has suffered."

"You think so?"

"Quite certain. But...yeah..." and she looks up from her ice cream with a huge grin, "It's reeeeeally cool!"

We finish our ice cream in silence, as I digest the words from this 8-year-old. Then I take her hand and we cross the street to the field.

"Did you have fun?" I ask her when we get back.

"Oh yes—it was divine!" she says then proceeds to teach me four German phrases, the correct pronunciation of the word "hyperbole," and read two chapters of Jane Austen's "Pride and Prejudice," before I fall sound asleep on the sideline all tucked in under my Shark jacket, weary from so much eight-year-old energy.

I wake up just a few snores later and find Charlotte distributing water to the players. She is delighted to run the cage of water bottles onto the field when Coach Rex yells for a break. Normally, an eight-year-old would be too young to handle the task, but Charlotte works the job to perfection—she sprints to the players, she stays out of the way, she refills the bottles after every distribution, and she loves it!

"Christine, this is God answering prayers. I don't need a babysitter anymore and we have an official water girl."

"Hey! H2O!" yells Eve from mid-field. "How about getting some liquid out heah!" Charlotte laughs and races with full water bottles to the thirsty Sharks on the field.

"We better hire her, buddy!" Turpie says with a big smile.

"This is the beginning of Shark nepotism." I answer.

When I finally get home, I am in need of food, so I eat my usual meal—I open the refrigerator door, pull up a chair and pick until I'm full. Tonight, I find one dozen macaroons. I down eight of them, before I spot the two leftover sausages and one slice of pizza. I am digesting my found meal nicely when the phone rings. It is Erin. "Janet thinks she has broken her ankle and is at the hospital."

"Whaaa? I didn't see her go down! What did Coach say?"

"He said she is remarkably under-equipped to deal with life as it is lived."

I laugh. "Ok. Please let me know what the result is if you hear first."

"I will." It's nice to have a friendship evolving with Erin. I am beginning to understand that she is a hero in her own storm, which is how she found a sense of value as a child. She was the EMT at the family wreck and, in her concept of the world, the more she carries, the stronger she is. Tasks, problems, lives...football teams...all piled up on her back while she folds herself into colorful, origamied layers for the outer world to see. We understand what we each don't understand, and she is a comforting friend.

I sit back down on the chair to pick at dinner, when the phone rings again. It is Dulce. She has a question and she'll be right over. When I open the door, she immediately gets to the meat of things.

"What kine o' sex life do you tink the average couple has?" There is a certain amount of anxiousness about her.

"I'd say the average couple hasn't." This is what I believe, although I understand from the other players that Dulce's is quite active. According to them, Dulce and her "Sweetness" outperform the average couple hands down. Or wherever their hands go. The entire team is aware of their actions. And reactions.

Today, as Dulce stands in my kitchen wearing tights and Sweetness's white, button down work shirt, she is perplexed.

"Who," she inquires "do you tink receives the most from our relationship?"

I answer as honestly as I can. "Your neighbors." She doesn't comment and is staring at my small T.V., which is showing a video of last season's game against the New York Galaxy.

"It's hard for me to say, Dulch," I continue. "Our love lives are very different. You have one. I don't." Plus—and I don't say this out loud—your erogenous zone starts several feet from your actual body. To me, an erogenous zone is one more place in New York not to park a car unless you want a ticket.

"Tha' was a great tackle I made!" she says, dropping the subject. For some reason, all Sharks are mesmerized by watching themselves on video. I offer her one of the remaining macaroons.

"Are they any good?" she asks, scooping several into her palm.

"Well, I can't speak for the ones remaining, but the eight I had minutes ago were superb. Why are you asking me this?"

"'Cause I dunt want to ea' one if they suck!"

"No...about you and your "Sweetness.""

"'Cause my Sweetness may not wan' me to play this year and I wa' wondering if he wa' worth it."

"Sweetness" comes to most practices since he and Dulce live minutes away from the practice field. "Sweetness" does everything he is not supposed to do from parking in the handicapped spot, to interfering with Coach Rex's practices. It is Turpie's job to keep "Sweetness" in line; "Can you please move your car," "Would you mind sitting in the bleachers until after practice," "The coaches have asked that you not shout advice onto the field during practices or games, ok?" "Gatorade is not allowed on the turf field." "Please drink that beer outside of the gates." "Sweetness" is a tough dog to keep under the porch.

Last week "Sweetness" stood in the back of the end zone at practice, defiantly feeding Dulce bites of pizza, despite Rex and the staff repeatedly asking him and Dulce to stop.

"The other players are hungry, too! Why should you get to eat and not them?" Erin asks Dulce in a semi-puffed state.

"'Cause they dunt have a 'Sweetness'!" Dulce says matter-of-factly with her mouth full.

"You aren't gonna have a 'Sweetness' either 'cause I'm gonna kill him if he ever does it again," Turpie jumped in and squelched the feeding. And now, if we lose Dulce because of "Sweetness," the entire team will kill him.

CHAPTER 75

TURPIE THE FIXER

Verbal commitment to the team is often easy
but when it comes time to show up, life happens.

I'm sitting at home playing Italian music, which makes me pine for Tuscany. I have to find Sharkie, our mascots uniform, which is hopefully in the basement though I didn't see it there the other day. After practice, things often end up in player's cars: "Can you keep this until next week? I'm taking the train home," one will ask, or "I can't be at practice Tuesday. Can you keep the balls?" Things like that. Turpie has found Kayla, a volunteer to wear the Shark suit this season and we are excited to have Sharkie on the field leading cheers.

In just days, Montreal will arrive in full force, with Scarlette, the owner, at the helm. We must beat them! We can and I really think we will. Dulce's return at halfback is paramount and moving Big Dot to guard and having Jade Max at receiver is huge! Dennie, a friend of Tanker's is joining the team and she will be a great defensive back.

An incoming phone call—right in the middle of Italian music—interrupts my reverie.

"Fuckin' Wanda!" Kim shrieks. "Now she says she's not going to play. Wanda has changed. A LOT! Wait 'til you see how she dresses! She had a purse when we saw her in Atlantic City the last time." Kim and the Coven spend a lot of time at the casinos in Atlantic City. "Now I'm fucked and it's my own fault because I counted on her and I shouldn't have, and I know better, but she said she was gonna play. She's the one who contacted me! I didn't go beggin' her!...."

Spit a period Kim. Deep breath...

"You gotta call her. The film is downloading...." she tells me, loudly clanking the phone down to cross the room and check the computer. I can still hear her yawping. "Eight more minutes, then I can watch and I'll have every play Montreal has ever run since their first game. Now Wanda quits? We don't have a defensive baaaaack! And Dulce won't move to inside linebacker. She's scared she'll get killed, but she's a BEAST!"

The word "beast" is so pronounced it must have winded her because she pauses ever so slightly to refill the lungs. I quickly slip in the edgewise word.

"Why is Wanda not playing? Can she not get cleared?" I ask, knowing she had minor surgery on her knee from playing softball and has gone through recent rehab.

"She says she's fine," Kim squeals back, squeaking out the word "fine" in a voice that is so high and strained she must have refilled with helium. "That's just it! She came to me and said she'd rehabbed and wanted to play football. And now she won't!"

"Isn't there anything we can do?"

"I don't know! I'd show my ass in Macy's window, if it would make her play but... God's gotta help us, Christine! I mean it!"

I had to chuckle. "I'll call her."

"Now?"

"Yes." And I do. Wanda answers. "Wanda. It's Christine from the Sharks."

"Hi Christine!" Wanda answers.

"Hey. Listen, I just got off the phone with Kim who got your news and blew a gasket." She laughs softly. "And if you don't come play," I continue, "She's gonna swerve off the road and flip upside down." I hear a snarf on the end of the line.

"I know. It's just there's a lot going on in my life and I can't make a full commitment. Plus, I don't have a car anymore."

I heard you traded it for a purse.

Verbal commitment to the team is often easy but when it comes time to show up, life happens. The traffic in and around NYC is often outrageous depending on the time of day and public transportation can be difficult to manage. Especially when one is carrying large bags of football gear and still wearing work clothes. So when someone says they can't commit, it's usually not because they don't want to play but more about the huge effort it takes to show up at all the practices and events.

"Don't worry! We can hook you up with a ride."

"Yeah?" Wanda hesitates.

"Listen Wanda; we're all back together for Sarah. We have a great team and if we win it in her honor and you aren't a part of it, you're not gonna be happy that you didn't play."

"Naw, I wouldn't be," she admits, laughing a little.

"You think about it and let Kim or me know by Thursday, ok?"

"Ok. I'll let you know." We hang up.

Meanwhile, an e-mail from Erin who has taken over all medical organizing and correspondence for the team, tells me Erica, one of our linebackers, has not only pulled a calf muscle, but broken the ulna bone in her forearm. Then Piper sends an e-mail telling the team her BBM is 503962 which spurs a flurry of e-mails giving BBM's. What the hell is a BBM? A double poop? I can't keep up. I just got used to the internet.

My phone is going off. Kim again. "Jade Max isn't coming to practice tonight. I'm gonna have a stroke. I'm gonna kill someone."

"How do you know she's not coming?"

"FACEBOOK!" she screams so loud her parrot squawks in the background. "Can you believe it? I found out on FACEBOOK that one of my receivers is not coming to practice! Actually, Big Dot saw it and passed it on. I don't even have a Facebook page! Mother fucker! She's our only other chance at receiver and she needs to be there both nights this week to know the system. We can't lose to this team! We are better than them! Like in Key West when we lost to the Queen Mother-Fucking Bees! Remember?" Their full name was the Queen Bees, but Kim has installed a middle name. "We were better than them, but Wendy didn't do what I told her to do and was out of position and they scored. Oh...I can't——"

"I can't either. Don't talk about it."

"It's Wanda calling! I'll call you back!" Of that I have no doubt, but Erin beats her to it.

"Janet has left the hospital in a wheelchair. The doctors told her to stay off it, but it's not broken."

"So, she can play in a few weeks, I suppose."

"I suppose," is her dry answer.

"Gotta go. Other line."

Kim's turn. "Good news and bad news. Fuckin' Wanda is now playing, but only for Sarah. Thank you Sarah!" She holds the phone only inches away and yells. "Then, I get a call from Dulce and—listen to this— 'Sweetness' said Dulce can't play! And she is listening...to...him!" Kim is stroking out.

"Call Turpie."

"Why?"

"Because she will kill 'Sweetness' and then Dulce can play."

"Let's just kill Dulce!"

"Seriously, call Turpie. She can fix things."

"I am going to kill everyone! I'm going to watch film. Good bye," and, for the moment, she is gone.

Dulce's dilemma is real. 'Sweetness' is taking a stand and telling her it's "them or me." She is sobbing at a Tuesday practice. In spite of her 'girly' ways, Dulce is a tough football player and she is key to both offense and defense. Losing her would have a huge impact.

"Why woo' he wanna tay' this away from me when I lub it so much? Why woo' he wanna do tha' to me?" It is frustrating to think that he would impose such limits on the one he loves. My life loops into a wider world and it hurts to see my friend snared in this man's selfish ultimatums. Some people get stuck in a way of life that seems to me like a beautiful library stocked with only one book.

Turpie, the fixer, is more patient than I, and very wise from her overlapping world. Unexpectedly, she arrives with 'Sweetness' in the car, something that Dulce and I are both shocked to see.

As they walk up, Dulce is trying to remove all signs of her tears and runny nose with the front of her Shark sweatshirt.

"Hey, Baby," he says to her. "Meet your Assistant Gameday Manager!"

Turpie is beaming that she has found a solution. We walk away, while Turpie goes over the details. I give her a big hug for averting disaster, and we see Dulce and 'Sweetness' kissing, as Dulce dresses for practice. Shark nepotism expands..

CHAPTER 76

SHARKS HOORAH FIVE ONE

This is the season we will dedicate to our lost friend.

It is never far from our minds that the 2002 season is dedicated to Sarah. Our chant after every offensive and defensive huddle honors her jersey number with a loud "FIVE-ONE!" and after every practice and game, we never leave without gathering in a tight circle with hands reaching skyward and voices boldly shouting "SHARKS-HOO-RAH-FIVE-ONE!" With all of our actions and determination, the season is all about her and opening day is a declaration of such. As names are announced in numerical order, the players whose numbers fell on either side of Sarah's number 51, carry her jersey onto the field. There is barely a dry eye amongst the 400 or so in the crowd on this April Saturday. Her presence, though not seen, is felt now. The first play of our dedicated season, we take the field with only ten players on defense, leaving a hole at her position of linebacker.

"She used to touch my back before every play," Janet says sadly as she comes off the field three plays later. "I waited for it...being without her feels so strange."

We miss Sarah and the peppery words she scattered all around us in her non-stop chatter. Her father Thomas cries like a baby along with Tanker, who wraps her big arms around him, until Coach Rex calls for Tanker to "Get the hell on the field and launch someone!"

CHAPTER 77

LEE'S WEB WRITE-UPS

The Sharks officially retired Sarah's jersey.

Game 1. Queens, New York, April 20, 2002. The Sharks started the 2002 season in a brand new style. They joined a new league, hired a whole new coaching staff, had a new home field, and were now sporting brand new uniforms. On the left side of the chest was a small blue Shark emblem and on the right side was a blue football emblem with the number 51 on it to honor Sarah Parham.

New season. New League. New Uniforms. New coaches. New offense. Same old results, a win.

In honor of their much-beloved teammate Sarah Parham who tragically died on Christmas Day last year, the Sharks have dedicated the 2002 season to her memory. Throughout the day, the Sharks held tributes to Sarah. For the Star-Spangled Banner, Sharks center/punter Jan Piper played the anthem on her flute.

Montreal won the coin toss and elected to receive. As another tribute in the memory of Sarah, on the first defensive play of the game, the Sharks ran onto the field with only ten players. A time-out was then called and a moment of silence was held.

As part of the halftime ceremonies, the New York Sharks officially retired Sarah's jersey. A presentation of the jersey and a bouquet of flowers was given to Sarah's mother and father by Sharks owner Christine Davis. As part of the halftime entertainment, the New York Sharks as a team sang, America the Beautiful to the fans.

As the game was winding down, the Shark players and Sharkie the mascot dumped a bucket of Gatorade on their head coach, Rex Richardson to commemorate his first win of the season, the score; 45-6. Rodriquez and Edwards received game balls for their play on both sides of the ball.. SHARKS-HOO-RAH-FIVE-ONE!

Our next game unfolds in similar fashion. We play the Massachusetts Soldiers and the final score—with Dulce scoring three touchdowns –is 40-0. And as we do with every game of the season, we dedicate it to our missing teammate, Sarah.

An e-mail to the entire team comes thru minutes before I leave for Tuesday's practice.

Can someone give me a ride?

from King of the Sea

"King of the Sea," otherwise known as Gloria is, to quote my grandmother, "toting water with a leaky bucket," but we love her. Except when she fails to arrange rides with her teammates until the last minute and then sends a last ditch e-mail plea. I respond by sending an e-mail to the team.

Can someone PLEASE be Gloria's ride to ALL games and practices before we have to shoot ourselves! Please, SOMEbody. Quickly....ANYbody?......a ride for Gloria....?

Christine

Erin replies to me only:

Someone needs to have a talk with her. These players expect us to do everything for them and if she can't be responsible enough to—Delete. I can't.... Really, I can't.

No one responds about a ride, but it does inspire several unrelated replies.

It's all in the attitude Sharks. You can't just go out there wanting to win and expect the opposing player not to feel the same way! You must HATE TO LOSE - hate it like you never hated anything ever before or ever will again! You gotta hate losing on every play... hate it so much that two blockers can't beat you, that three tacklers can't take you down, that your blocks become inescapable - do everything you can to keep from losing! It's not enough to want to win. You see ladies... everyone "WANTS TO WIN ... YOU GOTTA HATE TO LOSE!" So, in the end ladies... it means you've got to hate to lose MORE than you love to win.

see everyone at practice,

Coach Rex

Then, miles away from football altogether, comes a message from the wheelchair of Janet:

Ladies!!!

I want to THANK everyone for coming to the party last Sunday. I had a terrific time and I truly love hanging out with ALL of you! You ladies are the best!!!

I greatly apologize for the hot tub being out of commission for the weekend! It honestly just died Friday. I called the spa service guy out Saturday and obviously, it wasn't a same-day fix. Being a woman of my word, I was very upset that I made a promise I couldn't keep to my teammates! BUT... we found a reason to strip anyway. Hedonism Dot... I can still see that black booty walking through the patio doors! Burned in my memory FOREVER!!! LOL.

Alyssa, thanks for lending an ear and a shoulder when I needed to vent. Now tighten up those knees so we can play in a game together!!! I don't know how long I'm gonna last... I'm falling apart like Mr. Potato head. LOL.

Love you guys!

Janet

Then Jade's head reared;

We have come to that time again and I'm still allowed to have a barbecue at my parent's house. Amazing. We apparently have not caused enough noise, had enough participation in nudity and enough alcohol-related in the incidences to be banned. So that only leaves one thing left to do-turn it up a notch! Their dog is fat enough and does not need to be fed anything. Please don't put cigarettes on the floor either there will be ashtrays. Do not be alarmed if you see my parents, they usually hang for a little bit and are used to this. My mom has been known to do a Jell-O shot or two. Also, I'm sure my 87-year-old grandmother will be around. No worries either, we caught her drinking a beer on the couch last year.

It's early in the season. They are still relatively nice to each other.

Then Turpie calls with news from the Giants meeting we had a few weeks ago. "Buddy, it looks like they are going to let us wear our jerseys and work in the bubble before all of their home games. They will pay each player $75 bucks and a ticket to the game!" she is thrilled by the news. "They said they are going to put us on their web and all Buddy—like we are their little sister organization." It does seem like a good deal and when we tell the players later, they are quick to sign up. The NY Giants have actually acknowledged us and it feels big.

CHAPTER 78

THE INVISIBLE OPPONENT

Is the idea of pitting us against the boys simply a way of putting us in our place?

There are a handful of men that I love, but I can't think of many that I like. Our coaches are not helping to break this pattern. Because we have a bye this week, they have insisted on scrimmaging the high school boys that they coach. I am not comfortable with it but the players talk me into agreeing. Shortly before the scrimmage, Kim calls my cell from the field. Turpie and I are almost there but I answer the phone anyway. Rasping, she says Coach Rex brought a guy to help and informs me with vehemence, that "He's a dick!"

"This is why you called?" I ask.

"I just thought you should know."

"We just pulled in. Be there in a minute." I hang up as Turpie and I park the car and go into the stadium. Before going onto the field, we lean on the railing and listen to this new guy lord it over everyone. Kim's assessment appears to be accurate. I walk out onto the field to meet him and he is no less subdued.

"Christine, my friend Leo came to help us today," says Coach Rex.

Leo gives me a quick, perfunctory handshake and tells me in a sturdy voice how he likes to put his "signature" on what he does. He doesn't make eye contact once and quickly spins away onto the field toward a group of players.

"You! You in the Jet's jersey...what is the matter with you? You dumb or something? You don't block the 'A' gap on that play! Fifty sit-ups. Now!" He must be "signing" his name now. Spraying like a goddam cat. Spraying commands and utterances all over the field! His signature is getting on all of my players.

"Where did he come from?" I ask Coach Rex.

"He coaches at the high school with us. He's really good. I asked him to help us today."

"He's not making a good impression." I say which provokes a "So what?" look from Coach Rex, as he returns to the offensive practice huddle. I take a breath and wade onto our ego-humid field.

The scrimmage begins, but nothing feels right to me. My gut says we shouldn't be playing these boys. They are too big and have too much ego to let a "girl" make them look bad. I am suited up but am busy watching to make sure I don't see any cheap shots when Coach Rex puts me in the game. He calls three QB keepers in a row and I know he's trying to kill me, but I run tough and survive. Then he calls a sweep to Dulce who makes it to the outside when one of the boys blows her up knocking her upside down and air-born. My helmet flies off and I am yelling at Rex to stop the scrimmage!

"Are you out of your mind? My players are going to get hurt!" I am outraged and am walking towards Rex on the sideline when "Leo Signature" gets in my face and says if I don't shut up he's benching me. His words are so ludicrous, I laugh out loud. I stop and unleash mama bear who stands upright and leans into his face. "You...STUUUU-pid ...muh-ther... fuh-ker!! Get out of my face before I swab your head with this helmet." I start swinging it and he backs off slightly, but his attitude is still aggressive.

"This scrimmage is OVER!" I am furious. Kim is trying to calm me down for a change. The players are hovering around Dulce who swears she is Ok, but Piper, also a paramedic, is afraid she may be concussed. "She hit her head hard when she came down, Boss," she says to me.

Coach Rex doesn't appear concerned at all and indicates in a soft, patronizing voice just inches from my face that I owe the team an apology for not believing they can play with the boys.

"Since when does defending something I care deeply about require an apology? It is, in fact, you and your "help" who should apologize to me for making me protect my players from our own staff!" He walks away and tries to regroup and continue playing.

"Ok, Sharks. Let's run some more plays. Let's get some good work done!" His hands are in his front pockets and the glower on his face shows his anger.

"It's done, Rex!" I yell across the field. "Where was I unclear? You can have a practice with Shark players, but the scrimmage is over!"

He steps abruptly over to the coaches on the boys' side of the field and says something unrepeatable, I am certain. Then he dismisses the Sharks. No practice. No goodbye.

Invisible enemies, these coaches. Mentally camouflaged, so you never know who you are fighting. What statement are they making? Are they taking us to battle to show the world that we are as good as the boys or are they scoffing at us, intentionally pitting us against the boys to "put us in our place?" Do I fire him for putting us in this position or praise him for offering the opportunity to prove our skills? Honestly, I don't know. I want to believe Rex has good intentions, but the arrogance and condescension he shows to me says otherwise. I sit in my car to try and process all that just happened.

The confusion I feel takes me back to fresh summer nights at my grandparents' summerhouse in North Carolina. A gray, split level home, it sits on the upslope of a scenic mountain, full of windows and open doors, a yard full of dahlias, tall mint for the fresh ice tea and low-growing evergreen shrubs that cascade over a tiered, grassy shelf. The adults converse in rockers on the slate patio, drinking bourbon and enjoying a wide-open view of the Great Smokey Mountains. At a certain time each afternoon, a train can be seen so very far off, breaching the gaps of the forests, the chug-chug of its engine pushing swirls of smoke, just like my grandfather's pipe, into the shrouds of mountain air.

It is on these pitches and under the shrubs where the neighborhood gunfights take place with Hugo, Kurt, and Luke. Carrying pistols as well as bows and arrows, sometimes we are the cowboys, sometimes the Indians. Either way, our opponents are always invisible. If they "Get you," you're dead, but you can come back to life after you count to 100. The four of us are peeking from under an evergreen bush. We are cowboys today, chewing on a sassafras root we yanked out of the terraced side of the driveway. According to Hugo, we are surrounded, then "Whoops!" he says to me. "You're dead. Go lean against that tree and count to 100." Why just me? I wonder, but I don't argue. I can't see the Indians. Perhaps they did shoot me. I lean without protest against the tree, eyes closed, chewing sassafras and slowly counting towards my rebirth.

I try this now to avoid wanting to kill these coaches and when I open my eyes again, everyone has gone except Erin and Turpie who stand centurion-like near my car. I get out. We hug and just shake our heads back and forth in unison.

CHAPTER 79

WINNING AGAINST THE ODDS

Without confidence, running is out of the question, no matter what you're running towards.

Turpie and I lean on the stadium railing and talk of days gone by. Of the flag championship we won in November, 1997 when we beat Kim's team against all odds. Her team, the River Rats, had been undefeated for years. Kim had stacked her team until they were virtually unbeatable but, as the saying goes, "On any given Sunday."

"We won 'The Big One' buddy. You and me," reminisces Turpie.

"I will never forget that day," I say.

"You are right about that buddy. It's an athletic career high. I think that's why I love these fuckin' Sharks because I can still get high watching even though I can't play anymore. Plus, we're helping others to win their 'big ones.'"

She is right.

"That's so important," I say and my mind travels off to reminisce with hers. "I was playing in a softball game my senior year in high school. I can see it like it was yesterday. My orange and black jersey—No. 7—tucked tight into those white baseball pants. I loved those pants. I was on third base, holding my cap, ready to run home and if I scored, we'd win the game. The batter hit a fly ball to center field which gave me time to tag up and run home...but I didn't. I had a lot of swagger but in truth, not much confidence and I was scared the centerfielder would throw me out at home." I pause to look across the field full of Sharks.

"Whadja do?" she asks.

"I stood there like a complete idiot and listened to everyone scream "RUN, RUN!" The next batter was thrown out at first and that ended the game."

"Aw shit buddy, really? You didn't win the game?"

"Hell no. And to this day, I re-live that stupid play over and over. Not because we lost the game, but because I lacked the confidence in myself to take fate into my own hands and RUN. I was scared to fail, so I did NOTHING. In retrospect, I realize that she would have never thrown me out. I was too fast and the ball would have to have been thrown better than perfect. But without confidence, running is out of the question no matter what you're running towards." I have become prophetic. "The only thing that has taken the sting away was winning that championship in '97." My head turns and our smiles meet. "November 16th, 1997. Wantaugh Park, Long Island."

"The football league championship. We won 13-6!"

"And you remember what? I RAN both of them in on that damn Quarterback Draw! Bless Hayden's heart! He knew how to use his talent!"

"...'Member, Gemma did that little out and I stalk blocked and when you saw that hole open up..."

"...I took my chances and by God, I RAN!"

"Twice we did it!"

"And it worked!"

"Both times!"

"Two sixty-plus yard touchdowns!" We are hopping around, whooping as if it just happened.

"Everyone was screaming!" she says.

"One sideline wanted us to succeed, the other sideline wanted us to fail."

"Oh man! That was a good day for us!"

"Funny thing is buddy, it was just a football game. It meant nothing to anyone except those of us playing in it."

"But, it meant everything to me!"

"Me too. It was my 'Big One.' It made a difference in my life that will last forever because somehow, it gave me validation. I understand that now."

"Me too. Being on a championship team made me walk down the streets of New York City six inches taller." We are slowly returning to the present.

"I felt more confident because of that one game. Isn't that what life is all about? Finding whatever it is that makes us a winner in our own hearts? Mine boiled down to a football game. That's when I learned the difference between standing on third base and listening to the world scream at you, or hitting that hole running with all your heart listening to the world scream for you."

CHAPTER 80

SCANNING THE BLEACHERS

But she isn't there.

Kayla was working out quite nicely as Sharkie, in the mascot uniform. She attended every game and even came to practice at times. She was very protective of the Shark suit and sent it to be dry cleaned on occasion. She also helped us raise funds and was very involved in everything the team did. She rubbed a few people wrong now and then, with her brusque ways, but it never seemed to be an issue. I liked her.

The winning streak continued with the Sharks beating the Detroit Bulldogs 80-0.

It was a beautiful day for a football game. The sun was high in the sky, the temperature a mild 65 degrees with a breeze blowing. A gorgeous New York day.

New York can match any city for the most type A personalities in the world. Most of my Sharks are Type A, and we all know what the "A" stands for. Many, including myself, are older than Europe and for some reason, we enjoy our own dysfunction which includes the verbal annihilation of one another. The unsportsmanlike conduct flag thrown against us during the Detroit game did not at all involve Detroit. It was on us for throwing foul-mouthed tantrums about each other as if we were alone in a Shark bubble with no other participants.

"You missed the block again," says Kim to Piper after an unsuccessful play.

"Shut the fuck up you old fucking fuck!" Jessie retaliates in true Jessie form, even though the comment isn't about her.

"Me old?" says Piper. "It's because of you, we now carry denture glue in the First Aid kit."

"You're a dick."

"But a dick with teeth that stay in my head." The whistle blows for flagrant cursing and delay of game.

"You need to retire," this from Little Toni, in her cover three position many yards away.

"You suck."

"Up yours!"

"Get a room." a gratuitous remark from Jessie.

"I'm gonna have an episode!" warns Coach Rex in a loud voice over the din of bickering. Episodes happen when he loses his patience and temper, and they usually result in a lot of sit-ups and running for the Sharks. Although he knew his stuff, sometimes it was clear that he was only there for the meager paycheck. He lacked patience and could be overheard complaining about our lack of football savvy to his friends who would stop by to watch the Sharks practice.

"What is wrong with them?" he would say, flooded with irritation. "They are playing football! They are linebackers, not startled bunnies!" he had said when Azure was clearly hesitant to attack Tanker roaring into the secondary. A linebacker is a linebacker and a bunny is a bunny and Coach Rex detested the blend of the two in one body.

"Everyone shut up before I have an episode!" he yells again through strained teeth. Sharks reduce verbal insults to rolling of eyes and middle fingers shaking in the air.

The other teams hate us for our self-involved behavior and we don't even realize it. The Sharks are past the point of needing anyone around. Players bitch about each other before the game, during the game and in the locker room after the game ends. The Walton twins, still called the Twin Towers since they flank the center as offensive guards, are so petrified of nippy Sharks and their crunching remarks, they take their showers fully clothed, while the rest of the Sharks make fun of each other's breasts.

I leave the locker room just as Erin is coming in. "I told Jade Max's parents they have to sit in the stands from now on. He's yelling things and I don't want them that close to the players."

I am shocked. Jade Max's parents are the most consistent fans we have and have been with us since flag days. What a mess.

"They yelled to Coach Rex that the receivers, other than Jade Max, weren't any good." Erin tells me.

Shit. Clean up. Aisle 3.

"Erin, Jade Max's parents (and that's the only way we have ever referred to them) have been around longer than St. Pats. Please! Ask me before you do things like this ok? They can sit close to the players. I'll just tell them to tone it down," I say. She gives me a look saying she clearly disagrees, then twirls and leaves. I walk towards Jade Max's parents with my bucket and mop and on my way, I scan the bleachers. I remain hopeful that one day I'll look up and see Ellen watching.

But she isn't there.

CHAPTER 81

BEGINNING TO BELIEVE

Like a parent, I want everything good for them—better than
I had in the world of football.

I sit at my computer with Dina and listen to music the Sharks would call "old-ies." Soon, I leave for practice. When I arrive, I can feel the energy is really start-ing to pick up. We are 3-0 and the Sharks truly believe in themselves. If we trounce Montreal this weekend and then beat Albany the following weekend, we will be ready for Massachusetts. We just have to stay healthy.

At least the Coach Rex episode about the scrimmage has died down. He and I avoid each other. I because, not sure of his motives and not wanting to ask, I don't know what to say to him. He because I've been monitoring him and he doesn't like that. But he always shows up, Sharks aren't complaining about him and we are win-ning. I did ban Leo from our presence. We don't need "help" like that, even if we only have one full-time coach and volunteers fill out the rest of the staff.

Besides, Kim acts as a coach whether any of us want her or not. She pleaded with Coach Rex to put Alyssa in against Detroit and she hurt her knee. Now Alyssa insists that it's fine. Erin, not believing Alyssa or the coaches, joins me in the stands and is calling Natalie, the trainer, to come give a real diagnosis before Alyssa is allowed on the field.

"She won't tell the truth. She wants to play and the coaches don't care. They need her, so they will put her in. I'm not going to stand for this."

Eat a pill, Erin. Someday God will use you but until then, eat a pill!

The fireflies on the field are not apparent until dusk sneaks in, then they begin to twinkle against the traces of Queens row-houses across the street. I am on the phone with Eve, who is explaining to me why she is late to practice. I really don't care and forget who I am talking to while I watch the fireflies slowly plugging into twilight. I love Summer. Warmth. Light. Everything is magical. In summer, even a bug's ass is charming.

Suddenly, the stadium lights click on and reveal Kim in full pads. "Oh my God! Is Kim really playing tonight? I thought she strained her hamstring?" I ask Erin.

"They don't listen to the doctors. You should tell her no, Christine. Just tell her no."

"I hope she doesn't tear that hamstring."

"How 'bout she tears that larynx!" Eve says, hearing Kim bellow something in the background.

"I gotta go Eve. Just get here as soon as you can," I say and slam the clam phone shut. Then Janet can be heard coughing, coughing, coughing. Her malady du jour can be heard all over Queens. "So glad Janet decided to show up." Erin remarks.

Coughing is fine, even hamstring pulls—just so none of them get seriously hurt. Tonight or ever. When I see one of them get hurt, all the disgust for the jaundiced existence I am so poorly coping with morphs into an odd and growing love.

Somehow, a female player's injury is more disturbing to me than seeing a male player down. Boys have such promise to better their lives through this game. The women will walk away with memories, personal bests, failures, disappointments, joy and friendship, but probably not with acknowledgment, a career or monetary gain. There will be no signing bonuses or buying big houses for mom. No TV cameras or slick endorsements. Only teammates, playing flip cup at Joyce's Tavern, taking bus trips and yelling, winning, losing, fighting, bonding and sharing the privilege of suiting up with one another simply for the experience. It's this I love about them, and all the negativity fades when they demonstrate the purity of their passion. Like a parent, I want everything good for them—better than I had in the world of football.

Remember, the Sharks are a love story. How do I tell them of this odd love I have for them? Or do I tell them? No, I will just continue to hug each shoulder-padded torso now and then, and say my prayers: "Oh please don't get hurt, my Sharks. Have fun and don't get hurt."

CHAPTER 82

BORDERS AND BOUNDARIES

Do not say one word to anyone about anything!

The bus to Montreal is to leave at 8:30 am from the parking lot of Jade Max's office in Secaucus, NJ. Turpie and I arrive at 8:10 after getting severely lost and not one Shark is there. Shortly afterward, they begin arriving in carloads. Packs of them. Texts from those who are late begin blowing up my phone. Janet has arrived on time and is seemingly free of illness, but has an unexplained anxiety attack and can't get on the bus. "I'll meet you at the field," she says, getting back into her car. Whatever. I don't want to know.

We leave Jade Max's parking lot at about 10 am. Not too late. We pick up our trainer at the Thomas Edison rest stop and begin our journey.

Shortly into the game, we dub it the Montreal Flag fest because of all the penalties called. One of the refs even yells at Little Toni and makes her cry.

"Go ahead, number 21, -- say something, so I can throw you out. You're atrocious!" he barks.

Little Toni, who is anything but a dirty or mouthy player, is wounded to the quick. She comes to the sideline in tears.

"He called me atrocious!" she wails.

"Who did?!" asks Tanker.

"Him!" Little Toni says, and points to the ref, who is clattering in French now to his fellow refs. Tanker, choosing some Ebonics she thinks will really level him, yells across the field.

"Do that again I'm a fole-u-up!" Tanker and Little Toni wait a few seconds for his response, Toni wiping her eyes with the back of her gloved hand and Tanker poised with ham hock-size hands on hips and eyes bugged in his direction. When no response comes, they decide to move on.

"Thanks, Tanker. That was sweet," Little Toni says, blowing her nose in her uniform sleeve.

The game lasts longer than the Spanish-American War. Dulce gets sandwiched on a tackle and we suspect she is concussed, as she lies on the field with chunks of Montreal hanging from her facemask. Jessie removes a few wads, peers through Dulce's facemask into her eyes and saunters towards the sideline.

"Huh fuckin' eyes are rolled into the back of huh head. Maybe the fuckin' trainer should take a fuckin' look," says Jessie in her usually crude but oddly detached voice. Natalie hears her and runs to take a look. Tanker and I hover with great concern, while the rest of the team takes a knee. Natalie holds up three fingers in Dulce's face.

"How many fingers am I holding up?"

"One an' it looks like this!" she says while thrusting her middle finger into the air and insisting that Tanker help her up. Tanker obeys and cranks Dulce upright. They wobble off, Dulce hanging from Tanker's strong right arm like a marionette. She deposits Dulce on the sideline, and goes back on the field, but the next play, she breaks a toe. She is trying to hide the pain as she lurches off the field, but does not disguise it well. Fuckin' Natalie takes a fuckin' look and tells her it's just a toe.

"It's gotta be the whole foot, Nat. I feel it all the way up to my cooch!"

"Well then, let's get you to the ambulance," she motions to the medics who pick up Tanker and start to carry her to the ambulance. Then they put her down. They suggest picking up the ambulance and carrying it to Tanker. It is easier.

Tanker, embarrassed that no one can carry her, hobbles to the bench and takes a seat near the water cooler.

"It's just a toe. I'm good," she lies. And the Spanish-American war continues without her.

It feels like days have passed when we are finally on the bus and approaching the US/Canada border where we have to go back through customs. The Sharks are performing their usual banter; being cruel to one another with love and affection.

"That was deep," says Big Dot about a remark from Janet.

"What do you know about deep?" says Eve. "I've taken baths deeper than you."

"Heh, heh." Is Wendy's contribution.

"Are we gonna stop to ea' now?" asks Dulce for the fifth time in as many minutes. "I can tas' that pizza already."

"You'll have a hard time tasting that pizzer where I'm gonna put it. Shut the hell up already." Jessie's charming post-game banter warms us all.

"I'm starved," declares Kim.

"You need to starve. You look like a tight end gone to seed." This from Cooper, of all people. The Sharks were clearly ruining her and her educated mind. Yuna, our Japanese player, lets out a slender chirp of a laugh that reminds me of a small, extinct bird.

"Someone play some good music that I actually know please!" I say. "They played good music in that bar we went to the other night. Reminded me of my high school music."

"Gregorian chants?" Eve again.

"Heh-heh," Wendy again.

"We closed that bar in true Shark fashion!" says Erin "We set the bar. We raise the bar. We close the bar."

"Sharks!" I say over the bus microphone with authority. "Do not say a word to anyone who gets on this bus. I will do all the talking. No funny comments, no strange noises, or feigned afflictions of any type. Nothing! Just show them your passport if they ask and keep quiet!"

The bus pulls up to the booth, but there is no attendant peering out of the window, so the driver puts it into park and we sit. And we sit. And sit. The tired Sharks begin to squirm. It has been 16 hours since we left home this morning.

"Let's fuckin' GO!" yells Wendy, unable to hold another word in.

"Just drive, man. No one cares!" says Jessie. I feel the same way, but am trying to be a sensible leader.

"There's no one there. Must be a free day. I say we go," says Turpie. I can't believe she is suggesting this. But I like it.

"Stay here with them. I'm going to check the booth. Maybe they are in the back and don't know we are sitting out here."

The bus door swings open and I step off the bus feeling like Neil Armstrong on the surface of the moon. One big step and I'm looking into the open window of the booth, which appears to be free of attendants in any shape or form. There is the chair. There is the computer. There is the entrance door, the floor mat, the clipboard and pen. But of booth attendants, there is a complete shortage. I walk closer to a gray building about thirty yards from the booth. Perhaps there is human life inside, but it is dark. I touch the hood of the cars parked in front to see if the engines might be warm, signaling a recent arrival. They are cold. I go back to give the report. When the bus door opens, I hear a cacophony of Shark voices: "Just drive! Let's go!"

Wendy croaks from one of the back seats, "I'm too tired to say the whole 'Let's fucking go'.....just LFG! LFG! LFG!" A chant begins. The bus is rocking: 'LFG! LFG!'

I tell the bus driver to hit it. He does.

"We are blowing customs buddy," I shout to Turpie above the players' whooping and she grins.

Erin is unexpectedly enjoying herself. She is all smiles, watching the players in the seats behind us rolling with laughter. At first I am a little nervous, but after ten miles, I relax and settle in.

I find Piper, the detective, a few rows back wondering if she has an opinion and is willing to give it up. But she says nothing and we shrug our shoulders at each other. "You can't make this shit up," I say.

"Nope. Nope. You sure can't."

At eleven miles, Lee delightedly announces that the cops are behind us. "Cool! They have their lights on!"

Fuck me naked...

The Sharks suspend their naps, chats, and book reading and are ecstatic to hear we are being chased. Lee hustles to get his video camera out and is filming the scene from the back window of the bus.

"I've never seen a real American chase scene," chirps Yuna, polite excitement in her accented voice.

Kim, delighted by the disturbance we have caused, starts singing a round of the song from a TV cop show, substituting the word Sharks for boys.

"Bad Sharks, bad Sharks, watcha gonna do...

watcha gonna do when they come for you,

bad Sharks, bad Sharks, watcha gonna do...

watcha gonna do when they come for you?"

The whole bus is singing along. Lee is filming the red lights behind us, and getting commentary from the players. Turpie is still grinning, but it has turned to a nervous sort of grin. Erin leans over and says one word, which stops my heart: "Yuna!"

Fuck me naked...

She is not an American citizen. She has a visa but...we just blew customs.

Fuck me naked...

I stand in the aisle and yell "SHARKS! Listen to me, NOW! When they board the bus, DO NOT say ONE WORD about anything or anyone and DO NOT offer your passport unless asked. Quiet! Complete silence!"

The twittering slowly dies down as the bus pulls to the side of the road and a large US Customs agent steps on board. There is a silence that has never been heard from a team of Sharks. It is so quiet, Lee's rolling camera is the only noise on the bus.

"Where you headed?" the customs agent asks the bus driver.

"New York City," he replies.

"Is this a team or something?" he asks me.

"Yes. The New York Sharks Women's Pro Football Team. We just played Montreal and are going back to New York City." He is looking past me at the faces of my Sharks as I speak.

"You know you should have stopped at the border to be cleared?"

"I do know. We stopped, but there wasn't anyone in the booth and we waited for quite some time, but no one came out, so we just thought it was Ok to go." He is still quietly looking at us.

"You all US citizens?"

"Yes." I answer.

And then, as if someone stuck a pin in her, Cooper shrieks, "Yuna's not a citizen."

I then hear about a dozen odd-sounding emissions from Sharks up and down the aisle, and I turn around to see that Yuna's terrified eyes have taken over her entire face, and someone is slugging the shit out of Cooper, who looks more surprised than any of us. In speaking those words, she has blown our cover. She has called attention to the tiny Japanese aspect of the matter, just when it was vital to stick to the citizens, the whole citizens and nothing but the citizens.

"Everyone take out your passports and show them to me when I walk down the aisle," the cop demands.

We do. He does. We wait.

"You'll have to turn around and go back to customs," he finally says. "It shouldn't take long, but I have to clear Ms. Tanika's visa."

We do. He does. He gets off and the driver cautiously turns the bus back towards Montreal.

"Hey Yun Yun," shouts Eve. "For having slanty eyes, they sure are round right now!" Yuna bows slightly. Yes. Yes. About forty-five minutes later, Yuna is cleared and released. We drive off towards NYC, watching Lee's replay of the video and singing 'Bad Sharks.'

CHAPTER 83

RETHINKING THE INNER WARRIOR

I am telling you—we will not win unless we all
show up to practice and actually practice!

Tuesday opens with the usual e-mail from Mabel:

From: moutzen@earthlink.net

Subject: feeling slighted

The last few days were miserable. With total sleep deprivation, I have been spending much of my time:

1. *Schmoozing with the guy who does the PR for the dumpling contest and the Hong Kong Dragon Boat Festival. They are certainly going to want to get their dumplings sold at the football field and I want them to sponsor the Sharks before they decide on other teams.*

2. *Writing the NY Sharks' song, of which I get that no one, except me seems to care about. The song will involve the fans as well. Believe me, getting credit for writing the team song is not going to get me anywhere in my career.*

   And then, after doing all I did for the team, the only name that gets omitted from the program is mine. Wouldn't you be unhappy?

I am going to lose my mind. Mabel is a mood assassin. I don't reply. I know I should but I don't care about the team song and I just can't fake this one. I head for practice.

There is a lazy gene in the Shark tank and attending practice is not at the front of their pointy heads. Sometimes we only have twenty show up which makes it impossible to practice effectively. Others show up, but declare injuries and the need to "rest," or that they can't put weight on a foot or lift a shoulder. Come Saturday, however, every Shark is miraculously healed.

Unless you are Dulce, who, at today's practice, is promising that Natalie cleared her of the concussion and gave her the Ok to get on the field.

"But Dulce," I tell her. "You have to have a written letter."

"I do!" she says. "I left it at home." She is pleading and I am trying not to give in. I, too, would be risking my health to get on the field and I am being a player, not an owner. Just as Dulce becomes tearful with frustration, gross reality arrives in that devastating, show stopping form of Erin.

"Dulce, I just spoke to Natalie and you aren't cleared," Clipboard in hand, she whisks past us to the large group who is dressed and ready to play. She does a roll call and the Sharks reply in crisp, eager voices, then Coach Rex takes over and practice begins.

In the middle of it, I receive a visit from the concerned husband of Rosie, one of my players. I leave the practice field to talk to him.

The husband Martin, a "petite" man of 6'7" and 429 pounds, wags his head at me like a Mastiff and declares in a shaky voice that, "Rosie shows up to every practice and she just wants to play. Why can't she play?" It has taken a lot for Martin to approach me and ask why Rosie isn't playing. I feel so bad for this sweet giant of a man who loves his wife.

The first time Coach Rex put her in a game, he gave her a pat on the shoulder pad and a slight "good luck" shove onto the field. Rosie tripped over the down marker chains and spread-eagled onto the field.

"Martin, Rosie's a second or third string player. We all love her because she's Rosie, but as a player, she is not a starter." The song "Cruel to be Kind," plays in my head. He wags his Mastiff head again.

"Ok." He stares at the ground—which is a very long way down—for a few fraught seconds. "I can't tell her that." His face registers sadness for a few more fraught seconds, and then he says, "Thanks for being honest." Then he pats my shoulder pad with a hand the size of a Christmas ham, and silently moves away.

Turpie appears to see what the visit was all about and I tell her. We both want to cry. "Buddy, can we find a place for him on this team? I have room for him on game day. Can he be the grill-master?"

"He's hired." And Shark nepotism continues.

This particular day produces a good practice where almost everyone shows up. There appears to be a unified energy and I like it. Unified or not, I feel a speech is still necessary before we go home.

"Sharks, I hate to put a damper on this past Saturday's win," and I really do. They are sitting cross-legged in a semi-circle, all seven rows of Shark teeth glistening through satisfied grins. I expect to see shreds of multi-colored Montreal Jerseys still hanging from some.

"There are five or six really good teams in this league. Our schedule for the rest of the season is against those teams. Unless we change our practice ethics, we will not win. Simple as that. Our goal is to win the Championship and we have a good coach in Rex, despite the "episodes," and all the talent we need. I am telling you—we will not win unless we all show up to practice and practice! Montreal was a great win! I am very proud of you! Now, let's change our practice ethics and take it all the way!" I turn it over to Coach Rex, but Kim wants to say "a quick something first"...again. Doubtful it will be positive and certainly not short, the Sharks groan as she takes her position in front of the group. I hear the first words of her "quick something."

"The definition of a star is a self-contained mass of gas..."

It's an appropriate start, but I leave for home to take care of other Shark related things. When I drive past the field the next afternoon, I look to see if they are still trapped there listening to her.

CHAPTER 84

YOU'VE GOT MAIL

*I can't heal our pain, but I can allow them to
experience a freedom we all long for.*

From: moutzen@earthlink.net

Subject: Re: feeling slighted

I'm not sure if you understand how much time and effort goes into getting accolades for everyone and yet, one article...the only article that I wrote......does not get recognized. Do I feel like shit? What do you think?

They say if you dig deeper, you find truth. The deeper I go with the Sharks, the more mental illness I find so I think our team is the sanatorium of the league. That's what I think.

It is a rainy week so Coach Rex calls a chalkboard practice inside at a restaurant named "The Salty Dog." It is successful. Tanker sweeps through the room like a bear in a campsite, grabbing food. Everyone is chatty. I notice Janet is sans wheelchair. Yay.

"How you feeling Janet?" I casually ask. She immediately stands up and drops the velour pants of her matching sweat suit to proudly show me a bruise.

"I got one against Montreal, but it finally went away and then this one popped up." Her mouth betrays a slight grin as she hoists her shirt up one side of her ribcage to display another trophy bruise under her arm. Nasty. "I have a book of bruise pictures at home showing all of them I've gotten since I first started playing. I'm going to add these two to it." It is now a full-fledged smile.

"I think you should." I remark. "Plus, they are Shark colors." Figures that bruises are black and blue.

"Let me know if you can see Jesus' face in one of them. There's gotta be some way to get people to the games," I dryly add, as Dulce shimmers into the room. Beautiful, buffed Dulce dressed to kill. Big Dot and Kim follow, and last is Jessie. Listening to their chatter always amuses me.

Kim spots a rookie in one corner. "Now there's a lesbian waiting to happen."

"Snap. Snap," answers Big Dot as they swagger in and choose a seat at the long table. I notice how healthy many of them eat. All except Janet who orders a hamburger and fries. Alyssa orders an egg-white omelet. Jade Max, a turkey burger. The others decline fries and only drink water. They begin a bruise showing event in which Janet wins, but not without competition from Dulce who places her svelte thigh next to her dinner plate and pulls the flowing chenille pant leg up to her crotch for inspection. The players "ooh" a little, thinking nothing of the half-naked woman draped across the dinner table.

Amazing, but no grace.

The next morning is the day of the Albany game and it's foggy. I lie in my bed on this cool May morning and stare out my bedroom window at the lilacs in bloom. They are shrouded in mist but I open my window for their fragrance, which slices through the fog and fills my bedroom. I am excited for the game and wonder if DeeDee, the owner, brought her team down last night or left Albany early this morning.

If I got rid of the team, I think to myself, I could be taking weekend jaunts to the Catskills, Newport, Greenwich, all the places that have been woven into my years in New York. I would miss those Sharks, but not the violence of the sport or the injuries. Even the competitiveness of the game does not agree with me like it once did. Every time one of my players goes down, I literally panic until I know they are not hurt. Most are bigger than me, but I still want to cradle them in my arms like newborns and make them Ok. This is not a good thing. For one, they would think I am a madwoman for even admitting this. For two, my inner-warrior is dying. I feel like Ferdinand the Bull who wanted to sit in his pasture and smell flowers all day instead of bullfighting.

When you are connected to a group so large, everything each one goes through affects the whole. Many of my players have experienced emotional pain while playing for the team. Felicia's son tried to commit suicide due to bullying. Theresa's house burnt down, and we all collected money and items to help her and her family. Grace discovered cancer after the mandatory physical and is not doing well. Laci's son was killed in Iraq. Irene's father died in a car accident. The list of personal tragedies goes on and this too, makes me want to help them, give them big hugs and a kiss on top of their sweaty little Shark heads before sending them onto the field to play. Is this why I bought the team? I can't heal our pain, but I can allow them to experience a freedom we all long for. If the self-expression playing football provides is healing for me, why not for them? But when did the experience of freedom start feeling like war? And when did I become Ferdinand wanting to be left alone to smell the flowers?

The freedom from pain the game once delivered has re-shackled me. I used to be buffed and bull-headed, ready for any battle and considering it already won. Age is a funny thing. The molten red warrior in me is turning lilac.

I rinse the coolers while the early May sun seeps through the potted cedars on the roof deck. What would my loyal Lee do with no Sharks? After all, Lee put us on the map with his innovative and content-filled website. Would he find another team and transfer his talents to them? Or would he simply become a fan, traveling to games, seeking out the quirky food stops that he loves along the way?

I throw the coolers and two game balls into the back of my Jeep. Even the game ball routine pains me. I feel sad for the players who haven't the athletic ability of an avocado and will never get a game ball, but still stand on the sidelines and cheer for their teammates, wishing it were them doing the hero-works. I would give game balls to the less talented players and they would suddenly grow taller and straight shouldered like Turpie and I did when we won the flag championship. Lives would be altered if only for that moment. And isn't that when so much is seeded? In a moment? Yes, of that I am sure. I wish for them...moments.

The Sharks have almost everyone healthy. Alyssa has been cleared. Dulce will be able to play, Janet, at this moment, has no maladies and both of her "broken" arms are back in full service. Only Stella (broken bone in left hand) and Jessie (self-diagnosis: smashed fuckin' kneecap) are not suiting up today. I will be kicking extra points.

And now, we are ready for kick off. I'm kicking and as I line up I look each way to make sure the line of players is ready. Each Shark is watching me, eagerly awaiting their cue to run down the field and tackle the ball carrier and I say softly to myself "Fucking Sharks." I smile out loud remembering lilacs and fresh coffee and realize how much joy I get from this team.

When I come off the field, I remove my helmet to talk to Turpie and Erin. We have walked away from the usual bitching and cheering on the sideline, while our offense drives towards another score. Sharkie, when not leading cheers for the small group of fans, is swimming smoothly among the Sharks on the sideline. I notice several of the rookies are winded and have sat down on the bench. Big Dot, not winded at all is helping to stretch out Kim's quads. It is an extraordinary thing that anyone who has had such good times as she has, can be so amazingly healthy. Dulce has just stopped a run with a beautiful tackle and is on the field proudly puffed up like an adder.

"Her ego has gotten away from her," says Erin.

"She does have the big head, but at least she can back it up," Turpie replies in agreement. Shortly after that a large explosive sound is heard in the middle of the Sharks.

"There it is," I say. "Her head finally burst." and oddly enough, the head of Sharkie's suit is spotted in the air over the bench where the Sharks are sitting. The three of us hurry to the sideline.

"What happened?" I ask Cooper, who is wringing her gloved hands and staring wide-eyed at the scene. According to Cooper's account, Wendy had tried to get some water from the cooler when she came off the field and Sharkie was filling water bottles to take to the players during the next time out. Wendy shoved her out of the way, so Sharkie pulled her hand out of the Shark suit and gave Wendy the bird. Wendy replied with a bird of her own. Sharkie returned it.

"They kept shooting birds at each other for about ten seconds until Wendy threw the cooler on the ground and took an upward swing..." she says while demonstrating in slow motion... "and then the head of that thing popped off and flew over the bench." Fortunately, shock prevented other Sharks from joining in the fray. Sharkie left the field in a headless huff and I would have gone after her, but Kim began screaming from her prostrate position on the field. Turpie and Erin and I run to her next while Natalie, our longstanding trainer follows us to the noise. From her cries, she is in severe pain. The trainer is trying to talk to her but Kim's hair has covered her face. Several Sharks come closer, propelled by curiosity, and watch as the trainer burrows through tangled masses of hair so she can hear better.

"Kim, what hurts? Where is the pain?" asks Natalie.

"Aaaaaaeeeeeiiiiiiiiiioooowwwwwwww!" is Kim's reply and one hand is holding the other as she rocks from side to side.

"Look at all that hay-uh." Says Eve, peering over Natalie's shoulder. "...disgusting..."

"Oh dear," Says Cooper. "I think it's her hand. Kim, show us your hand." Kim unrolls her fingers and we see the knuckles on her ring finger pointing in opposite directions.

"It's huh finguh." croaks Jessie. "All this noise over a fuckin' finguh." Eve and the other Sharks walks off, while Natalie coaxes Kim off of the field to splint her finger. Turpie the fixer, says she will return Sharkie's head to Kayla and try to get her back.

CHAPTER 85

SHARKS ADVANCE!

If we win the next game, it will clinch a
play-off berth for this team of Sharks.

It is Wednesday and I am at home. I am getting used to dining alone so I shower and head off to a restaurant down the road, for a glass of wine and calamari. They are closed, so I get a pizza at Scotto's and go home to a bottle of Cabernet and Dina who digs her little parrot feet into her half of the pizza and helps herself to a pepperoni slice.

By Thursday morning, Turpie has convinced Kayla to fill the Shark suit once again. Kim is back to simple complaints, stating that everyone sucks and we have no players to fill the appropriate positions. The rest of the Sharks are spending time thinking of ways to avoid practice tonight. At least it is finally warming up and by Saturday, the weather is supposed to be cool and partly cloudy. It snowed in upstate NY yesterday and I hope I won't be sweeping "partly cloudy" off my doorstep come Saturday morning.

I arrive at practice in time to see Kim call the Sharks together to give one of her infamous pep talks before Coach Rex arrives.

"Ladies. A few weeks ago, when we started, we stunk. Today, we stink less."

If we all show up on time and practice hard, we might, in the future, become just a faint odor.

"Now, until coach gets here, break into your groups and let's do tackling drills."

"I want them to take me off special teams," moans Rosie to Kim. "I can't tackle. People just run past me no matter what!"

Jessie, making herself part of the conversation, proudly recalls a play she made in the last game. "One kickoff last week—I hit someone and knocked her flat. I just saw a body and hit it."

Rosie acknowledges the play with wide eyes. "I saw that girl go by—I said "Where are you going so fast?"—then Jessie hit her. They're just too fast for me. Gotta get me offa special teams. I ain't that special."

"Why won't Killer Miller get out of the car?" asks Erin.

"She's listening to P. Diddy," reveals Cooper.

P. Diddy. Sounds like a bodily fluid mixture of number one and number two.

"Turpie, did she get that new helmet? She cracked that other one and it's not safe."

Erin's version: "Piece of shit and she's gonna get concussed!"

"She told me she did, but I'm not sure."

"She's lying!" Erin hisses. "All these players think they can get something over on us, but not this one! I'm on to her. I'll bet you she doesn't come up with it. I'll bet you!"

"Well, let's hope she does," I say. Erin stands with arms crossed ogling the Sharks suspiciously while they do their practice drills. Coach Rex arrives and places Wendy at defensive end while the offense runs some plays. She gets to the QB every time, which is a good thing if you are not on our team but unfortunately, she won't slow down which results in head-thumping crashes with Eve.

"If she hurts Eve, it will be the last day she walks on this earth," says Coach B, one of our volunteer assistant coaches.

"Kim, get her under control, before I have an episode!" Coach Rex yells emphatically knowing Wendy is uncontrollable. Kim rasps a threat to her, then comes over to join our group standing behind the offense as they run plays. "She's gotta learn to break down and not over-run her target."

"She needs a parachute to slow her down, like those dragsters have. She's a beast!" says Turpie.

"I've told her a million times. I don't know what else to do." Kim replies.

"I say we drive her way out into the woods and release her back into the wild," I suggest, as I watch Janet, my favorite hypochondriac, lumber over and interrupt.

"I know this is TMI, but for two weeks now, everything I eat comes out and this morning, it was green." The coaches are horrified. Kim offers Kaopectate. Erin stomps away. We are ready for Massachusetts, but Massachusetts is not ready for us.

CHAPTER 86

THE TEAM EPISODE

Massachusetts, watching us closely,
has abandoned any game plan and is very focused on hating us.

Game six goes well in Wakefield, Massachusetts, on June 8, 2002. The "Goddam" New York Sharks (6-0) were looking to get a step closer to winning the IWFL Eastern division by taking on the Massachusetts Soldiers (4-3).

The score was New York 14, Massachusetts 0 as the first half ended and when the game was over, the Sharks had recorded their fourth shutout of the season. Most importantly, the win clinched the Eastern Division title. SHARKS-HOO-RAH-FIVE-ONE!

During the game, the Sharks also performed their own team episode. It starts when we are warming up. It's rainy and chilly and Sharks are slipping around in the mud complaining bitterly about each other, unaware of the utter disgust forming on the far side of the field by the other team. Finally, it's kick-off time.

"Game time!" yells Kim. "Pass out the Geritol! Let's go ladies!"

Eve turns to Kim. "Careful leaving the locker room. You could slip and break that hip."

Massachusetts watching us closely, has abandoned any game plan and is very focused on hating us. Their coach stands with hands on hips staring at us. The announcers in the press box are sharpening their tongues, eager to mar our fins.

"LFG!" Wendy crosses her eyes at me then rolls them to the corner in mock boredom. Since she shortened "Let's fucking go!" to LFG, she uses the term frequently. Other Sharks have adopted the new expression and are coating the field with "LFG's."

The game kicks off and Sharks are doing typical Shark stuff. Ragging at each other, dropping a ball or two. Rag more at each other. Mouth off. Massachusetts's players are distracted by our uncouth behavior and the Sharks score easily. This compounds Massachusetts's irritation and that of their coach after Eve, perched safely behind Piper playing center, encourages one of their large O-line players to "Have another doughnut, number Ninety-two!" The large player glares at Eve and threatens to pull Eve's vital organs out through her ear hole. The Sharks are too busy snapping at each other to notice. Eve turns to Jade Max. "Maxer, you got hands like feet today!"

"Kim, you see what I mean?" Jade Max shouts to Kim on the sideline. "She shouldn't be yelling at us! The ball is wet and slippery!"

"You shoulda had it," Kim yells back. "You all suck!"

The press box adds to the commotion by taunting us over the mic.

"Sharks can't swim in water!" says the announcer loudly and the words drip into the rain-soaked helmet holes of the Sharks on the sideline. Trouble brews.

"I think they took a shot at us!" says a rookie.

"Who?" asks another.

"Those people up in that box!"

"What did they say?"

"I'm not sure, but it was a shot!"

Kim is yelling at Cooper to get aggressive.

"Hit someone. Anyone!"

"Hit Eve!" Big Dot says.

"Fuck you, Huge Dot." Eve retorts. The Massachusetts coach has walked onto the field and gotten close to Eve's face.

"Fuck you number two!" His voice is loud and aggressive and suddenly, the earth's rotation shudders and all Sharks become aware that there is someone besides themselves on the field!

"Look!" I hear one of them say. "Who just said "fuck you" to Eve?"

Oh my God! There is another team here and for some reason they seem hostile! It appears to be a discovery previously not had by Sharks. Fins snap up straight and razor-sharp. Sharks can curse at each other, but no one can curse at a Shark!

The offense has grouped around Eve and Shark teeth are snapping at the wet air. Eve, usually the one with the perfect comeback, yells to the coach who is walking off the field:

"The fish stinks from the head!" The finned ones are expecting a more caustic comeback and look quizzically at her.

"You have carte blanche to say anything you want and that is what you say to him?" Big Dot's hands are perched on her hips and her fin visibly droops. She has been let down hard.

The clock is running towards the end of the first half and Kim, sidelined for her chronic hamstring pull, is now screaming for Eve to just spike the ball. Time is running out. Eve, flustered after spouting a lame comeback, does not spike the ball. Again, a loud, scratchy-throated plea from Kim, "Spike the ball!"

Still no spike. Kim is crawling in wet grass, begging. The clock is ticking...

"Spike it! Spike the ball Eve!" And then time in the first half runs out.

"Why are you freaking out, Kim?" asks Coach Rex who has given up on trying to shut Kim up. "We are winning 36-0."

"Yeah, but..."

"I kept you out because of a hamstring. If you keep screaming like that, you'll pull a jaw-string. Get back in the game the second half and shut up," says Rex.

Halftime is not spent by either team making adjustments or adding strategies. The Sharks' time is spent discussing, "What the hell could be the problem with those asshole Massachusetts coaches and why was that one on the field yelling at Eve?"

Massachusetts spends their halftime glaring at the small room that the Sharks have sardined themselves into, jabbing each other with insults.

"Cooper, you have to get mad! Hit them!" says Rex.

"I can't Reeeeex....I'm too Zen."

"Think of something that'll make you get aggressive!" says Kim. "They killed your cats, Cooper!"

"Up yours, Kim," says Cooper in a monotone dismissive voice.

There is a demur knock on the door and I open it to find Cooper's parents standing there. Cooper's stock is Upper East Side, boarding school, Ivy League. Her parents are unaware that NYC continues south of Grand Central. Her mother stands in the crooked framed doorway of the shabby little room where we are. She has emeralds clasped, slid, pinned or pierced on every appendage. It looks as though the Jewel of the Nile has exploded on her.

"We were hoping to say hello to Cooper."

"Mom?" pipes Cooper from a sea of smelly Sharks.

"Cooper?"

"Is that you?"

"Yes, is that you?"

"Yes, it's me."

Anything in the nature of misunderstanding is immediately cleared up. It is both of them.

"We've a picnic prepared for you. Come join." At this juncture, Coach Rex had had enough, something which he was having more and more of lately.

"Cooper! You will stay with your team until after the game!"

Mrs. Cooper twitches slightly and says to no one in particular that they will "see her directly after the game." Then she leans towards me. "Isn't she an angel?"

"The Sharks' leading seraph," I assure her and gently click the door shut.

The second half goes no better for Massachusetts score-wise and no better for us behavior wise. Cooper, inspired by her parents' locker room appearance, clocks one of the Soldiers after the whistle is blown and draws an unsportsmanlike flag. Instead of retaliating, the Massachusetts player flings her head back and yells in a highly penetrating tenor that "Number 71 is pure trailer trash." Hearing this unflattering mention of their daughter, "Lovie and Thurston," picnicking in the stands, congeal into living statues filled with alarm and disapproval. The taunt also sets off Wendy who reminds the Massachusetts team that it was they who were "late for the flag tournament in D.C. because a tornado hit their trailer park." She further illustrates the unfortunate incident by alluding to their trailers as "fucking tin ducks" that popped off their tie-downs and took off.

"There's gonna be a fuckin' fight." says Jessie, who stuffs her mouth guard into her mouth and re-positions her arm pads.

Coach Rex is hollering for everyone to "Shut-up, Goddammit, before I have an episode!"

When the game ends, I tell the Sharks the bus is in a hurry and to shower quickly. We really must leave. They ignore my request for the most part, but we are finally kenneled up and drive away without further incident until the bus driver gets us lost five times while trying to leave Massachusetts.

"You want to point the bus south in case you were wondering Ricky Retardo!" says Eve to the Latin driver.

"That's more like it, asshole." Big Dot says and mutters "...the fish stinks from the head......" while sinking into her seat. She doesn't see Eve's middle finger raise up and shake in her direction.

"Who says I never lift a finger?" I hear Eve say to Wendy.

"Heh-heh..."

CHAPTER 87

AN AHA PRACTICE

We had to be labeled 'different' so Caitlin can be 'normal.'

I arrive at practice Tuesday and sit in my car listening to music. A rookie gave me a CD entitled Lesbian favorites. I look around before I push "play" on my iPod because I am embarrassed to see LESBIAN FAVORITES come scrolling across the little screen, but I love the songs, so I push the button. Annie DiFranco comes on with her rendition of "Mrs. Brown You've Got a Lovely Daughter." At my age, I wonder how lovely Mrs. Brown is. She would probably be more interesting to me than her lovely daughter.

Erin gets out of her car and is walking towards me. She detours when she sees Wendy arrive and runs to her car before it's even turned off. Her voice overpowers Mrs. Brown and her lovely daughter.

"Wendy, you owe forty-five dollars for the bag and NO, your jacket is not free!" She runs off to badger other players for owed money. She is very task-oriented and this is a task she seems to enjoy in spite of her grumbling.

Young Caitlin Moore walks up while I am listening to "Let Your Love Flow", a favorite of mine since high school. My God! That was back in the 70's. Sometimes my age is an embarrassment. I hear Caitlin tapping on my window, but I am spending time being 16 again, running down our neighborhood field, dodging, outrunning, scoring, winning. I am free and fast as the wind and would she STOP THAT INCESSANT TAPPING ON MY WINDOW AND LET ME BE YOUNG!

"Hi Caitlin!" I say, mentally crawling from my time machine.

"Hi Christine. Did you get my sponsor info?"

"Yes sweetie, I got it. I'll ask Lee to post it for you." Why do I call them "sweetie?" I sound like I'm a thousand when I do that, but I can't help it. I see them differently since this season for Sarah began. And often I see myself; the athlete, the defiant, the competitor, the mediator, the young, the aging, the innocent, the devious—fearless and frightened all in the same breath. They are precious to me despite the constant aggravation they cause and I can't go giving them hugs all the time, so out comes the word "sweetie." Eww! I hope they aren't grossed out by that!

"And I need their ad for the program, too." I yell after her. "I sent the dimensions to you in e-mail. Tell them to send it in jpeg format, ok?" She shakes her head in acknowledgment as she walks to the locker room, her long dark hair hanging down her back and her jersey encased shoulder pads and helmet swinging beside her feminine figure. Today, in 2002, this sight is a symbol of strength and sexiness. In 1975, she would have been ridiculed, ostracized by her peers and would have to sue to play. I guess that is the price my generation of athletic women paid. We had to be labeled "different" so Caitlin can be "normal." I re-start "Mrs. Brown You've Got a Lovely Daughter." How wonderful it is that times have changed, even if not nearly enough.

CHAPTER 88

EXPECT SUNNY WEATHER

Owning the Sharks is getting better.

Game Day. Queens, New York, June 15, 2002. After a month of playing away from the Big Apple, the New York Sharks (7-0) finally came home and with a mission. With one more win, they would clinch the IWFL Eastern Division title and propel them into the Championship Game in Redmond, Washington on July 6th.

The home field concession stand was fired up and Gameday Manager Turpie Evans had Martin Delany, defensive tackle Rosie Delany's husband and Marco Scalini, halfback Dulce Rodriquez's longtime boyfriend grilling hamburgers and selling beer. Everyone was part of the Shark family.

The Vermont Hawks (1-7) were the Sharks unlucky next victim. Things started going right for the Sharks from the start and didn't really end. The defense shut the Hawks down, and quarterback Christine Davis piloted three touchdown passes. Final score another shutout: 34-0. SHARKS HOO-RAH-FIVE-ONE!

I am in the rooftop garden reading Lee's account and listening to "Here Comes The Sun," my all-time favorite song. Maybe I'll play it at the end of each game. I used to play "New York, New York" until we went through such hard times, and now I play nothing. But things are changing. Owning the Sharks is getting better and better! Here comes the sun indeed.

I begin watering the marigolds and petunias when the phone rings. It's Kim. For the eighth time today.

"I talked to Sneed. She is depressed."

"Why?" I ask.

"She said she is starting to think about 9-11 again and her fiancé. I didn't ask if he died in 9-11. I didn't think that was right."

"Mmmm." I add.

"I told her that we were there for her and to take it easy. I wanted to tell her she shouldn't have a male fiancé and to shave her mustache!" It's mean but I can't help it—I laugh out loud. She continues. "I need to get Montreal's tape of our first game. Our film guy was eating a hotdog and not paying attention to taping."

"He wasn't paying attention to the hot dog either. It was all over his nice, new, WHITE coach's polo." I say, remembering the red stains. Pig. "I will e-mail Scarlette and ask her." I continue to listen as I compose the e-mail to Montreal's owner, Scarlette:

Hi Scarlette,

Is it possible to purchase the game tape of when we played you last time? We use them to do stats. Our coach was taping and eating hot dogs and scratching and whatever else and our tape looks like The Blair Witch Project. If you could bring a copy with you this weekend, it would be greatly appreciated!

Thank you,

Christine

NY Sharks

I push send as Kim drones on: "I don't want to play Jacksonville the last game! I don't even care if we have to travel. I know you do from an owner's viewpoint, but I would rather play Maine. Then I want someone to come limping to us!"

"Limping would be nice. I'll see you at practice."

"Alright. I'm going to watch more film."

"Of course, you are!" I smile and hang up to get ready for practice. I play "Here Comes the Sun" again because I can feel the sun coming rosy-fingered through the window of my soul. Maybe I am healing. Maybe I am finally coming to terms with things that terms desperately needed to come. Maybe I should check my e-mail before I leave.

From: moutzen@earthlink.net

Subject: Re: feeling slighted

I know that you are quite busy and have much on your mind, but I need to get this out to you. I realize that it's important when the NY Times publishes an article or when we're on TV and that gets up on the Sharks website. An article gets published about Debbie and that gets up on the website. And yet, I wrote what I thought was an excellent article at no pay (as usual) and nothing happens with it. You said that you read it and liked it and you did not ask Lee to have it up on the website. But, somehow there seems to be time for other articles and now for photos of the new field.

How do I feel? I feel like shit.

I toy with the options before me. I can go to practice and club her like a baby seal in the middle of the field. Or I can administer compassion and ask her to be reasonable. I will start with the latter, so no one can accuse me of being short-tempered. No one means any disrespect but some things fall through the many cracks. She does a lot for the team, but her combative attitude is wearing thinner than the skin on a sausage. I, once again, ignore her e-mail and trot off to practice where I can chat in person with our disgruntled volunteer PR person.

When I arrive, Jessie is picking at a slice on her hand she got from hitting the buckle on a helmet. She has taken two of the nine stitches out. I tell her to wait and Natalie will take them out when she gets to practice. Natalie, the professional trainer, will give her professional attention and professional opinion.

The thought of stitches takes me to my life back when I was nine. The stitches in my chin, evidence of a roller-skating accident, are becoming itchy. My mom tells me the itching is caused by its healing and that in a few days we will return to the doctor's office and let the nurse remove them. I happen to know that Phyllis, the thin, white-haired nurse with the long face and the lopsided smile, lives just down the road from our house. Walking distance.

Why, I wonder, do we prepare ourselves for a doctor's office visit and drive halfway across the world so that Phyllis, who lives just down the road, can take my stitches out? I prefer to walk down the road, knock on her door, point my chin skyward and let her extricate them right there on her doorstep where there is no smell of medicinal goings-on, no babies squawking, no frightful white uniforms elevated to unnatural heights by tall, noiseless nurse shoes which approach silently and pry the Highlights Magazine from my defiant grip. Wouldn't it be simpler to just walk down the road? I close my eyes, a Buddha with a migraine. This thinking shit has got to stop.

Erin comes in for a landing and clearly, the contents in her overhead compartment have shifted during flight. Given the slightest bit of info that she disagrees with, she goes "phffoooooot" before my eyes and puffs up like a blowfish. It takes time to calm her down and reduce her to her normal size. And then, over nothing, her voice becomes tight and "phffoooooot," there she is again, four times bigger than she was two seconds ago.

Her current agitation is with the league CEO. "I just found out from Kate that there will be a random drug test before the game," she says. This news has stirred her up like an egg whisk. "They shouldn't be able to do this without some warning! This can't be legal!" she barks. I tell her it's probably just a scare tactic to make the league look more professional.

"I don't think they will follow up on it. We'd lose half the players!" I chuckle but she does not. "You and Turpie and I would be full of wine!" I add.

"We would," she confesses and begins to de-puff.

"We cannot pee a lie," I say and chuckle again and then she chuckles and de-puffs two more sizes. "You might want to check on Jessie's stitches. Natalie isn't here yet."

Erin finds Janet hunkered over Jessie's hand with a straight pin trying to pick the remaining stitches from her skin. Several other Sharks are poised nearby watching Janet's handiwork. If she can't be the ailing, she can administer aid to the ailing.

"Did you sterilize that needle Janet?" Erin asks. All Shark heads turn towards Erin like puppet heads strung to the same wire.

"No," says Janet. "Big Dot—I can smell alcohol on your breath from here. Come breathe on this needle for us." Even Erin laughs and Natalie arrives to save us all from a malpractice suit.

CHAPTER 89

LEE STAYS THE COURSE

Game day.

Queens, New York, June 22, 2002. The Sharks had already clinched the IWFL Eastern Division title and are going to the IWFL Championship Game on July 6th, so this game had little meaning. Nobody told Massachusetts.

It was a very warm, muggy day with the temperature in the mid-80's. A typical New York city summer day, better suited for going to Jones Beach than wearing 25 pounds of football gear and running up and down a football field. The team physicians were concerned about the heat and humidity, and ordered extra ice and even filled up two trashcans with water and ice so they could dunk a player in it if they were showing signs of heat exhaustion. With less than 2 minutes left to play, the Sharks were called for "icing." With New York coach Rex Richardson facing the field, the Sharks dumped a bucket of ice water on him to celebrate the team's 8-0 record.

The Sharks finished the regular season winning every game they played. Game balls were given to Piper for her strong blocking game at center and to Big Dot who had a spectacular day on defense. And the last game ball was given to "H2O", Charlotte Rodriquez, the team's water girl and daughter of Shark player Maria "Dulce" Rodriquez.

The Sharks have a perfect regular season record and are looking to win just one more game and bring another championship title to the Big Apple. SHARKS-HOO-RAH-FIVE-ONE!

CHAPTER 90

A PITCHFORK AND
A TICKET TO RIDE

*"It's not the will to win that matters -- everyone has that.
It's the will to prepare to win that matters."*

My QB has been a topic of interest since our inception. When Kim calls to say Eve has been arrested, I am not surprised.

"She finally got caught, but at what?" I ask. Allegedly, explains Kim, according to the Massapequa police who were called by Eve's boyfriend, Eve is guilty of domestic violence.

"Eve?" I ask. This does surprise me. Allegedly, according to Kim and the Massapequa police, Eve and her boyfriend "were having an altercation of sorts and Eve threw a pitchfork across the yard. And hit him!"

Of course, she did, she's a quarterback with a 101.8 rating!

A pitchfork protruding from his back, prompted his call to the Massapequa police.

"Well fuck me naked!" I deadpan. "Kim, you gotta get her out. Do something."

"Mother fuckin' Eve..." mutters Kim as she hangs up.

Our other obstacle comes in the shape of dollar bills. We don't have enough to get to Redmond, Washington, where we are slated to play the Texas Bandits for the IWFL Championship. The plane tickets are about three hundred dollars per person and there are sixty-eight of us. Fundraising for the Sharks is like trying to raise the Titanic with a pair of salad tongs. We haven't produced enough to fly even a half-dozen of us and driving is out if the question. I call Melinda at the New York Giants office to tell her of our plight. I don't expect anything but I don't know what else to do.

"You know, Christine, the NFL gives matching grants to organizations that past or current NFL players support. Do any of you know a player or past player you could ask for a donation?"

"No. I wish I did." I answer. She is sympathetic and promises to ask the player personnel director of the Giants. I thank her and relay the conversation to Turpie.

"Buddy, wait—we do know someone. Oh, yes, we do! Johnny Belmont! Our first coach!"

"Turpie, once again, you have saved the day."

"Tanker has his number from when he coached. I'll see if I can get to him."

The "fixer" gets to Johnny Belmont, who donates three thousand dollars.

"I don't remember that we had to worry about that in the NFL," he tells Turpie with a laugh. He calls other former NFL players who donate and soon we have about fifteen thousand dollars.

Melinda, even though Belmont is a former Jet, makes sure we get to the right person at the NFL to receive the matching grant. The money helps propel the Sharks on to Redmond.

My God, my heart is pounding at the thought of the Sharks in the Championship. I envision all of us leaping into each other's arms as time runs out. I haven't felt that pounding-heart adrenalin rush in years.

The e-mails start coming through about unity and believing in ourselves. Cooper sends some informative info on geese.

Hi guys.

I read this about geese and think we should learn something from them.

Scientists have determined that the V-shaped formation that geese use when migrating serves two important purposes: First, it conserves their energy. Each bird flies slightly above the bird in front of him, resulting in a reduction of wind resistance. The birds take turns being in the front, falling back when they get tired. In this way, the geese can fly for a long time before they must stop for rest.

The second benefit to the V formation is that it is easy to keep track of every bird in the group. Flying in formation may assist with the communication and coordination within the group. Fighter pilots often use this formation for the same reason.

If we stick together and use the 'V' attitude, we will beat anyone we play!

Cooper

Geese. Then Coach Rex clocks in:

Sharks,

We will be working on the listed formations at practice. Be there!

Offense: a lot of 'I' and two back, trips and empty set. We want our TE in to block on passing plays

Defense: 3-5-3 cover 2 man under

I will leave you with this quote from Bear Bryant, a great football coach from before the time of cable TV;

"It's not the will to win that matters - everyone has that. It's the will to prepare to win that matters."

Coach Rex

Jessie adds this:

You know what? All this "Redmond this" and "Redmond that" shit is making me nauseous! F@#$ Redmond! We should treat every team like the enemy. I sleep on NO ONE! Everyone has to pay for making me wear those hot ass long socks on Saturdays! We should play like it's the Championship EVERY TIME we get on the field regardless of the team.

By now, we are all able to decipher her e-mails. Jessie was pumped and ready to hit Washington for the big game!

No one was as pumped as I am when Kim calls to say Eve has been sprung from jail.

"God has helped us," she says before saying hello.

"Tell me," I say.

"She is free to throw another pass. And it better be with a football this time." We both laugh. "The judge was so young, he couldn't believe that someone with Eve's sweet face could throw a pitch fork at anyone." She mock coughs after the word "sweet."

"He must have been very young."

"I have shit in my fridge older than him."

Truly, God must be wearing a black and blue jersey.

CHAPTER 91

NO ONE CAN SLEEP

'Twas the night before the Championship and all through the hotel...

Big Dot is pushing Eve on the luggage cart from room to room. They are wearing colorful PJ's and eating candy. Janet is holding a handful of pills trying to discern which is Claritin, to give to Erin, who is puffed so tightly she's about to pop.

"What you got?" asks Eve, thinking it might be candy. Big Dot, lying in her bed with the door open sees the cart go by and hears the banter in the hallway.

"I love how we prepare for a game!" she shouts. Wendy is rollerblading up and down the hallway to warm-up even though the game is 22 hours away. Little Toni is standing outside of her door in her underwear yelling that she has forgotten her game socks, so Erin calls a group who has gone to Modell's and asks them to get her a pair of long black socks. Eve is in black tights, a huge Packers long sleeve shirt, and fur snow boots.

"If anyone did a pregame show, no one would ever take us seriously again." says Kim.

"Until the first snap! EH!" says Eve.

"Did you say snap or nap?" asks Wendy. "Heh, heh. You're fuckin' old."

"We may be old, but not on Saturdays!" her usual reply.

Walking the halls, I peek into some of the rooms where the Sharks are preparing, each in their own way. Piper is smoking, quietly reading a novel by flashlight in her darkened room. Occasionally, her hand moves, the cigarette glow like a snake in the dark. Wearing her oversized, ground-mopping, Shark blue sweat-suit, she smiles at me with a rarely seen ear-bending grin. I am always surprised to find her reading some heady book when we ride the bus to games. Piper is such a dichotomy.

"Number seven," mocks Cooper in her monotone voice as she approaches. "I'm number sixty-three. Nice to meet you."

"And you, number sixty-three." I reply in a serious manner. "May I call you by your first digit or is that too personal?"

"By all means." She curtseys and makes way for Little Toni who is now on her razor-scooter racing Wendy on her rollerblades. The Sharks as a whole, were incapable of relaxation. Our blood was flowing fast, our brains were glowing and even those sitting in chairs or sleeping seemed to be in motion. The hall of rooms vibrated long after the lights went out and when the sun rose, we plunged into the delight of chance and dreams and our quest for the championship.

CHAPTER 92

GAMEDAY

And 25,000 Good Thoughts

Redmond, Washington, July 6, 2002. IWFL Championship game. Against a picturesque mountain background, the day is bright and warm with the game time temperature expected to be around 90 degrees. I spot a few ducks slicing through a sky buttered in shades of blue. Humidity is low to make the conditions bearable, but it is still going to be tough to play football in the dry heat. I worry that the heat will be too much for Tanker and the larger players on the line, but our trainer assures me there will be large amounts of ice and ice water.

I have called my mom and dad and kept them informed of all we are doing to prepare for the game. I didn't expect them to come, but, things have changed and I can feel their support in unspoken ways; how my mom laughs when I tell her stories of the players, and when my dad asks what formation we are running, or how our front line is holding up against the defense. But it is my sister Annie, who happens to be at the house, who spills the beans and lets me know just how much they all support my team and me.

I just wanted to wish you good luck today Toad," she chirps into the phone.

"Thank you." I respond. "I wish all of you could be here but I know it's a long way to come."

"Well, you just remember that Mom and Dad and Grandma and Jan and I send you good thoughts. Twenty-five thousand of them to be exact."

"Thank you." I say and tell her I have to hang up because Coach Rex has called a film session in the lobby of our hotel. I don't think about why Annie sent "twenty-five thousand good thoughts" until Coach points out to the team the dedication and "cost" of getting here today. He is not talking about monetary costs, but my mind returns to Bank Street and the day the check fell out of the envelope. There was no address or any indication of who it was from. It was for twenty-five thousand dollars and it said "from Sarah for the 2002 season."

I let out an audible gasp. The players turn to look at me and I stare at them for a second, before I excuse myself and run outside. I always thought the check was from someone who loved Sarah. Someone who knew the value of what the team meant to her and what the team means to those of us here and those yet to play. What we do is so much bigger than football and I figured it was from someone who felt the same way I did. I figured if they wanted me to know who they were, they would let me know. Some people prefer to support anonymously, so I didn't pry. But it had been my family all along. My mother who said women shouldn't be playing tackle football. My dad who "Hmmmmphed" at my purchasing the team and called it a bad business decision. My grandmother--always trying to bridge family gaps--and she support-ing both points of view. My sister Annie, who agreed with Ellen that playing tackle football was an aberration, and Jan who was strangely silent about the whole ordeal.

I have no breath in my lungs as I kneel under a huge cottonwood tree and weep for the joy I feel because it was them, for the stupidity I feel for not suspecting it was them and for the near "wholeness" I am experiencing for maybe the first time in my life. Turpie and Erin cautiously appear and I motion for them to come closer.

"They sent the check...my family. They sent it. I just figured it was from Sarah's family..." I can get no more words out but they understand. We hug as gratitude for so many things about women's football melds us into one.

Coach Rex is still talking when we return to the team meeting. Heads turn, including his, but I motion that all is good so he continues.

"Everything that needs to be said has already been said, but since no one listens, it all needs to be said again. I'll start with this: We have to jam up the alley or the receiver will split the seam and get behind Little Toni, and we all know what happens if someone gets behind Little Toni."

"Yeah. Big Dot shoots them," comes the pat answer from the candy-crunching gallery which Coach Rex ignores.

"Dulce," he says. His flat head is tilted downwards and he focuses intently on her.

"Yes Coach," she answers.

"You know what 26 left and right are now, right?"

"Yes, Coach. I block the A gap and..."

"NO!!!" He snaps. "NO!!"

"Oh, right! I fake to the opposite side..."

"NO!!!" He's gonna have an episode.

"I dunt understand Coach 'cause you said..."

And then, in an anger-choked voice that sounds linguistically handicapped, he says, "You're getting the BALL!" His hands are twisted together and his fingers and thumbs are bent in odd shapes to further illustrate the point. The Sharks begin to howl with laughter. Dulce smiles and swings her hair behind her head. "Ok, Coach. I got it now."

Everyone tries to act calm, but their numerous trips to the bathroom betray them. Because she is perched on the "throne," Tanker is late getting on the bus to the field again. The Sharks chide her as she crawls on, but the ride is fairly calm. When we finally arrive, we go straight to the locker room. It's surprisingly quiet as players claim lockers around the small, rectangular room. We are nearly dressed and ready to take the field for warm-up when Jessie stands in the middle of the room, solemnly looking at us, one at a time and finally says, "Someone else has got to fuckin' notice this besides me."

"What?" asks Dulce.

"Look around the room. Which is the only locker that isn't taken by one of us? Look around the fuckin' room..."

She has our attention. We stop whatever we are doing and scan the room. Tanker spots it.

"Fifty one ... no one took locker number 51."

It has just become clear that Sarah has claimed her spot like the rest of us. She should be here, lacing and buckling and snapping on the garments of the game we all love. We are silent and reverent and sad and introspective as we finish prepping to take the field.

But once out there, we change. I can tell our feelings about her absence, the game, this life we've chosen to carve out for ourselves and experience is animating us. Ratcheting us up. Like I've said, this is a love story.

"Tanker," Coach Rex says. "Remember, we are moving you to nose guard. Their QB takes a straight drop. I want you to blow that middle up! Wendy, at middle linebacker, you should be able to walk in behind Tanker and have your way. Don't show blitz! Delay three counts, then, follow Tanker in."

"I'll be right on your ass, Tanker," says Wendy.

"Nobody is touching you, girl. You WILL be able to have your way! Let's GO, now! Let's GO!"

Minutes later, Sarah's father, Thomas, stands on the field with the Shark captains as the coin is flipped for the 2002 IWFL Championship game. Sarah's championship. As the team stands in a horseshoe-shape holding hands and waiting for the captains and refs to signal the result, glances are exchanged. Hands are squeezed. A few tears slide down our faces. I hope we can get into another frame of mind to win this game. The empty number 51 locker discovery reminds me that, though she may be here in spirit, Sarah is gone forever. Time skips a beat, and I hear Tanker shout.

"Look at that. Look over there!" Tanker's arm is raised and pointing to the sky as a pink balloon floats gracefully earthward and settles onto the field near the goal line. "That's Sarah!" yells Tanker and runs across the field towards the balloon. I am too stunned to move or comment. Any other color of balloon wouldn't have made an impact, but pink... we all knew that everything Sarah wore and loved had pink in it.

"Holy shit buddy..." says Turpie.

"Sarah's here..." Erin agrees, her voice trails quietly off in disbelief. Tanker is gamboling towards the balloon, a dainty battleship with purpose. Just as she draws close, a puff of wind lifts it back towards the heavens. Tanker stretches out to it, arms and fingers unfurled, her face tilted towards the cerulean sky. "You are here with us, mother fucker. You are here. I love you so much! I miss you..."

When the balloon is out of sight, Tanker turns back to her teammates with an elated grin. Sarah has injected us with that needed voltage of faith and now we are ready.

The Sharks are considered the visiting team, while the Western Division Winner, Texas Bandits are considered the home team. This means that the Sharks have the opportunity to make the call for the coin toss. Eve calls tails, but the coin turns up heads. For some reason, the Bandits elect to kick-off. Taken aback, the referee asks if he heard correctly and they answer he has.

So, the game starts with Wanda catching the ball on the New York 35-yard line and returning it to the 50. Coach Rex sticks with his game plan that got us to the championship and keeps the ball on the ground. On the first play, Dulce picks up 15 yards. She gets the ball again for a 5-yard pick-up and again for only a 3-yard gain. On the third down play, Piper and Eve fumble the snap, but Jessie recovers making it fourth and 5 yards on the Bandit's 30-yard line.

G-ma J is standing by me and we are clasping each other's pads. "Poop just rolled down my leg." She says as the play clock runs down, Dulce runs Coach's play in from the sideline and we are going to go for it. My heart pounds when it looks like Texas is going to stop us, but Eve scrambles to her right with five Bandits on her tail. She turns to make a pass down field and starts to slip. As she is falling to the ground, she tosses the ball to Wendy who is able to move the ball down to the 12-yard line. We are about to score.

I cannot believe how nervous I am! With a first down, the Sharks go back to the ground game. After 3 hand-offs, we have a fourth down situation with only inches to go on the 3-yard line. It is up to Tanker and her line to come through big. Calling her own number, Eve not only gets the few inches, but the three yards to score a touchdown.

Thank you, God!

Then she tosses the ball to Cha-chi who runs to her left for the two-point conversion. *Thank you, God!*

Less than 5 minutes into the game, the Sharks have drawn first blood to take an 8-0 lead. Everyone high-fives and hugs as the offense comes off the field and the kicking team goes on. I am counting players to make sure we have eleven out there. Nine, ten...where is the damn kicker? Oh shit! That's me! I'm the kicker!

I hunt frantically for the kicking tee until Erin shoves it into my hands and I run onto the field trying to focus on the task at hand. Or foot. My God, I'm nervous!

I get a decent kick off and the Bandits return it for about ten yards and have fair field position at their own 43-yard line. Trying to take advantage of their good offensive line, they attempt to move the ball on the ground but their half-back fumbles, and 'Killer Miller' recovers the ball. I'm a little less nervous, until Eve overthrows Jade Max and Texas intercepts.

"God DAMMIT EVELYN!" she yells at herself as she comes off the field and the defense goes out. I realize that even Eve is nervous and I am happy to see Turpie telling her "It's all good" as she slaps Eve's shoulder pad and thumps her helmet.

Our defense had stopped Texas from scoring, but it is short-lived. The Bandits defense stifles the Shark's possession and we are forced to punt deep from our own end zone. Not wanting to risk a miscue and possibly give the Bandits a touchdown or the ball in great field position, Coach Rex orders Eve to run to the back of the end zone and take a safety. This makes the score 8-2 in our favor.

Ok, I'm nervous again. At least halftime has arrived. The heat is taking its toll but the Sharks determination is pervasive. Still, Coach Rex feels the need to remind us during his halftime speech that "This is it," that we should give it our all as "There is no tomorrow."

"There's 30 minutes left in your season, don't leave anything in the tank here." The talk is truth, but the real truth is, we don't need more inspiration than what Sarah has provided. The expressions on our faces are confident even though Tanker heads back to the bathroom and Eve and Wendy are filling their fins with candy.

The Sharks receive the ball again to start the second half and keep the ball on the ground, letting Rodriquez and Wayne move the yard markers. To keep the Bandits on their toes, we mix in one pass play, a big 30-yard gainer from Eve to Jade Max and the scoring play is a 7-yard run by Dulce. We convert the 2-point play on an Eve pass to Kim. It has taken a little more than 4 minutes and 9 plays for New York to stretch the lead to 16-2.

Texas is starting to feel the pressure of the championship slipping away. No one has scored more than 6 points in a game against the Sharks and Texas now has to score 14 in less than half of a game. On the ensuing kick-off, the Bandits kick returner tries to get them back into the game. She has a great return, getting all the way to the New York 45-yard line but fumbles the ball. The Sharks, who have feasted all season on turnovers, feast again. Shark ball!

Going to the air, Eve hits Jade Max for a 25-yard pass and again from the 19-yard line for our third touchdown of the game. The 2-point conversion pass is complete from Eve to Kim to make the score 24-2. I am feeling less and less nervous as the fourth quarter is ticking away.

The Bandits do get on the board one more time after the Sharks create another turnover. Eve, who is replaced by me at QB, goes in at safety and picks off a Texas pass on the Shark's 20-yard line. When Texas sacks the quarterback, moi, number 7, the Sharks face a fourth down from our own 12-yard line. On the punt play, Janet, our long snapper, snaps the ball over Piper, our punter's head and through the end zone for another safety making the score 24-4. Then we kick off to them.

Texas does not want to let this opportunity slip away and continues handing off to their running back, who sweeps the end all the way to our 9-yard line. Coach Rex, annoyed that our outside linebackers look soft, tells Jessie to go to outside linebacker for the next play. As the Bandit back gets around our ends and into the secondary, Jessie engulfs her in a blanket of black and blue jersey. We hear a muffled Bandit grunt as Jessie drops her to the ground and unclamps herself. She stands up, pulls her jersey up to reveal a pink undershirt, points to the sky and says "That's for you, Sarah."

The Shark sideline roars and an intimidating energy covers the field. At this moment, my team has no limits. Ignited, we are flying around the field, each emotion divulging a story and each story, unique and singular.

Texas has to punt and our offense takes over with me at QB. I am elated to be sharing the energy that has enveloped the sideline and the Shark players on the field. I hand off to Dulce for a short gain. I throw a quick slant to Diane 'Azure' Holt for a first down. With less than 2 minutes left, I see commotion on the sideline when Eve, Jessie and Cooper ceremoniously dump a bucket of water over Coach's head. The game is close to being over and all of us are celebrating. We need one more play so I line up under Piper, take the snap and take the knee.

CHAPTER 93

I HEAR MY VOICE

...how did this ever happen...

I have the ball in my hands. I hear the whistle blow and I know the game is over. A game that just moments ago had been orderly and recognizable is now an emotional smear of colors as the jerseys of players and the bright clothing of loyal fans are no longer separated by down markers and sidelines. Tears run down dirty faces. People embrace in joy, disappointment and disbelief. I see Turpie and Erin coming at me with fixed stares and I am not sure how to decipher their countenances. When they get close enough, I wrap my arms around their necks and I can't hold back the tears and I say to them over and over "It came through...it came through..."

I drop the ball to the ground as I cling to my best friends and I cry like a baby and I think to myself: how did this ever happen...

EPILOGUE:

WINGS OF FREEDOM

"Mind the gap," said a page in one of the books I was reading. "It's the distance between how you dream life and how it really is." Sometimes I still think women's football is a dream. And on certain days, it is a peace-shattering nightmare! One night, one of our starters broke a bone in her leg at practice. With the snap of the small bone, came the shattering end to her season. I confess I sat down and asked myself "Why do we play this game, any of us, male or female? Is it some primitive need to demonstrate physical prowess? Or is it more simple than that...the joy of simply doing something for which we have an affinity?"

My receiver's leg was in a cast along with her heart, but her reason for participating outweighed the risk of possible injury and inconvenience. The bigger risk was to deny her heart those few seconds of flight derived from a six-month season of football games: the mere 22 hours of actual game time and approximately 330 plays we will run. How trivial the risk of a broken bone seems to these women when the alternative is sitting in the stands, remaining so chronically unseen!

A woman passed by me once wearing a t-shirt that said: "Women Fly When No One is Looking." And it is true. In my team's most illustrious of flights, hardly anyone has looked. But as the years pass, the hard work of both my staff and players lessens the gap between dream life and reality.

Do mind the gap, it's true. But sometimes the gap is the best place to grow. And sometimes the only way to bridge the distance is to fly. Someday, someone is going to look. And somewhere in that gap, between our dream and our reality, lie our stories. And our reasons.

Every person who has come to this team has had a different reason. As many memories as we take with us from our struggles and triumphs, we leave some behind to seed new wings for others; powerful dreams of unprejudiced equality, benevolence and generosity. We release them like winged wishes towards a new horizon of hope.

To each of you, my "Sharklettes"...here's to your reason, whatever it may be, and to our vision, our dreams, and having the courage to fly.

"SHARKS-HOO-RAH-FIVE-ONE!"

Forever.

A native of central Florida and a graduate of Florida State University and Pratt Institute, Andra Douglas has been a National Champion athlete in rugby and women's tackle football, a Vice President/Creative Director at Time Warner, the founder of the Fins Up! Foundation for Female Athletes, a non-profit to benefit at-risk teens, (**www.womensgridironfoundation.org**), the owner of the New York Sharks Women's Pro Football team for 19 years (**www.nysharksfootball.com**) and a known artist. She lives with her parrot, 'Pie' in New York City where she spends much of her time working from her rooftop studio in Greenwich Village on her mixed-media artwork. (**www.andradouglasart.com**)